She Reflects

A Spiral Journey for the Feminine Soul

Erica Ross

She Reflects: A Spiral Journey for the Feminine Soul. Copyright © 2018 by Erica Ross

Published by Erica Ross, www.EricaRoss.com

All rights reserved: including copy, photos, drawings and playlists. No portion of this book may be reproduced in any form without permission from Erica Ross, except as permitted by Canadian Copyright Law.
For permission, contact: erica@ericaross.com

Artwork by Erica Ross

Cover art, book design and graphics by Erica Ross

Photographs by Erica Ross

Author Photo: Vanya Laporte

Disclaimers:

This book in its entirety is designed to provide inspiration and support. No warranties or guarantees are expressed by any of the content. You are responsible for your own choices, actions, and outcomes - physically, psychologically or emotionally.

All personal stories are true, recalled from my perspective and to the best of my ability. Some names and locations have been dropped or changed out of respect for others' privacy.

The use of the words 'she,' 'her' and 'woman' in this book applies to anyone identifying with, or wishes to know, the feminine soul, regardless of gender or sex.

ISBN: 978-1-926926-95-7   *She Reflects: A Spiral Journey for the Feminine Soul* (pbk)

ISBN: 978-1-926926-96-4   *She Reflects Journal & Colouring Book* (pbk)

ISBN: 978-1-926926-97-1   *She Reflects: A Spiral Journey for the Feminine Soul* (ebook)

To Caya, and to my sisters near and far...

May you feel inspired, nourished and validated.

May you find infinite curiosity, creativity, compassion and courage.

May you pass the flame on, so no one is left behind.

May you know you are a blessing.

I'm with you. For you.

I love you.

Contents

Homage to Mariam / 8

Introduction / 12

    Playlists: Uzume / 20
                    Amaterasu / 21

First Turn: Listen / 23

Story: Soul Speaks / 24

Reflections / 29

Pausing Practices: / 32
- Breathe / 33
- Linger at the Threshold / 35
- Be in Silence / 37

Relaxing & Softening Practices: / 39
- Be Kind to Yourself / 40
- Slow Down with Body Flow / 42
- Pamper Yourself / 45

Listening Practices: / 47
- Listen for Answers / Ask Questions / 48
- Listen for Signs and Synchronicities / 50
- Listen to Your Yoni / 52

Playlist: Slow Dance / 56

Second Turn: Follow Your Impulse / 57

Story: Part 1. Mr. Pudding Shop / 58
           Part 2. Burkas, Barbers and Borders / 67

Reflections / 71

Practices: / 73
- A Day of Curiosity / 74
- Meander with a Pen / 78
- Be Moved / 81
- Become a Wanderer / 83
- Dare to be Impulsive / 86
- Divine with Oracle Decks / 89

Playlist: Follow Your Impulse / 94

 **Third Turn: The Partner Dance / 95**

Story: Part 1. The Set Up / 96
Part 2. The Dance / 102
Part 3. The Healing / 109

Reflections / 112

Opening to Love Practices: / 115
- Create an Altar for Aphrodite / 116
- Design Vows of Self Devotion / 119
- Dance with Love, AKA 'Love Comes Dancing' / 122

Partnering Practices: / 124
- Listen Compassionately to Another / 125
- Consciously Collaborate / 128
- Nourish Your Relationship / 131

Moving On Practices: / 134
- Boast Your Way Out / 135
- Let Go with De-Cording / 137
- Forgive with Metta (Loving Kindness) / 141

Playlists: Opening to Love / 144
Partner Dance / 145
Moving On / 146

 **Fourth Turn: Collective Joy / 147**

Story: Saturday Night Fever / 148

Reflections / 152

Practices: / 155
- Find Your People / 156
- Be a Mirror / 160
- Get Playful / Laugh Together / 162
- Throw a Dance Party / 164
- Form a Healing Circle / 166
- Know Your 'Group' Self / 170

Playlist: Collective Joy / 172

 **Fifth Turn: The Magic of Letting Go** / 173

Story: Mama Ocean / 174

Reflections / 180

Practices: / 183
- Be with Your Exhale / 184
- Shake it Loose / 186
- Free Your Voice / 189
- Transform Your 'NEVER!' / 192
- Become an Open Vessel / 195
- Tell Your Future Self / 197

Playlist: Shake it Loose / 199

 **Sixth Turn: Touch the Wild** / 201

Story: Spreading My Wings / 202

Reflections / 208

Practices: / 212
- Live Life Unscripted / 213
- Touch the Wild / 216
- Encounter the Wild Goddess / 219
- Connect with the Gifts of Animal Wisdom / 224
- Create Beauty / 228
- Dance Your Wild / Dance Yourself Free / 231

Playlist: Touch the Wild / 235

 **Seventh Turn: Return to Self** / 237

Story: Into the Soup / 238

Reflections / 243

Practices: / 246
- Create a Gratitude (List &) Collage / 247
- Accept What Is / See Life as a Sacred Experiment / 251
- Keep Your Heart Open, Regardless / 254
- Support Your Expanding Heart / 258
- Trance Dance with Love / 261
- Appreciate Your Unique Light / 264

Playlist: Return to Love / 267

Eighth Turn: Share Your Light / 269

Story: She is My Prayer / 270

Reflections / 276

Practices: / 278
- What's Your Soul's Offering? / 279
- Pass the Flame / 283
- Heal Our Sisterhood / 285
- Get Solar Powered, Sun Goddess / 288
- Show & Tell / 291
- Share Your Light in Amaterasu's Circle / 293

Playlist: Share Your Light / 296

Epilogue: Holding it All / 297

Playlist: Holding it All / 300

Index of Practices / 301

Other Women's Voices / 303

In Praise of Juli / 305

More Gratitude / 306

About the Author / 307

Homage to Mariam

Beginnings are important.

It's where we set our intention and set the stage for what is about to unfold.

The beginning of my story starts with Mariam, my grandmother - my Bubbie - who was born in Poland in 1903. She was born into a religious Orthodox Jewish family, living in a small town outside of Lodz, one of the bigger cities in Poland. The story of Bubbie is where my story begins.

Mariam's parents divorced when she was ten, and that's when her mom and the kids still young enough to be living with her, moved to Lodz. It was a big deal because husbands, by Jewish law, didn't have to grant their wives a divorce. The men held that power. Lucky for my Bubbie's mom, when she asked for a divorce, her husband consented. We're not exactly sure why she asked for one - nor why he granted her one - but she did.

Bubbie's upbringing followed all the strict traditions of being orthodox. By far, the most difficult rule for her was the one about dancing – no dancing with boys. Girls could dance with girls, but never girls with boys, and NEVER on a Friday night, the holy night of Sabbath.

But, like me, my Bubbie was born to dance. She was bursting to do it.

There was a community hall in Lodz where every Friday night the local teenage boys and girls would meet to dance - together. When Mariam turned 16, she had a girlfriend who had gone to the dance hall and wanted her to go too.

My Bubbie said yes, knowing full well she was breaking three taboos - going out on the Sabbath night, going on a streetcar on that Sabbath night, and maybe worst of all... going to a dance hall to dance with boys. Sacrilege for her. But, she didn't care. She had to dance.

At the time, Bubbie was an apprentice for a seamstress. It was a place where wealthy women would come to have their fancy dresses repaired or refitted. My Bubbie, with her strong resolve, and nothing pretty to wear, took one of their client's dresses home when her boss wasn't looking and altered it to fit her. (And, after the dance, she unstitched the dress and returned it back to the shop without her boss ever knowing!)

That Friday night, she snuck out of her house, in her specially stitched dress, and secretly made her way to the dance hall with her girlfriend. For the first time in her life, she danced with a boy. She loved every second of it. It was pure joy. And, it was absolute sacrilege.

Bubbie waited for God to strike her down. Surely, God would mete out some kind of punishment after such a brazen act. She told me she was waiting for a brick to fall from the sky, or a car to hit her. Something was going to happen that would end her life because God would know she had danced. She waited an entire year for God's retaliation, constantly watching over her shoulder, certain she would die.

But nothing happened.

No brick. No car. No punishment. Nothing. For that entire year.

'Well,' she thought, 'maybe God doesn't actually mind if I dance. I break the law of faith, and nothing happens? God must not care.' And that's when she decided, 'I will dance.'

And dance she did, still secretly, still sneaking out the house because God may have let her off the hook, but her mother certainly would not. For the next year, she went to the dance hall every chance she got. It made her heart sing. It was utter joy for this young woman, this teenager, this rebel.

By the time she was 17, my Bubbie was leaving to go to Canada with her older sister who was 25. Three of their older brothers were already in Canada and paid for their passage. Their mom was to join them later. Bubbie and her sister took a ship called "Canada" from Liverpool to Halifax. With the cheapest tickets their brothers could afford, they slept on the deck at the bottom of the ship.

My favourite story from that crossing was when Bubbie met a girl her own age who also loved to dance. While Bubbie's sister was sleeping (she had terrible seasickness and slept a lot), Bubbie and the other girl snuck up, more than once, to the first class deck where an orchestra played, and danced together outside the door of the big ballroom. That image delights me!

When Bubbie arrived in Montreal everything changed. She had a new country, a new city, a new language, and a new name. Mariam became Mary, and Mary soon fell in love and married a man also from Lodz, named Issac, Izzy for short.

Together, Mary and Izzy built a life for themselves in Montreal. They started a family, bringing two daughters into the world, Rita and Honey, both, as it turned out, were born to dance: Rita with her jive and cha-cha-cha, and my mom, Honey, with her ballet and modern dance. (Mom is in the archives of Ottawa as one of the dancers of the 'New Dance Theatre,' the first Canadian modern dance company documented to dance barefoot on stage!)

Those two daughters had three daughters, (and two sons), and I'm proudly one of them. All the women in the family - including my own daughter and my niece (the last ones in the line, for now) - love to dance.

Whether it's dancing professionally, as a dance teacher, in a healing practice, or simply for the joy of it, we all danced. Mariam gave each one of us the gift of dance, and we have pursued it.

Sometimes, I imagine the long line of women in my family born before Bubbie, born into the tradition of religious Orthodox Judaism, who never dared to do what they loved. Then, along came brave Mariam, who at just 16 broke with tradition, defying her God and her family in order to do what she felt born to do.

Because of her, everything changed for us. The lineage of dancers in our family leads right back to my Bubbie. We owe her, now, for four generations of dancers.

Mariam-Mary-Bubbie liberated herself, and, thereby, all of us. She opened the door for dance to come alive in us. Even more, she showed us what it means to be brave. She showed us what it is to follow your heart's true desire.

This is my beginning. This is my heritage. Dance. Courage. Love.

Thank you, bold, beautiful Mariam.

"There are two ways of spreading light:
to be a candle
or the mirror that reflects it."
Edith Wharton

Introduction

Dear one,

I offer these pages as both a love letter *and* a call to action - for compassionate and courageous healing and reflection, for you, for me, for us. Born out of a full heart, broken-down body and weary soul, with much asking and listening in for guidance, *She Reflects* is living proof that pain, loss and vulnerability can (and will) be transformed into art, creativity and healing. (See **'Into the Soup'**.)

Before I go further, I'd like to place these words like sacred stones at the gateway of our journey:

Acknowledgments

I acknowledge the sacred land, which I call home, and on which I wrote this book, as the territory of the Huron-Wendat and Petun First Nations, the Seneca, and most recently, the Mississaugas of the Credit River.

I acknowledge and honour the countless teachers, mentors, wisdom-keepers, muses, musicians, goddess stories, cultures, communities, friends, experiences and influences (seen and unseen) which have shaped and nurtured me through my 63 years around the sun. (See **'More Gratitude'**.)

I acknowledge that the practices offered here are not drawn from one path or tradition, or specifically from my lineage, but rather, from the myriad of people and places mentioned above. Many practices have been with me for decades making it difficult to distinguish their original or exact structures or sources, while others are drawn straight from my muse (inspiration). In all cases, they are rooted in personal experience and shared with you from a place of respect.

I acknowledge my privilege and power - and how it has afforded me unearned benefits and opportunities. With this knowing, I vow to stay awake to learn/unlearn, challenge, and change the beliefs, attitudes and behaviours, internally and externally, of oppression, bias, separation, racism, and discrimination of all kinds.

I acknowledge my deep love of, and embodied relationship with, the sacred feminine and her mythology for over 30 years. For me, goddess myths are wisdom teachings and belong to us all, regardless of where we're from. They remind me of our divinity and carry messages for self-healing, wholeness and empowerment for all women (CIS and trans alike).

++

And now, grounded in gratitude, reverence and love, from the oldest religion in Japan, I give you a miraculous story which weaves its silver threads through the book, beaded with mirrors and luminous pearls of other goddess myths big and small. Here we go...

Amaterasu and Uzume

It's one of my favourite myths, the story of Amaterasu and Uzume.

Two powerful expressions of the divine feminine, rooted in ancient Japanese mythology: one, a goddess - the most powerful goddess of them all - and the other, a shamaness (a female shaman), who together held the fate of the world in their hands.

The story of these two women has been told across the centuries, and in countless ways. It is a story of love, community and light.

This is my telling of their story, as I have learned it over the years:

Beautiful, beautiful Amaterasu was the Shinto Goddess of the Sun, the most powerful of all the gods and goddesses in the land, beloved by all, but one.

Her brother, Susanoo, was the God of the Seas, a mighty god, but not nearly as powerful, nor as revered, as his sister, and that made him jealous to his core.

One day in a drunken rage, he attacked the palace where he and his sister lived with their parents. It was a home of exquisite beauty and he ruined it, destroying every single, precious family heirloom.

Amaterasu was devastated. How could her brother destroy all that she held dear? How could he betray her? Heart-broken and outraged, the Goddess of the Sun withdrew into her sanctuary, a deep cave high in the mountains. She placed a giant boulder at the mouth of the cave, vowing never to leave. With that, Amaterasu retreated into the 'Cave of Heaven,' taking with her all her shining light.

Her disappearance was catastrophic for all the gods and goddesses of the land. Their beloved source of light was gone. Their crops would wither, their animals would die, their way of life would change forever.

As the great land plunged into darkness, the gods and goddesses tried everything to lure Amaterasu out of the cave. They tried coaxing her, wooing her, arguing with her. Nothing worked. The Sun Goddess stayed deep within her cave, and the great land remained shrouded in darkness.

A young Shamaness named Uzume (pronounced, Oo-zoo-may) said, "I know what to do! Come. All of you. Meet me in front of Amaterasu's cave and bring with you a piece of mirror. We must let Amaterasu see herself. We must remind her of her beauty. We must show her how brightly her light shines."

Uzume climbed onto a humble, overturned washing tub just outside the entrance to the cave and she started to dance. She pounded the wooden cask with her feet, and danced with total abandon - joyful and alive. She opened her kimono, baring her naked body, allowing her breasts and hips to swing wildly, along with her arms and legs, hands and feet. Hundreds of deities were gathered around her, and they roared with delight at her wild and outrageous dance.

The more Uzume danced, the louder the crowd became. Their jubilant voices enticed Amaterasu to the door of her cave. She was so curious. Why was everyone laughing? Why was there so much noise? She had to take a peek.

Amaterasu pushed the boulder aside just a crack to have a look.

Suddenly, a shard of shining light burst through the gap in the door. The crowd gasped and cheered and Uzume began to dance more wildly, making the crowd laugh more loudly, all in the hopes that Amaterasu would thrust the boulder completely aside.

Amaterasu could stand it no longer. To satiate her curiosity, she did it. She thrust the boulder aside and her beautiful, bright light poured out of the cave. Immediately, Uzume urged the gods and goddesses to hold up their fragments of mirror. For the first time in her life, Amaterasu saw her reflection. She witnessed her own great beauty. She saw her glorious light.

In that instant, everything changed.

Once the Sun Goddess saw her light, she burst into blissful laughter and she danced her way out of the cave, clapping her hands, swinging her hips and pledging never to hide again.

Uzume's plan had worked - the gathering, the dance, the laughter, the mirrors - all of it served to restore Amaterasu's light to the land and heal her heart, making her whole again.

+++

This story so moved me when I first heard it many years ago, I've never forgotten it.

Haven't we all been Susanoo at some point in our lives? Feeling dissatisfied and impetuous, consumed by envy, anger and jealousy?

And, haven't we all been Amaterasu? Heart-broken and hurt by the world, withdrawn from life, lost to our own beauty and light?

And, haven't we all been Uzume, too, working in community with others to help someone through a tough time, offering humour, joy, and playfulness to shift someone's mood and lift their spirits?

Haven't we all been a mirror - a divine reflection - to a loved one, or even a stranger, in order that they might see their beauty and shine their light again?

Like Uzume, I am a dancer. I grew up in a home of dance and art and creativity, and much love. As long as I can remember, dance has been my great joy. Dance is where I found my friends, my community, my lovers, and my freedom.

I've danced in wild nature: on the shores of the Indian Ocean, in the forests of Canada, the mountains of Peru, and along the cliffs of Wales. I've danced in the discos of New York City, the go-go clubs of New Jersey, in an opera in Toronto, and in improvisational dance performances in Bali.

Dance is my devotion. It's how I pray. It's my doorway to the divine and to what's sacred. It's my bliss.

Like Uzume, dance has also been my elixir - my way of calling out the light in myself and other women, goddesses in their own right. This has been my work.

- For 20 years, I've worked with women across Canada, from every walk of life, serving as a guide to sacred feminine knowing, embodiment and joy.

- I've served women seeking to connect to their own radiance through the creation of "Dance Our Way Home" and "RADICAL RADIANCE", two programs and healing processes that facilitate the discovery and re-discovery of women's own unique gifts, power and voice.

- I've served women affected by eating disorders and body image issues struggling to reconnect with their bodies, and find a sense of belonging and home.

- I've served families, teaching creative movement to parents with their children.

- I've served my local community, co-founding "The Move," which is one of the largest ecstatic dance communities and events in Toronto, if not all of Canada, and which inspired the blossoming of a myriad of other ecstatic dance events.

- I've served a global community, co-founding "DAILY DANCE", a 21-day virtual ecstatic dance program for women and men (and their families).

- I've been honoured by the Canadian Dance Assembly with a national dance award as an 'Outstanding Individual and/or Organization Promoting Dance as a Tool for Healthy Communities.'

Dance and unveiling the power of the Divine Mirror has been my life's work. It's my calling.

(Dance as prayer and ritual has been and continues to be practiced as a tool of liberation and celebration by cultures across the globe, across decades and centuries. I'm grateful for this inspiration.)

The Eight Turns of the Spiral

Life unfolds more like a spiral than a straight line, doesn't it? We move forward in our lives as though around and around the curves of a spiral. Being. Becoming. Being. Becoming.

As we make the turn around each curve, we evolve. We move from selfhood, to partnership, from our inner life to interaction with the world, from innocence to discovery; from inexperience to wisdom, each turn providing a new vantage point from which to look inward at ourselves and outward at our lives.

As part of my work in Dance Our Way Home, I created a process of healing and discernment, of shedding the old and celebrating the new. The process takes us through eight turns of a spiral. **Each turn is a chapter in this book.**

1. At the **First Turn**, we slow down, linger and pause. We soften, relax and listen. We tune into ourselves, creating space for our inner voice, body and heart wisdom, to be heard. We ask and receive. We open to the exquisite dialogue only we can have with the world around us.

2. Through the **Second Turn** of the spiral, we become the wanderer journeying out into the unknown guided by our inner impulses, instincts and rhythms. This journey is a solo one, inviting us to be curious, innocent and present. It's a deeply personal and daringly courageous adventure.

3. We then move into relationship with another. Into Heart. Into Aphrodite's realm of Love and Devotion. At this, the **Third Turn**, we prepare to meet and be met. We nourish our partnerships and conscious collaborations, and learn to lovingly dance our way out. We learn to move on with compassion, kindness and forgiveness.

4. In the **Fourth Turn**, we shift our focus from one-on-one relationships to being in community. It's about finding our people, and sense of belonging. It's the healing of collective joy and play. Here, we become both mirror and mirrored, to amplify our gifts and celebrate the circle. We gather, unite and shine.

5. The **Fifth Turn** of the spiral is about the magic of letting go and its healing power. We learn to yield and shed what no longer serves. It's here where we let powerful Oya, the Goddess of Tornados, sweep us clean, and release the grip of our inner critic and perfectionist. We give it up. We let go. We do it with, and for, love.

6. At the **Sixth Turn**, we arrive after the release, ready to invite Wild Woman, and all that is wild, to guide us to a life with abandon - feral and free, spontaneous and juicy. Without script, apology, or regret. To be free, to feed our soul. To howl at the moon; run with the wolves.

7. And then, at the **Seventh Turn** - having met ourselves, another, and the world - we return to self, to love. Here, we bring back home the wisdom we've gathered, and integrate the experiences and lessons of our journey. We find the truth of who we are. We find acceptance. We find gratitude. We see the sacred.

8. At the **Eighth Turn**, our personal experience of the return to self longs to express and fulfil itself outwardly. We become of service. We share whatever goodness we've found, to be a source of light, solidarity and healing for others. To radiate and reflect, and be the divine mirror we are born to be!

And as we prepare to enter the process and cycle back around, we come to a potent liminal space. (Check out the **Epilogue**.) Here, we take a moment to pause, reflect, and honour the ways in which we can and do hold it all - the dark and the light, the tender and the wild, the mundane and the mystical. Everything. Feel it. Know it. Be with it all.

There it is - *the full spiral*. We begin with soft curiosity, and complete with gratitude, being a loving witness to the sacredness of our journey. But keep in mind, as spirals go, this ending is really just the beginning, the pre-requisite for the next whirl around the sun. The spiral dance keeps going. And so it is!

How to use the book:

Every part of this book has been carefully crafted to support you in exploring what that 'turn of life's spiral' might mean, or has meant, for you. They are 'mirrors' intended to reflect back to you your own glorious light! This is YOUR book.

At each turn - in each chapter - I tell a **personal story** which illustrates my own experience, sharing some of the geography of my own journey, from exploration and adventure, through love and forgiveness, from letting go to freedom.

Each personal story leads to **reflections** on that turn, and a collection of my finest, **well-loved practices** - expressive, healing and **inspirational prompts** and exercises.

I've enriched the journey with visual and acoustic experiences: **Artwork** (sent straight from my Muse), found here and in the companion *She Reflects Journal & Colouring Book* as **colouring pages**, and personally designed **music playlists** hosted on my website at www.EricaRoss.com/playlists. (I normally don't share my playlists. You're welcome!) *If you find artists you love, please show your appreciation by buying their songs.

Although each turn flows from the one before it, they are self-contained. You can read the book from front to back, or pick a chapter that calls to you and start there. Go at your own pace, and adapt or modify the practices as you need.

Work with whatever sections of the book resonate with you. LISTEN for a nudge, a wink or a YES. Let your gaze land on ONE or a combination of practices that feel right for you today. Some days you'll want to take a bath and read a book. Other days you'll feel called to walk in nature, or listen to a sacred chant.

Get creative:

- ◎ Print out copies of the colouring pages from the *She Reflects Journal & Colouring Book* and invite friends over for a colouring party. Share your creations on social media with #SheReflects. (Please credit Erica Ross for the original artwork. Thanks!)

- ◎ **Start your own She Reflects Book Club** - for support, partner and group practices.

- ◎ **Go to www.EricaRoss.com/playlists** and dance, dance, dance - alone, and with friends and family.

- ◎ **My personal favourite:** Make a cup of tea, pull out your *She Reflects Journal &*

Colouring Book, start the playlist for the part of the book you're on, and get cozy. Let the tunes and nourishment infuse your senses as you read and spiral your way home.

If you ever feel that what I suggest or say is out of your reach or even outrageous for you, please go ahead and turn the page! Take it or leave it. Trust your own wisdom. (And if you leave it, consider circling back around to it at a later date to see if there might be something of value there to investigate - a shadow piece to be healed, a perception to shift, a belief to let go of. Who knows?)

And always, always, <u>seek support</u> from a trusted therapist, friend or family member if and when 'stuff' comes up that feels too much for you to explore alone. (You don't need to do it alone, or be superwoman.)

Whatever you do, however you do it, remember... All paths lead us home if we ask for them to do so! All ways are sacred. There's no right or wrong, just here and now.

This is a sacred laboratory for your consciousness and a playground for your aspirations.

Because, here's the thing...

We are each of us extraordinary and brilliant.

In forty years of practicing creative, healing and spiritual arts, spanning four continents and countless countries, I have come to learn that we are the experts in our own lives. Each of us, individually, have our own innate wisdom which we can call upon to bring ourselves into the light. We have wonderful counsellors, yogis and teachers in our lives, sharing their wisdom. Yet, for each one of us to shine our own, unique light, the search begins within.

I believe we need to be, like Amaterasu - curious. And, we need to turn that curiosity inward on our own lives to find the answers we seek. In my experience, through the process of self-investigation, I've fallen in love with my own life and my place in it, and I've come to believe in limitless possibilities, in miracles, and in the magic of letting go.

May I take you for a delicious dive, a spin and a whirl? (Did I mention that Uzume means whirling?)

May this book, as Uzume does for Amaterasu, serve as a divine mirror, a mirror that will remind you of your radiant beauty and light, regardless of your race, mental or physical abilities, religious beliefs, colour, place of origin, gender, sexual orientation, size, age or income. May it validate your experiences - past, present and future.

After all... my beloved...

You are precious. You are perfect. You are powerful beyond measure.

You are LOVED.

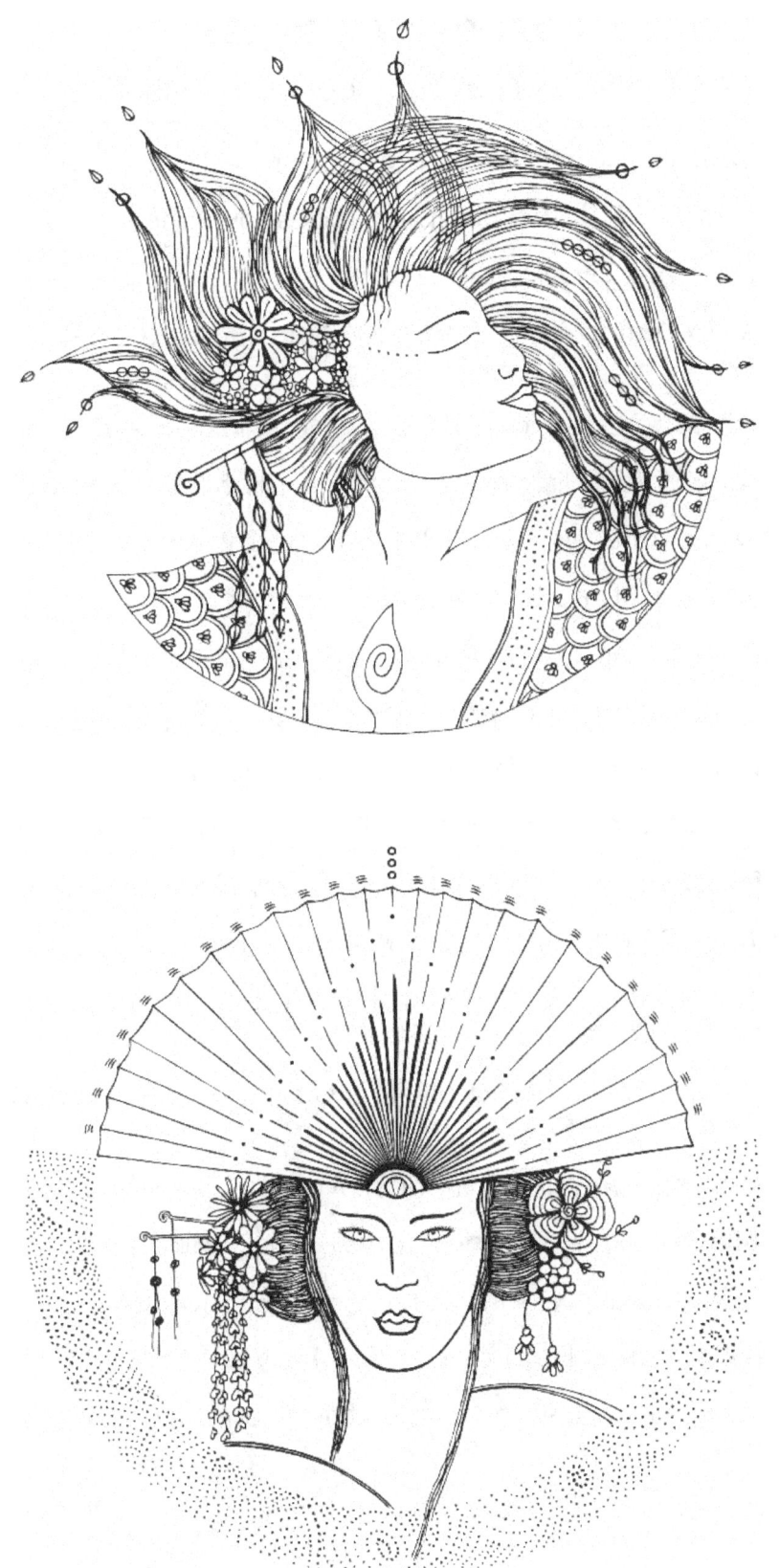

"Beauty is eternity gazing at itself in a mirror." Kahlil Gibran

Uzume's Playlist

Dance with love, laughter and abandon. Be the mirror. Serve.

1. **Ain't No Sunshine**, Bring It On Home, by Aaron Neville
2. **Nothing Compares 2 U**, The Hits/The B-Sides, by Prince
3. **Frozen**, Ray of Light, by Madonna
4. **Lose Yourself to Dance** (feat. Pharrell Williams), Random Access Memories, by Daft Punk
5. **Stomp** (Remix), The Essential Kirk Franklin, by Kirk Franklin
6. **Holy Mountain**, Vale's Nirvana Lounge, by Michiko Tanaka
7. **Pump Up the Volume** (UK 12" Mix), Pump Up the Volume - EP, by M/A/R/R/S
8. **Pump Up the Jam**, Pump Up the Jam, by Technotronic
9. **Gypsy Majik**, Frequency, by Naked Rhythm
10. **Temoine**, The Center of the World, by Ekova
11. **Eatnama Heagga** (Earth Spirit), Mannu, by Angelit
12. **Sisters** (feat. Northern Voice), Nation II Nation, by A Tribe Called Red
13. **Children of the Sun**, Buddha-Bar Clubbing, by Cosme Martin, Christian Vila
14. **The Sun Rising** (LP Version), The Sun Rising, by The Beloved
15. **Earth to the Sun** (Srikalogy to the Earth Remix), Rising: EarthRise SoundSystem Remix Project, by EarthRise SoundSystem
16. **Sing It Back** (feat. Samatha Sam), Slow Down, by Cesar de Melero & Mr. Claude
17. **Mouth** (Brad Peep's Remix for Friends), Mouth, by Iz & Diz
18. **Joro Boro** (BBB Remix), Nu Made (Remixes), by Balkan Beat Box
19. **Chacarron** (Radio Edit), Chacarron - EP, by El Chombo
20. **The Awakening**, Indian Electronica, Vol. 1, by Sharaab
21. **Hangappella** (ft Manu Delago), The Hang Drum Track (Miami Mixes), by Timo Garcia
22. **You Are the Sunshine of My Life**, Talking Book, by Stevie Wonder

Go to: www.EricaRoss.com/playlists

Amaterasu's Playlist

Dance yourself out of your cave.
Find and shine your divine beauty and light. You are never alone.

1. **All We Do**, Oh Wonder, by Oh Wonder
2. **Don't Give Up,** So, by Peter Gabriel
3. **Asia Experience,** Asian Lounge, by Skin 4
4. **Deliver Me**, The Sun Rising, by The Beloved
5. **Rise and Shine**, Later That Day…, by Lyrics Born
6. **Becoming More Like God** (feat. Holly Macve), by Jah Wobble & The Invaders of the Heart
7. **Dusted**, A Final Hit - The Best of Leftfield, by Leftfield & Roots Manuva
8. **Looking for the Sun**, Strange Flower, by Aya
9. **Higher Ground** (feat. Michael Marshall), Om Lounge, Vol. 13, by Shiny Object
10. **Divine**, Divine Operating System, by Supreme Beings of Leisure
11. **Wednesday Night**, Bryant Street, by Dubtribe Sound System
12. **Summertime** (Original Radio Mix), by Wass Feat. Earl T
13. **Flawless** (Italo Disco Mix), Flawless - EP, by The Ones
14. **Walking On Sunshine '82** (feat. Donnie Calvin), The Streetwise Sessions, by Rockers Revenge
15. **Sun Goddess**, Sun Goddess, by Ramsey Lewis and Earth, Wind & Fire
16. **The Creator Has A Master Plan**, Cool And Steady And Easy, by Brooklyn Funk Essentials
17. **Thank You For Hearing Me**, Universal Mother, by Sinéad O'Connor
18. **Let Your Light Shine**, Keep It Simple, by Keb' Mo'
19. **Golden Lotus**, Monsoon, by Asiabeat, John Kaizan Neptune, LAM, Lewis Pragasam & Ottmar Liebert
20. **Found My Light** (Acoustic Mix), Found My Light - Single, by Imaani
21. **Everybody Loves The Sunshine**, The Best Of Roy Ayers, by Roy Ayers
22. **I Am Light**, SongVersation, by India.Arie

Go to: www.EricaRoss.com/playlists

First Turn

Listen

"If speaking is silver, then listening is gold." Turkish Proverb

Soul Speaks

I was up to my ears in renovations. It was 1999 and I had just bought a house that really needed some tender loving care. My boyfriend was helping me out, thank goodness – it was my first venture into DIY.

My beautiful daughter was just seven at the time. While she was at school, I'd chip away at the renovations and, in the in-between times, I'd teach dance classes at the YMCA. It was the usual juggle - raising my daughter, building a career, creating a home. It was an exciting time, an intense time, and it was easy, right? (I'm joking!)

In the mornings, I had my routine down. It would begin with driving my daughter to school. Once I dropped her off, I would head over to a local cafe where I would read and write and think, and get my morning coffee on, which is really important in my world.

Mornings were my time. Afternoons? Not so much. They were spent back at the house working on the renovations where, note, there was no kitchen and no possibility of coffee!

At the Y, I was also teaching dance classes. I was the Program Director of their dance program and I liked it there. They were generous and supportive, providing everything I needed. I had a beautiful studio and license to create the programs I imagined. I created three dance programs: one for parents and their babies, one for parents with their toddlers, and one for parents and their kids, aged three to five.

Now, don't get me wrong; it was a great experience and I was grateful. But, honestly, I didn't love the work. It just wasn't my passion. What I really longed to do was be in community with WOMEN - to dance, celebrate and connect in a meaningful, spiritual and healing way with other women. Not to mention, I also wanted to be with people who had an attention span.

Dance and ritual were something I was already using in my life. I especially loved rituals that honoured Mother Earth and the Divine. I was practicing my own version of the Celtic Wheel of the Year.

In the 80s and 90s, I explored the body-mind-spirit connection, alternative healing, and Eastern and Indigenous wisdom teachings - from chakras, angels and crystals, to past lives, essential oils and breath work. I was initiated in Reiki and Kriya Yoga, and practiced Buddhist meditation, guided visualizations, Tai Chi and Qi Kung.

Above all else, I had fallen in love with the Goddess in all her expressions and traditions. The Great Mother. The All Encompassing One. The Divine Feminine. The Goddess Who Dwells Within and Without.

She became a beautiful teacher and guide for me. Through her embodiment and teachings, I felt - and still do - whole, complete, and deeply connected with the rhythms and cycles within and around me. The Goddess has helped me see my own and others' radiance and beauty, and the preciousness of ALL beings and all life around me.

My deepest desire for my work was to create a circle of women where together we would dance and heal, play and pray, explore and express ourselves. We would go deeply into delicious processes and get spiritual.

And, of course, include The Goddess, to support our re-awakening and re-membering of our true worth - that we are all sacred, beautiful and precious, in all our shapes, colours, sizes and expressions. To see each other as a goddess.

I absolutely longed for this. But, I held back.

I didn't have any kind of therapy background and I was concerned that if someone was triggered or had a kind of a breakdown or meltdown through the process, which can happen in this work, I wouldn't know what to do.

Even though I truly wanted to be doing this work, I wasn't confident in my ability to hold space for women in a deeper way. So I didn't (or didn't let myself) pursue my dream. Instead, I continued to teach dance to parents with kids who had short attention spans.

In the spring, I decided to learn to play the djembe. The djembe (or jembe) is an animal-skin covered, goblet-shaped drum played with bare hands. It's originally from West Africa. A six-week course was being offered by my friend at a local mall in Toronto. There were just four of us in the class, all women.

We were learning the very basics, from how to hold it, to how to create different sounds with different parts of our hand, to how to create different rhythms. It was inspiring and fun. The four of us really enjoyed playing together in our tight knit group. But when the course ended, the four of us went our separate ways.

Summer arrived and so did all the music festivals which I was planning on attending – of course. The first festival that summer was Afro Fest and who did I run into but one of the women from djembe class. Her name was Nancy.

I didn't know her well, or, really, at all. We were at different ages and stages of life. I was a mother raising a daughter. She was a good fifteen years younger than me, in her twenties, and she didn't have kids. We happily remembered each other from class and had a quick conversation and reconnection.

Delightfully, I bumped into Nancy again at the next festival. And the next. I would bump into Nancy at all the festivals that summer. Every. Last. One.

When autumn arrived, I was back into my morning ritual. I'd drop off my daughter at school; I'd head to the coffee shop for my cherished, can't-start-my-day-without-it cup of coffee; and I'd settle into my morning of reading and writing.

One day while I was reading, quite suddenly and out of the blue - and I mean right out of the blue - I heard this big, booming voice. Make that BIG and BOOMING. "Call Nancy," it implored. "There is something for you to do with her."

Actually, it sounded more like this:

"CALL NANCY. THERE IS SOMETHING FOR YOU TO DO WITH HER."

I thought, 'What the hell was that?' I had never in my life heard a voice like it. In fact, I'd never heard a disembodied voice, period!

And here was this one. So directive. So clear. And so loud!

I had to pay attention to it. More than that, I had to do it!

Of course, after all those chance encounters, I had Nancy's number.

I called her right away, and she picked up.

"Hi, Nancy, this is Erica from djembe class," I said. "This may sound very strange but, I just heard a voice tell me to call you, that there is something for me to do with you." (Yes, I told this woman, whom I hardly knew, that I'd heard a voice.)

I asked her if she would meet with me to explore what this might mean.

How did Nancy respond? "I am so honoured," she said, immediately.

We met just days later, at a neighbourhood restaurant. Sitting across from each other, I said, "Well, let's figure this out. Why don't we share our dreams, and see what happens?"

I told her about my dream of creating a Circle of Women.

"I have a strong dance background," I told her, "but I don't feel I have a strong enough background in therapy."

As I described my dream, her eyes grew bigger and brighter.

"My dream," she said, "is to have a women's group, which includes dance and ritual and prayer. I am a therapist, but I don't feel I have a strong enough dance background."

There it was. We each had the same dream. We each were the missing pieces for the other. Together, we could bring the dream into being. It was pure magic, and we knew we had to do it.

(Oh, can we just pause here for a moment? It has to be said: My higher self - or whomever that voice belonged to - is really, really smart! Okay, pause and due acknowledgment are complete.)

You won't be surprised to learn that Nancy and I got right down to business. We named our work "Transcendance: Dance as a Healing Path," a movement-based practice incorporating goddess mythology; voice, yoga, and ritual; archetypes and the elements.

And, all of it was combined with ecstatic dance - a free-form dance where we move from the inside out, without judgment. It was unlike anything else being offered in the city. We rented studio space in downtown Toronto. It was the perfect spot for us, down a long flight of stairs into a large room in the basement. It had a dance floor and high ceilings, and not a single window. We filled the dark, mysterious space with fairy lights and altars laden with images of goddesses, beeswax candles, scarves and shakers. The space was like a womb – contained, sacred and safe.

We spread the word through our own circles of friends, colleagues and clients. In just two months, quite effortlessly, we were up and running. Two almost-strangers met for coffee and literally weeks later, we introduced a new program. It was incredible.

Three weeks after our doors opened, the dance critic, Deidre Kelly, of the *Globe and Mail* called me. She was writing an article about Ecstatic Dance and someone had given her my number. She came to the studio to interview both of us and take pictures.

We recreated the ambience of the sessions with the fairy lights and an altar we'd set up and shared all the details of our new sessions. Ms. Kelly's article came out on October 23, 1999. People were calling us from Vancouver to Ottawa, and within weeks we were full.

It felt like divine timing. It felt like the universe was saying YES. YES to the work we were doing. YES to the classes we created. YES to our partnership. It all felt effortless and perfect, like we were doing exactly what was needed.

As it turned out, we were just getting started.

Nancy, who eventually shortened her name to Nan, suggested we create something for Sheena's Place, a sanctuary for people who struggle with eating disorders and body image issues. Two years after creating Transcendance, we co-created an 8-week program called Dance Our Way Home. Sheena's Place hosted us there for a decade.

Two years after introducing Dance Our Way Home, Nan and I co-created a new platform called "Expressive Healing," a series of programs in stress management and relaxation, and in expressive and spiritual arts.

It was a richly creative time for us. Nan and I worked so well together. Our classes were full, and our dreams were being realized. But, after five years of intense creativity and expansion, there were budget cuts at Sheena's Place.

We decided to split up the work. I would carry on with Dance Our Way Home, and Nan would go on to facilitate relaxation and chanting groups. Our paths were beginning to gently diverge. Our dreams realized, we could pursue what was next calling to us, each individually.

In 2007, I decided to take Dance Our Way Home beyond the walls of Sheena's Place.

With Nan's blessing and her full permission to take it in whatever direction felt right, I turned Dance Our Way Home into my business, and truly made it my own.

I created a website and rented space at a thriving three-story building of studios filled with dance of every description. I held workshops and regular classes. With love, clear intention and dedication, I built a community of devoted dancers. Just three years into it, I was offering facilitator certification training to pass the torch to others.

It's been almost two decades since I heard that 'Booming Voice' which implored me to "Call Nancy, you've got something to do with her." Little did I know a stranger would become my best friend and, together, we would create programs that would inspire and bring healing and joy to so many women.

Who knew it was the beginning of what's been my life's work for almost twenty years, which is to be a mirror and a facilitator through dance to help women see and shine their own light, much like Uzume.

That day in the restaurant, when I met with Nan, I felt a giant YES to dive in with both feet, even though we barely knew each other, even though we were entering uncharted territory. We both decided to follow the YES and trust.

At every step of the way, Nan and I *listened*, to both the loud and soft voices, to the external signs and the inner prompts that guided us; first, to come together to create, then, to diverge when the time was right, and, finally, to create our own work individually that continues to fuel each of us all these years later.

In the end, listening is a way to start any journey, the journey of a single day, or the journey of a life's adventure. To 'listen' means to pause, relax and soften, and then listen to whatever it is that gets your attention. It's an invitation to lean in.

What wisdom is coming to meet you where you are right now?

Give it space. Give it attention.

Listen for the signs. Listen for your YES!

Listen with your full and soft body.

Listen with your mind and heart.

Ask the question, "What would love do?"

Then, watch the magic happen.

And so it is!

Reflections

"Think of the world you carry within you...
Be attentive to that which rises up in you and set it above everything that you observe about you. What goes on in your innermost being is worthy of your whole love and attention. You must somehow keep listening
and responding to the inner call." Rainier Marie Rilke

LISTEN.... Shhhhhh....

What do you hear?

Do you hear birds singing in the distance? A buzz in your mind? Your breath? The wind blowing?

Listen up.

The universe (life) is talking.

It's talking to you all the time. It's a special conversation that only YOU can have with life, within and around you, seen and unseen.

Listening is how that dialogue happens. Listening is the way.

Sometimes it comes from deep within us, flowing out towards the world, like when we ask, "Where am I to go now? Show me the way, dear universe." And then we listen for the response. A sign. A doorway. A calling.

And other times, it flows directly from the world to us, from the outside in, like when we encounter, usually unexpectedly, an animal or person who seems to be speaking right to us. We sense they've come to offer a gift, a message, a teaching. It feels synchronistic. It feels right. And we respond in kind, with a fresh new idea, a question, a clear knowing, a bow of gratitude.

This exchange, this interaction and conversation, is vital to our journey.

Every moment of every day is an invitation to LISTEN. Inwardly. Outwardly. Separately and together. To practice, to honour, and trust in your own knowing. To listen compassionately to yourself and others. To listen, understand and respond to your own body-wisdom, to have the conversations that only you can have with the world.

If you don't prioritize the practice of listening - intentionally, openly and curiously - imagine what you might miss.

Will you hear the song of love? The call of the wild? The sound of opportunity knocking?

What soul relationships, magical encounters and genius ideas will be unrealized? What deeper feelings, profound truths and sweeter revelations will go unnoticed?

This goes for all of us. When we don't listen, we miss the deeper meaning. We miss the information needed to say yes, no or maybe. We misunderstand and misinterpret.

Because listening is the genesis for it all: For a life of meaning, for navigating a journey, for seeing in the dark. (We hear before we see, in fact.)

Listening is the connector to everything. To our own nuanced feelings. To others' heartfelt stories. To all of life's offerings.

Through listening, we find home. We find love. We find the divine.

It doesn't matter how you do it - whether you listen in solitude, by a river, in meditation or through doodling…

What matters is that you do it.

For me, dance, and especially my practice of ecstatic dance, has been one of my best ways in. To listen. Every time I touch the dance floor, I listen to my breath and impulses. I listen to the music, earth and spirit moving me. I hear all life dancing with me.

This is the power and magic of listening. It shapes and transforms who and how we are in the world through receptivity and reciprocity. It's not something you can force. Its power has nothing to do with that. Pausing, relaxing and softening have everything to do with it.

And so… as you dive into this Practice section, you'll see it unfolds through three steps, three doorways into fuller listening:

1 **Pause**
2 **Relax and Soften**
3 **Listen**

May these practices arouse your own conversations with the world.

May they carry you into the sweetest of moments.

May it be so.

Practices for the First Turn

Pausing Practices:

- Breathe
- Linger at the Threshold
- Be in Silence

Relaxing & Softening Practices:

- Be Kind to Yourself
- Slow Down with Body Flow
- Pamper Yourself

Listening Practices:

- Listen for Answers / Ask Questions
- Listen for Signs and Synchronicities
- Listen to Your Yoni

Playlist: Slow Dance

Pausing Practices

"Learn to pause ...
or nothing worthwhile will catch up to you." Doug King

Breathe

Breath is our constant companion. So constant, in fact, it's easily forgotten, especially when we're looking outside of ourselves for support or healing. We forget, unless we have challenges with it, that it even exists. And yet, our breath is one of our greatest allies if we let it be.

Conscious breathing is used universally in meditative and mindfulness practices, for inner awareness, peace, and presence. It's also used as a medical and therapeutic tool for improving breath function, accessing nonverbal memories, and opening to non-ordinary states of consciousness.

Yogis, Buddhists, therapists and trance dancers use it in Pranayama, Vipassana, Rebirthing, Holotropic and Integrative Breathing, and Transformational Breath, to name a few.

It's a beautiful practice to do when you're feeling scattered and overwhelmed and your mind is all over the map. And if you have worries, pain and stresses, consciously breathing can facilitate a kind of 'forgetfulness' - allowing your mind to forget about your concerns for a moment. This gives space for healing and renewal.

What I love most about utilizing the breath is the fact that you can do it for free in your own home, in your own time, in your own way. It's available to you right now. Conscious breathing, even for one minute, can change the quality of your day. Being with your breath offers a sweet pause.

Join me in a simple conscious breathing practice as a way to pause and give space to your mind and day. We'll do this in three rounds of four breaths each, counting as we fill up and empty out with life-giving breath.

In the first round we'll breathe with equal measure of inhale and exhale. Second round we'll lengthen the exhale. And third round we'll make the exhale audible with sound. And we'll complete it with an affirmation.

Everything that needs attending to will get done, but for now, let go of your to-do list, and JUST BREATHE.

(And here's a tip: As you bring attention to your breath, see if you can feel it moving vertically up and down to engage your parasympathetic nervous system, which is designed to naturally support rest and recovery.)

Here we go: 3-4 minutes

1 **Slowly breathe and inwardly count** with me, 4 full breaths.

Inhale, 1, 2, 3, 4   Exhale, 1, 2, 3, 4

Inhale, 1, 2, 3, 4   Exhale, 1, 2, 3, 4

Inhale, 1, 2, 3, 4   Exhale, 1, 2, 3, 4

Inhale, 1, 2, 3, 4   Exhale, 1, 2, 3, 4

2 Now, **lengthen your exhale** an extra count for the next 4 breaths.

Inhale, 1, 2, 3, 4   Exhale, 1, 2, 3, 4, 5

Inhale, 1, 2, 3, 4   Exhale, 1, 2, 3, 4, 5

Inhale, 1, 2, 3, 4   Exhale, 1, 2, 3, 4, 5

Inhale, 1, 2, 3, 4   Exhale, 1, 2, 3, 4, 5

3 Now, **on your exhale, make a sound, sigh or 'ahhhhh'** instead of counting, for the next 4 breaths.

Inhale, 1, 2, 3, 4   Exhale, 1, 2, 3, 4, 5

Inhale, 1, 2, 3, 4   Exhale, 1, 2, 3, 4, 5

Inhale, 1, 2, 3, 4   Exhale, 1, 2, 3, 4, 5

Inhale, 1, 2, 3, 4   Exhale, 1, 2, 3, 4, 5

4 Now, **end with chanting.** Chant an affirmation, silently or out loud, a few times. Use one of these or make your own:

Breathing in… "I am at peace." Breathing out… "I let go."
Breathing in… "I love myself." Breathing out… "I trust myself."
Breathing in… "I am loved." Breathing out… "I am loving."

This, my friend, is conscious breathing. Enjoy the afterglow. This is practicing PAUSE.

+++

"Pausing is the doorway to awakening." Patricia Donegan

Linger at the Threshold

In Esther de Waal's book *To Pause at The Threshold: Reflections on Living on the Border,* she describes a simple daily act in Japan:

"Before entering the house, the Japanese stand on the lintel in order to remove the shoes worn outside in the street. Upon entering the house, they put on slippers placed inside the door. This forces a very deliberate and conscious way of standing still, even if only for a moment, in order to show respect for the difference between two spaces, the outer and the inner; the preparation for the encounter with another person, another household."

I love this! I love the deliberate pausing, and honouring of the in-between, the liminal space. It speaks to me on so many levels, so much so that I have a session in Dance Our Way Home, 'Dancing in the Doorway,' inspired by this practice.

Thresholds feel like temples to me - sacred spaces of transition, mystery and decision making. Dwellings of the not-yet-known. Womb-like. Ambiguous. Inviting. Potent.

They are doorways between time, neither here nor there, between past and future. Between ending and beginning, between the feeling and acting. It's the moment of NOW, a potent place for inquiry and possibilities.

Musing on the potency of liminal spaces, I'm reminded of the Goddess of Crossroads and Thresholds, Hecate (Hek-uh-tay). It is there at the crossroads she lives - at home in the threshold places through which we pass.

Hecate was worshipped by the Greeks, Turks and Amazons, from pre-Olympian to Classical or Hellenic times, as a Goddess of midwifery, protection, ceremony, magic and divination. Her devotees ate and talked magic at 'Hecate Suppers,' and left food offerings for her at crossroads.

She's the Crone aspect of the 'Persephone, Demeter, Hecate' trinity. Sadly, over time, Hecate was degraded to the Goddess of Trivia (Latin for three ways) and her wisdom considered dangerous to the Christian faith.

And as she is a goddess after all, she is blessed with three heads - gifted with the ability to see three ways - past, present and future, to see the larger picture. She sits at the crossroads waiting to guide us with her vision, to see and share where we've been, and the possible paths we can take.

She is a silent witness at every major threshold of our lives. I've called on Hecate many times in my life when I've needed a wise counselor and midwife to hold me and sit with me in the dark of not-knowing until I could see the light. Until I knew the next move.

In this practice 'Linger at the Threshold,' the invitation is to pause, relax and wait awhile in the in-between space. This space is Hecate's home where it's still and spacious, like the silence between musical notes, like the space between words.

And, there, in that pause, wise Hecate will meet you and, perhaps, teach you the gift of larger vision, the ability to see past, present and future. You too can be Hecate - wise, magical and divine. Goddess without, becomes goddess within. Let this practice be a reminder of the magic and potency of pausing. Let the pause feel delicious.

Linger at the Threshold: 5 minutes or longer

1. **Find a threshold or doorway** you can pause in, without being disturbed for a while.
2. **As you are crossing the threshold or doorway, PAUSE.**
3. **Soften** your heart, breath and body.
4. **Make yourself comfortable** right there in the middle. Lean against the doorframe or sit.
5. **Close your eyes.**
6. **Invite a sense of spaciousness, timelessness.**
7. **Hold the mystery of not knowing** - the potency of this new moment.
8. **Have compassion and patience** as you rest in the doorway.
9. If you have a question or decision to make, **ask it now.**
10. **Call on Hecate to join you,** if you wish.
11. **Wait for divine guidance** to answer. Give yourself the time and space you need.
12. If you have no questions or inquiries, **just be where you are.**
13. **Trust whatever happens** in this magical in-between space.
14. **Listen for the inner cue** to complete and move on.
15. **Give thanks** to Hecate and to this moment.
16. **Cross over the threshold and carry on...**

Be in Silence

*"It doesn't interest me where or what or with whom you have studied.
I want to know what sustains you from the inside when all else falls away.
I want to know if you can be alone with yourself and if you truly
like the company you keep in the empty moments."*
Oriah "Mountain Dreamer" House, The Invitation

In this practice of pausing, the invitation is to *befriend silence*.

Befriend a silence which soothes the nerves, softens the heart, and relaxes the mind. Befriend a silence which deepens the capacity to listen more spaciously, to hear the unheard.

The kind of silence that's less about the absence of sound, and more about the quietening of inner clamour and clutter. A silence which empties us out, to be more open, available and present.

That's the kind of silence I'm talking about. Medicinal. Healing. Nourishing.

It's the antidote to busyness. Even when we love everything we do, at some point, without the counterpoint of silence, the goodness becomes too-muchness.

And that's when hitting the pause button is essential, to our wellness, our creativity, our soul, our peace of mind. Whether carving out ten minutes or an hour, this kind of silence (or pause) can dissolve the din of our lives.

Every dance needs its still point. Every life needs its silence.

There are many doorways to silence. You can enter from the inside out, by simply being silent, for example, or from the outside in by finding spaces of quietude. All that's needed is a desire for it, and your willingness to wait, be patient and often vulnerable.

When we become silent, our ears sharpen so we can - like the big bad wolf who exclaims, "the better to hear with, my dear" - better hear the still voice within, and the larger buzz of life moving.

Let's be in silence to join in on the symphony of the heartbeat, wind and swallow. Let's get quiet.

Let's get quiet. Deeply silent. Vast.

Doorways to Silence:

- Turn the **radio off in the car.**
- Turn **electronics off at home** (no TV, radio, music).
- Stay in **silence while doing chores**.
- When you wake up, **start your day in silence**.
- **Meditate.**
- **Gaze** - at a candle, a sacred object, a flower, your hands.
- Find **quiet spaces of solitude** - a park bench or church pew.
- Spend an **afternoon without talking,** everywhere you go. (Carry a pad and pen with you.)
- Go on a **week-long silent retreat.** THIS is a powerful pause.

First Turn: Listen   39

Relaxing & Softening Practices

"Be soft. Do not let the world make you hard. Do not let pain make you hate. Do not let the bitterness steal your sweetness."
Kurt Vonnegut, Jr.

We entered the pause between the notes, the space between the words,
and now it's time to relax and soften the edges
to further prepare the inner landscapes for deeper listening.

Be Kind to Yourself

"Go only as fast as your slowest part feels safe to go." Robyn Posin

I'm sure you've noticed how easy it is to be hard on ourselves. I'm pretty sure you've also seen evidence of it in your close friends and colleagues, in the people you love.

It's something we've all inherited, passed down through the generations, from our families, our schools, our communities, our culture, basically coming from the overarching concepts, guidelines and principles of patriarchy.

Life has taught us: Be tough, push hard, be aggressive, achieve more. It's exhausting. Harsh. Rough. Painful.

As if life wasn't hard enough, we amplify it by aiming our 'toughness' towards our own thoughts, hearts, bodies and deeds. Like a poison dart penetrating our heart and soul, it bleeds us. It's a recipe for illness, depression and stress. And it is contagious.

I know it's a difficult gig to give up, even when we intellectually and consciously know better. Old habits die hard, right?

But… even if it's wrapped deep around our bones, it's never too late to undo and release it. It's your responsibility and blessing to be kinder to yourself. It's in your power to be and act in devotion to yourself, with a compassionate and soft attitude. It's part of your personal healing, and part of the collective healing.

Because when you practice being kind to yourself, your boundaries will change around how you allow others to treat you and talk to you. When you speak and act kindly towards yourself, you'll want to do the same for others. And so it goes.

Your practice affects us all. We need you to practice, to be a way-shower and role-model for future generations to follow. We need you to utter kind words, and be a messenger of peace, love and kindness.

Having said that… please don't put pressure on yourself that you now MUST be kind. It doesn't work that way. That's the antithesis of what's needed.

Yes, my words are meant to spark you to get moving on the kindness path, for us all… AND to gently inspire you to **soften, soften, soften**. This is a gentle invitation. In other words, the last thing you want to do is push towards any goal here. It's all in the allowing and the relaxing.

As you engage with these 'kindness' practices, give full permission to yourself to take it slow. Be patient with yourself when you speak unkindly. Keep returning to love and compassion. You're doing the best you can.

Take it one day at a time. When you can, from moment to moment, remember, and slowly, over time, you'll return to your original self - the loving, kind and shiny being you were born as.

As all sages say... it starts with YOU! If you want love, be loving to yourself. If you want kindness, be kind to yourself.

Be Kind to Yourself:

- **Notice your inner dialogue.** Invite a curiosity and a listening to your inner voice, thoughts and feelings. Pay attention with love. When you catch a thought that undermines your sense of joy and self-love, pause and breathe. Give thanks to yourself for noticing, which is the first step in transforming it. If you are able, start a new inner dialogue.

- **Watch how you speak to yourself.** Your words carry weight. Tapping into kind words, especially when stressed, can be quite difficult. Be gentle on yourself when it's hard. And when you notice you're speaking harshly and disapprovingly to yourself, take a breath and drop into compassion. How would you speak to a loved one? That's the voice you need.

- **Be a loving witness to yourself.** Be a loving mirror for yourself. How do you hold loving space for another? Be that for yourself. See yourself tenderly and compassionately. With love, notice how you think, feel and act. Soften your judgments and criticisms.

- **Give space for mistakes.** Take the pressure off yourself to be perfect! No one needs you to be, and it's harmful to your sense of purpose and all that you have to give. Give yourself lots more space to make mistakes, to forget, to be out of balance, to be confused. Keep returning to love.

- **Invoke more gratitude.** When you're feeling hard on yourself, remember: You're doing the best you can! This may sound hokey, but really... there's only one you. Give thanks for being you, and give thanks in general.

- **Use affirmations.** Affirmations are powerful when repeated often. They help re-wire and integrate new ideas. It's good practice to say statements like: *"I love my big heart." "I am gentle with myself." "I am perfect as I am." "I am finding ways to be gentle with myself."* Or create your own.

- **Create a 'Words of Kindness' List.** What kind words can you write to soften yourself? Return to this list as a reminder and support on your healing journey. Use them to create your own affirmations.

"Kind words will unlock an iron door." Kurdish Proverb

Slow Down with Body Flow

"Do not push the river, it will flow by itself." Polish Proverb

Whatever it is that you are doing, consciously take it down a notch. Stretch out your pace.

Give yourself permission to ... do ... it ... s l o w l y.

SLOW it DOWN! At least from time to time. At least a little bit.

In Leonard Cohen's song, 'Slow,' Leonard sings of his innate preference (it was in his blood) to go slow - he never liked it fast. I appreciate this sentiment. I, too, don't like it fast. Never really have.

I've never found fast driving or speed reading exciting or appealing. I don't like feeling hurried to make a hasty decision. And being hyped up and supercharged don't work for me. I don't like rushing when I'm late, or when I'm operating on someone else's timing. It just doesn't feel good. I know that about myself.

Instead, I prefer to slow down and take my time. It's a choice. It's a way of being. And lately, since I've had pain in my body, it's become a need, not just a preference. (I had no idea I'd need to become a turtle.)

How about you? What's your favourite pace?

Regardless of your temperament, this invitation is to practice slowing down, to bring in a pause, to become a better listener. Even if zooming around feels more true to you than going in slo-mo, the suggestion still stands.

Because, honestly, there is a world of invisible and unheard life within and all around you, and it's impossible to really drink it in when you're moving at light speed. It takes time to simmer an idea, to receive a message, and to let things land. It does.

So why rush? Why not savour the moment. Conjure up a sense of timelessness, and trust there's more than enough time. Give yourself permission to soften, and meet the moment. With curiosity. Spaciousness. Openness.

Let's slow it down... with **Body Flow**.

Body Flow is part of the relaxation phase of my practice, Dance Our Way Home. We do this after a guided journey and BEFORE we go into the actual dances of the spiral journey, as a way of softening, slowing down, and getting out of the head and into the body. It's a simple process, like a body scan, moving from the head down to the feet, spending a few minutes with each body part.

Let's begin Body Flow: 20 minutes

Please note: Although these instructions suggest doing Body Flow in a standing position, moving through many body parts, please honour your own abilities: You can do this sitting or lying down, and with whichever body parts you can. (You can also use your imagination, if movement isn't possible.) In other words, do it your way, softly, slowly.

1. **Find 20 minutes of sweet slow music,** or play the **Slow Dance Playlist**.

2. **Begin your music** and stand somewhere where you have space to stretch your arms. You'll be standing mostly in one spot, but it's good to know you have room.

3. Start first by grounding yourself. Imagine that you are growing **roots** from the bottom of your feet. Feel them spiralling down past the floor, and into the ground below. Feel the energetic connection with Mother Earth, grounding and supporting you. This will allow you to relax and feel stable like a rooted tree in the breeze.

4. Once you feel grounded, begin to move your **head** in ways that feel good and right for you. Let your head be the lead while the rest of your body gently responds. Let your breath and face soften with each movement, and your neck and throat relax.

5. Now bring awareness to your **shoulders** and let them gently and easily move. Allow space in your shoulders. Let any weight or stress you might be carrying there float away. Find peaceful movements here. Let your shoulders lead the dance.

6. Now find your **elbows** and let them move and float. Love them. Feel them. Let the movement of your elbows melt your entire arms. Surrender them to movement and peace. Find flow in your arms.

7. Bring awareness down your arms into your **wrists, hands and fingers.** Soften your palms and let each finger melt and relax. Let your hands dance around you. Feel the space around your body. Bless yourself with your hands. Your hands and fingers are receptive and soft.

8. Find your **spine** now and begin to soften and relax your entire back. Gently stretch and bend. Invite fluidity and flow up and down your spine. Feel your entire nervous system relaxing with each movement of your spine.

9. Now, soften the front of your torso and let your movements come from your **heart** center. Feel your chest relax. Invite flow into your heart. Feel it relax open. Feel the flow of love moving in and out. You are loving and loved.

10. Bring awareness down into your **belly** now and invite a gentle softening of anything being held there. Do your own belly dance and honour whatever you feel there as you move. Feel a gentle uncurling and unwinding as your belly dances.

11. Now find your **hips and pelvis**. Invite an opening in your hips and relax your pelvis

with gentle movements of flow and peace. Feel the sweet power of your womanly hips. Find the natural flow of your hips in motion. Invite pleasure and peace there.

12 Move down into your **knees** now. Invite a melting of your legs. Feel yourself moving closer to the earth. Honour your legs and knees. Make spirals and circles with your knees. Let your knees and legs lead the dance.

13 And now, move all the way down to **ankles, feet and toes**. Soften your feet. Feel each toe relax and soften. Feel the gentle connection between the soles of your feet and the floor. Remember your invisible roots that ground you to the earth wherever you are.

14 **Come into stillness, close your eyes** and just notice what you notice, **OR let your feet begin to take you beyond your spot**, and enjoy moving freely with your whole body, as you please.

15 Give thanks.

Bonus Practice: Body Scan: 15 minutes

Lie down and get comfortable. Close your eyes gently. Invite a deep sense of relaxation by noticing the soft rise and fall of your belly as you breathe. Ground with the earth and drop into your body by imagining, sensing and feeling every part of your body softening. Begin either at your feet and flow up, or from your head flowing down. Take your time. Allow every cell of your body to be touched. Invite a melting open. When you are complete, give thanks. Slowly open your eyes. Welcome back!

+++

"Where are you hurrying to?
You will see the same moon tonight
Wherever you go!" Izumi Shikibu

Pamper Yourself

*"In every woman there is a Queen.
Speak to the Queen and the Queen will answer."* Norwegian Proverb

This practice invites you to give yourself, your inner Queen, full permission to treat yourself to something delicious - for your heart, body, mind and soul.

Your Queen within is a protectress and guardian of your wellspring, of your wellness. She wishes for you to feel warm, held and nourished. Especially after the daily grind, the pressures, the work.

She longs for you to say YES to bliss and all things yummy. To turn guilty pleasure into joyful pleasure. She says, "You can never have too much pampering. Life is meant to be lived with gusto, with juice."

She knows this life - your life - is not meant to be dry, dull or barren. Oh yes… she knows all too well what happens when you don't invite pleasure in, and deprive yourself of even the simplest sweetnesses.

You, dear Queen of Queens, deserve to be spoilt. You deserve to be indulged, and to feel delight, pleasure and relaxation. (Yes, *you*, who thinks you have no time or feel unworthy to receive such frivolities.)

Do you know what your inner Queen loves?

Do you know what gives her pleasure and delight? If you don't, then it's time you did. There's no time to waste.

Begin wherever you are, with whatever means you have. There's a full spectrum of delicious possibilities. Get creative. Listen to your needs. Ask the Queen what she needs.

Maybe it's going to a matinee movie in the middle of your work day, curling up with a book or treating yourself to really good chocolate. Maybe it's going to a flow yoga class, hiring someone to clean your home, or simply allowing yourself to sleep in.

And remember, a little goes a long way when it comes to feeling pampered. A bon-bon, a quiet morning, a foot rub. The Queen in you will appreciate it. She will gladly return the favour, anytime. So listen in. Listen to your needs.

Say yes to pleasure and play and comfort.

This is a soothing antidote to the daily grind, pressures and hard work of being a strong, capable woman. Relief for weariness, burn out and overwhelm.

This is self-care, baby. This is self-love. Isn't this the kind of practice you want to do EVERY DAY?

Here are some delicious pampering suggestions:

- **Wrap yourself in fabric.** Mmmmm. Regardless if it's a silk sari, rayon sarong, wool blanket or velvet cape, enjoy the pleasure of being wrapped up like a baby swaddled. It's a sensual and comforting experience.

- **Cuddle up with a loved one,** human or animal. There's nothing like cuddling with someone you love - to be touched, held and loved. It's healing for the heart and soul.

- **Light a candle** or two or more. Beeswax or soy is best. (Stay away from paraffin and artificial scented candles, please. They really are toxic. Enjoy the soothing and flickering dance of the flame and the wafting natural smells.

- **Wear soft clothes** that make you move and feel beautiful, relaxed and fluid. Choose colours and textures that bring out the Goddess in you. This is all about you feeling good in your own skin!

- **Take a long luxurious bath.** With bubbles, bath salts or essential oils. Light a candle, pour yourself a glass of wine, and put on some soothing music. Ahhhh....

- **Treat yourself to a bouquet of flowers.** You don't have to wait for someone else to gift them to you. Find a florist, a grocery store, or garden center, and go with the bouquet that lights you up. Treat yourself. You deserve it!

- **Get a manicure and/or pedicure.** It's such a simple thing, but go to a nail salon and feel like a queen. Enjoy the pampering - the cleaning, massaging and touching, and time for relaxing and receiving.

- **Create your own home spa.** Give yourself self-massage or a facial, have a beautiful bath, do your nails, whatever it is that feels delicious and relaxing. Take as much time as you can.

- **Book a massage.** Do you know a gifted and loving healer who offers healing touch, reiki, Swedish or Thai massage, Lomi Lomi, or reflexology? Book an appointment, and melt away! (Or invite a friend over to exchange massages.)

- **Go on a spa retreat.** Is there a local or far-away spa you've always wanted to go to? Treat yourself to this luxury, this healing, this rest. For a day, a weekend, or a week.

"Caring for myself is not self-indulgence, it is self-preservation, and that is an act of political warfare." Audre Lorde

Listening Practices

"There is more wisdom in listening than in speaking."
Nilotic Proverb

We softened the edges of body, mind and heart.
And now the listening truly begins.

Listen for Answers / Ask Questions

"Mind knows the questions, soul knows the answers." Amit Ray

Questions yield great power and mystery. They have the remarkable ability to close us down in the recoil of being touched by the answer, or to crack us wide open in the revelation of the touching.

In so doing, with the right question, it carries the potential to change your life. Veils drop to the floor, mysteries reveal themselves, and answers speak with a thousand tongues.

It's the terrain of the unknown, of deep reflection, vulnerability and honesty. It's provocative, life-giving and beautiful.

Anything is possible in this magical realm of asking, especially when we let the question live in us. There's extra potency in the holding. In holding the question for as long as is needed. As long as it takes for it to be understood in all languages. Body. Heart. Mind. Soul.

And so it is... in this practice of deeper, more active listening, let's start with self-reflection - questions to focus your heart and mind, to bring loving and soft awareness to the depths of your truth.

May they open you, and shine a light on your own unique and beautiful truth. Always.

We begin...

1   In your own way, in your own time, **find a place to rest and relax.**

2   **Tenderly invite any and all of the questions on the next page to inform and guide your way.**

3   **Give them space.** See what bubbles up. Hold and rest in these questions as long as you need.

4   **Notice what you notice.** Sensations. Impulses. Words. Colours. Emotions. Or perhaps nothing at all. Trust whatever comes.

5   **Record your answers and give thanks.**

Relax into these questions:

- How can I invite magic into my life?
- How can I soften?
- How can I listen?
- How do I love myself?
- How do I nurture my soul?
- What am I afraid to hear?
- What am I letting go of?
- What am I moving towards?
- What do I deserve, no matter what?
- What do I long to say yes to?
- What needs to be embraced?
- What am I waiting for?
- What is available for me today?
- What is most alive in me right now?
- What moves me?
- What new story am I ready to live?
- What would bring joy and meaning into my life?
- What would I like to see in my life?
- Where is my healing path?
- When was the last time I amazed myself?
- When was the last time I celebrated myself?
- Where do I dim myself in the face of external circumstances?
- Why am I here?

And my favourite... Apply it to a situation you find yourself in:

- **What Would Love Do?**

Listen for Signs and Synchronicities

For more years than I can recall, I've been acutely aware of signs and synchronicities.

At first I had no idea why or how this awareness came to me. Was it purely intuition, a hunch? I really didn't know. I only knew that I did, and that I couldn't *not* see them.

I also didn't understand why others around me didn't see them the way I did. My family and friends dismissed them as coincidence, disregarding what to me felt significant and purposeful. They saw them as merely a chance occurrence, nothing more.

But for me, these 'chance occurrences' carried weight. They held messages. They felt magical, meaningful and important. They were, to me, sign posts affirming my path, that I was in the right place at the right time. To keep going. Keep listening. Keep noticing.

And the more I noticed, the more they happened.

It wasn't until 1993, when I read the novel *The Celestine Prophecy* by James Redfield, that I found my validation. In the book, there are a series of insights, and to my surprise synchronicity was the FIRST!

It was a pivotal moment for me to realize I wasn't the only one listening to signs and synchronicities. And regardless of what you may think of the book, I am grateful to it for confirming my own truth, and discovering there were others like me!

Since then, I've met many who believe in listening to signs and synchronicities. In fact, I'd say that almost all my friends do! This awareness is part of our makeup, of my people. We see signs. We notice and pay attention to these magical moments.

And as I have evolved spiritually, I now see synchronicity in a clear way. I now consciously understand the relevance and necessity for it in my life. I see that life is always speaking to us/me, continually offering signs and synchronicities as a means of communication. It's part of that intimate conversation with life.

Do you experience these magical coincidences too?

Regardless if you do or don't, the invitation in this practice is to consciously recognize the flow and sequence of messages and signs that move you along your path.

Perhaps, give yourself a week of intentional engagement with the practices of your choice below. Follow the bread crumbs. Connect the dots. Stay open and curious, and trust your 'listening.' Let it be a sacred experiment, a divine flow.

Are you ready to practice connecting the dots and seeing the signs? Magic is afoot!

Here are some ways to connect to that magic:

- **Start your day with curiosity.** Ask yourself… 'Who will I meet today?' 'What signs will shape my life direction?' 'What event might lead me to an opportunity?'

- **Watch for anything that calls your attention.** Stay playfully alert. See what resonates and leaps out at you. Take special notice of signs on the sides of trucks, billboards, car license plates, songs on the radio, or the time on the clock.

- **Follow your intuition.** Think about an idea, vision or question you have about an aspect of your life. A new move, your job, travel. Then let it go. As you go about your day, follow your hunches. See what happens! See if they lead you right to that vision.

- **Connect the dots. Follow the bread crumbs.** With no specific question or idea in mind, playfully follow signs and synchronicities. This is all about practicing being in flow, listening, and keeping the feeling of your life unfolding around you.

- **Notice repetitions:**

    - **Themes and images.** You see a post on FB about *elephants*, then flip on the TV and there's a documentary on them. You go to a tea shop and they serve your tea in a cup with *elephants*! That's a good prompt to look up the meaning of *elephants* as a personal 'spirit animal,' or think about what elephants symbolize for you.

    - **Numbers.** I've been seeing 11:11 or 1111 almost every day, for over thirty years. I know many who do. Or they see 1234, or 222 or 333. What about you? Practice listening through numbers and see how it brings more magic, curiosity and adventure to your day.

- **Listen to nature.** All of nature speaks. Go into nature and find a spot to pause, rest and listen for signs and synchronicities. Sit by a river. Sit in your backyard. Or take a long meandering walk in a park or a wilderness trail. Open yourself, your senses and sense of self, to live more fully in the presence and reciprocity of all things, seen and unseen. Give thanks.

Track your experiences in your journal.

Listen to Your Yoni

The yoni* has been worshipped all over the world.

I'm referring to the Sanskrit word for female genitalia, the sacred symbol of the Divine Feminine, the 'Womb of the World.' Yoni is a sacred space, an energy, a portal.

It's a doorway to love and intimacy, the seat of female sexual power, the source of creativity. This knowing goes back for millennia. One of my favourite examples is in Ireland, where, prior to the sixteenth century, female figures with wide open yonis were carved above church doorways. (Look up 'Sheela Na Gig'.)

*Because of its sacred and spiritual context, I'm using the word yoni, rather than vagina. I've also chosen to use the pronouns HER and SHE.

Have you ever sat and listened to your yoni?

My intention for including this practice is two-fold: To use it as a tool for self-discovery and directly access the wisdom, truth and stories of your yoni, AND, as a remembrance and honouring of your sacred sexuality, your sacred body and temple. For healing. For knowing. For love.

Within the yoni is a wealth of information, past, present and even future. Past hurts, present loves, future desires. The more you know about yourself, the better the choices you can make, and better choices create a better life, yes?

And because your nature is fluid and ever changing, including your sexuality, it's essential to listen in, to shine the light on your yearnings, sexual preferences and rhythms, to know what's right for you now. No two days are you the same, and this practice is made for that reveal.

How will you know what you truly need or desire if you don't listen? Not just to your heart and head, but to your yoni.

As you dive into listening to your yoni, listen with respect, open curiosity and compassion, like you would to your heart. Be a loving witness, without judgment.

Hold sacred space for her veils to drop, to feel safe to express her truth. There's a remembrance in her fabric, in her being. You may or may not know consciously what stories are held there. And believe me, there are stories.

She may be shy and it will take patience and some coaxing. She may be chomping at the bit, having waited a lifetime to be heard. She has much to tell.

Every time I do this practice I uncover a new story, a deeper truth in which I feel a sweet appreciation and compassion for her. It also brings up many emotions and tears. It's a natural response to being with her.

The gifts of listening to your yoni are vast - A deeper love, kindness and appreciation for yourself. New insight, understanding and truth. More compassion, power and healing. It's a sacred road of self-discovery. It's at the holy womb of co-creation where you'll learn more about the essence of the Divine Feminine.

The yoni is a great teacher, for a woman learns true self-love, sovereignty and self-respect. Your yoni has been through a life of experiences, some of which are painful and wounding, while others are delicious and life-giving. Hold this listening with the gentlest gloves. Honour, acknowledge and send love to it all.

*Please read this before starting: Due to the deep nature of this practice, it may trigger past traumas and wounds you may or may not know about. If it ever becomes too intense, soften your breath. Come back to love. Know you are in control and can stop at any time. If you can, remember gratitude as you end. Don't hesitate to reach out for support afterwards - a friend, a loved one, or therapist. Know that you are held and loved.

Here's the practice: 20 minutes minimum

1. **Find a private space** where you won't be interrupted. **Turn off your phone.**
2. **Lie down or sit** comfortably.
3. **Close your eyes,** and rest or **cup your hands on your yoni.**
4. **Relax and breathe** softly into your hands and yoni for a while.
5. **Tune into your yoni. Begin a dialogue with her.** Tell her you wish to know more about her, and that you love her.
6. **Ask your yoni any questions you wish:**
   How do you feel? What do you need?
   What do you long for? What do you love?
   How can I be of service to you? What stories are you holding?
7. **Listen with deep love and compassion** for any stories, feelings, thoughts, impressions, images or words to emerge in your consciousness.
8. **Trust** whatever arrives. **Let your emotions flow.** Cry, laugh, moan. Be with her.
9. ***If it's feeling too intense,** slow it down. Come back to your breath. Come back to your heart. Return to love.
10. **Stay present** until it feels complete.

54   *She Reflects: A Spiral Journey for the Feminine Soul*

> **11 End with gratitude.** Tell her you'll protect, love and cherish her. Give thanks to her.
>
> **12 Give yourself three full breaths and open your eyes.** Slowly orient yourself back to the room.

You may wish to record your experience in your journal. And if you feel extra fragile or overwhelmed by painful emotions or memories, please be gentle with yourself. Find comfort and support.

May you continue to honour, know and love your yoni.

May you remember your Divine Feminine wisdom, beauty and power.

As we complete the First Turn…

May you honour the nudges, longings and desires that arose.

May you cherish what you found.

May you continue to listen to the deeper and sweeter guidance and truth.

May you act on your behalf.

May you keep pausing.

May you keep relaxing and softening.

May you keep LISTENING.

Slow Dance Playlist

Relax, drop in and melt into your dance. Listen within. Be in flow.

1. **Grounded**, Breathing Space (re-release), by Sacred Earth
2. **Spirit Connection**, Spirit Connection, by Brenda MacIntyre
3. **Matinal**, Existir, by Madredeus
4. **Above The Sound Of Gravity**, Above The Sound Of Gravity, by Michael Moon & Laura Nashman
5. **Sacred Beach**, Zen Notes, by Nadama & Shastro
6. **You and I Are Falling, You and I Are Free**, The Sails of Self, by Rising Appalachia
7. **Svetasvatara Upanisad**, Bliss, by Sarmila Ray
8. **Nana: The Dreaming**, Weaving My Ancestors' Voices, by Sheila Chandra
9. **Mystery**, Sugaring Season (Deluxe Edition), by Beth Orton
10. **Blow the Wind**, Blow The Wind - EP, by Jocelyn Pook
11. **Make Sacred Space**, Goddess Chant: Sacred Pleasure, by Shawna Carol
12. **Easy** (feat. Norah Jones), Breathing Under Water, by Anoushka Shankar & Karsh Kale
13. **Idé Weré Weré**, Love Is Space, by Deva Premal
14. **Har Mukanday**, Awakened Earth, by Mirabai Ceiba
15. **Ambar**, Ambar, by Maria Bethania
16. **The Way You Dream**, 1 Giant Leap, by 1 Giant Leap
17. **Lost In The Labyrinth**, Beyond This Plane Of Existence, by Deosil
18. **Om Shanti**, World Spirituality Classics 1: The Ecstatic Music of Alice Coltrane, by Alice Coltrane
19. **Get Back to Serenity** (Beach Mix), Beauty, by Vargo
20. **Divine Mother**, Calling You Home, by Samart
21. **Moments In Love**, Daft, by Art of Noise
22. **Slow**, Popular Problems, by Leonard Cohen

Go to: www.EricaRoss.com/playlists

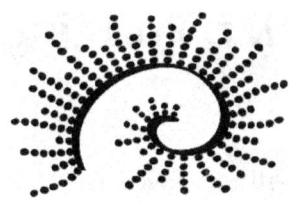

Second Turn

Follow Your Impulse

"Travel far enough, you meet yourself." David Mitchell

Part 1. Mr. Pudding Shop

I was ready for change.

I had just finished high school, something I was more than happy to leave behind, and I was way past ready to get out of the suburbs where I had lived all of my (18 years of) life.

I was a hippie and I wanted to be free. I loved adventure; I'd been a wanderer since the age of two and I wanted sex, drugs and rock and roll. It's true. I wanted that scene.

Yes, I was definitely ready for change.

I had my sights set on Europe. Well, my best friend and I did. Then she had to cancel and I had to decide: Do I cancel, too? Or do I go alone? Go alone. I didn't even think twice about it. It was time for me to spread my wings and, with the blessings of my family and boyfriend at the time, away I flew.

My destination was Greece. The Greek islands to be exact. My parents had been there years before and it had become my dream to see the islands for myself. Greece via Amsterdam was the plan.

When I boarded my flight that October, I was just days shy of turning 19. The year was 1973. It was the era of hippie trails and hippie buses. The 'American Express' office in Amsterdam was the hub for people looking for rides around Europe.

Once I landed in Amsterdam, I headed right over to American Express to see about getting a ride to Athens. Sure enough, I met a couple who had a van and were planning to drive through Athens to Istanbul. Perfect. I gave them a little bit of cash to reserve my seat, and in a few days we'd be leaving together for Athens. The couple seemed nice; the timing was right; I had the whole back of their van to myself. What could go wrong?

One day before we were set to leave, I got a call. "We've changed our itinerary," they told me. "We're going to go to Istanbul first, and then to Athens. Oh, and another traveller from Canada, a guy, will be joining you in the back."

Honestly, I didn't see that coming. I had two spontaneous reactions. The first: 'Damn. Now, I'm sharing the back seat.' And, then: 'Istanbul? I'm not sure I'm good with that.'

The back seat aside, I didn't know anything about Istanbul, and I knew even less about that part of the world. (It wasn't taught in school or featured in the media at that time.)

I expressed my concerns to them, that it kind of scared me to go to a place I knew nothing about. But they said it would be fine.

"We'll be with you," they said. "No worries," they said. "We're only going to be in Istanbul a few days, and then we'll continue on to Athens. You'll be safe."

And I believed them.

Second Turn: Follow Your Impulse

The drive was easy and smooth. We wound our way through Germany and Austria, down the coast of Yugoslavia, across northern Greece and down to Istanbul. It was a truly beautiful drive, and, along the way, I had my 19th birthday. In truth, other than a slightly annoying fellow passenger - a fellow Canadian no less - all went really well.

It took two full days and nights of driving before we arrived at the outskirts of Istanbul. We arrived around 9:00 p.m., and the couple decided they didn't want to drive all the way into the city that night. Instead, they drove into a campground. My back-seat buddy seemed fine with this, but I wasn't. It totally caught me by surprise.

"Wait a minute," I said, "I don't have a tent. I thought we were going to stay in a hotel. It's night time. We're in a campground. I can't stay here."

Without blinking an eye, they said, "Well, we noticed a bus stop on the road, just before the entrance to the campground. We're sure the bus will take you into town."

And just like that, they ditched me.

Yep. My worst fears were playing out. After telling me I was going to be safe, after convincing me it was okay to make the trip to Istanbul instead of Athens, all of a sudden, I was on my own.

Deflated, with my knapsack on my back, I hit the road. I made my way to the bus stop on foot, and stood there waiting in the dark for a bus that would, hopefully, take me to Istanbul.

And by the way, this was not the days of Google maps and iPhones. I had no idea where the hell I was going! Did I know the city? Did I know anything about it? Nope. Nothing. I really had no idea what I was getting myself into.

Sure enough, a local bus to Istanbul arrived within the hour and I got on - by myself. I was scared out of my mind - I didn't speak the language, I didn't know where I was, I didn't know what to expect. As we made our way into the city the bus stopped often, allowing people to get on and off.

As we travelled, I realized I had no notion of where tourists would stay in the city. I mean, once we got to the city, I really had no idea where to go. Luckily, but thankfully, after about an hour, the bus took me to the tourist part of town, and to my great relief, I found a decent hotel.

I had a restless night, to say the least. When I got up in the morning, I made my way over to a place called the 'Pudding Shop,' which was right around the corner. It was famous at the time, not that I knew about it.

It quickly became obvious it was like the American Express office of Amsterdam. It was the place where tourists, travellers, and especially hippies would congregate, share stories, and make plans to travel. It was the meeting ground.

That very first day, I met the manager of the Pudding Shop. I don't remember his name but I had a nice conversation with him. "I'm from Toronto," I told him. "I'm new. I'm going on to Athens." And then, I told him that I love to dance.

Well, that seemed to get his attention right away. "Dancing?" he said. "Me and some of the travellers from the Pudding Shop are going out dancing tonight to a club. Come with us."

I was over the moon. A dance club in Istanbul - fantastic! We made a plan to meet back at the Pudding Shop later that evening, and the whole group of us would go to the club together.

I looked forward to it all day. Dancing makes me feel grounded and at home wherever I am. At the designated time, I returned to the Pudding Shop to find not a single soul waiting to go dancing. No one, that is, except for the manager.

Mr. Pudding Shop said, "You know what, the others are meeting us there. Let's take a cab and go."

"But my hotel has a curfew," I said nervously. "It closes its doors at midnight. I absolutely have to be back by midnight."

(I should have said, are you kidding me?! I'm not getting into a cab with you. I don't know you. I don't know where we're going. No, thank you.)

"Don't worry, I'll get you back on time. You can trust me," he said. "I'm the manager of the Pudding Shop. You know where I work. It will be fun and I'll get you back on time. No problem."

'You can trust me.' Famous last words.

With that, I climbed into a cab. And for the second time in a matter of days, I got into a vehicle with someone who said, "Don't worry, it will be fine."

The trip seemed endless. We drove and drove and drove through the city, further and further away from my hotel. Suddenly, the reality hit me that we were heading to a part of Istanbul that I knew nothing about, not to mention I didn't have the address or phone number for my hotel. I couldn't believe I'd put myself in such a predicament.

At last, we arrived at the dance club. It was more like a restaurant with a dance floor carved out in the middle between all the tables and chairs. The club was filled with locals, no one was speaking English, and there was not a single traveller to be found.

Mr. Pudding Shop said to me, "They're coming. They're coming! Don't worry. The other travellers are coming."

Perhaps they were coming, but at that point it didn't matter. I felt really uncomfortable. I was in an unknown part of the city and I was with a guy I knew nothing about. I realized I'd made a huge mistake. A huge mistake. I decided that all I could do was make the best of it and hope he was telling the truth.

Thankfully, there was the dancing. The music was American and Turkish pop and disco, and the dance floor was packed. The two of us got up and started to dance. Nothing slow. Just fast. What a relief to be dancing. It took my mind off my worries.

We must have been dancing for about an hour when, out of the blue, he loudly said to me, and I'll never forget this, "While you're in Istanbul, you'll only go out with me."

"What?" I was completely shocked. "But I'm not going out with you. This was just supposed to be a bunch of us going out dancing. This wasn't supposed to be a date, or anything like it." I couldn't believe what I was hearing.

He got really angry with me and said, "You bitch! You don't go out with me one night and another man the next night."

It was soul-shaking. I had never in all of my 19 years had anyone call me a bitch. I didn't understand what was going on. I was frightened, confused and unsure of what to do. Then I had a flash. I remembered the couple from the van. They would save me. I only had another day or two at the most. We would be leaving for Athens in no time, and leaving this horrible man behind.

Then, Mr. Pudding Shop switched gears and said, "Some people here want to go to a house party. Let's go."

"Sorry, but I can't," I firmly told him. No way was I going to a party with him. "It's getting close to my curfew and I have to get back to the hotel."

He didn't listen. He just got angrier, I could feel it. I knew I had to get out of there. He kept insisting we go somewhere else. That was it! Now, I was pissed off.

I told him, "I'm not going to go anywhere else with you," and I walked off the dance floor and onto the street.

As I got into a cab, Mr. Pudding Shop jumped in beside me. He said something in Turkish to the driver and we took off.

"Where are we going?" I asked anxiously.

He said with a serious face, "I'm taking you to my place."

"Stop the car," I demanded. "Let me out of this car!"

Mr. Pudding Shop looked at the cab driver and said, "Stupid Americano," and he waved his hands as if to say, 'Ignore her. Ignore her.'

I started to scream at the driver, "I want to get out. I want to get out of this car now!"

And that's when it happened. He hit me. Hard. He slapped me right across my face. I was stunned. I wasn't even sure what had happened. I started to cry.

In a quiet, shaken voice I told him, "I don't want to go back to your place. I want to go back to my hotel."

From that point on, I didn't say another word, except to myself. I said, 'Oh Erica. You really screwed up this time. You're probably going to be raped tonight. You might not survive the night.'

I sobbed. I moved as far away from him as I could in the back seat while he and the cab driver carried on laughing and talking. It was two against one.

Quite a few minutes passed by. Actually, I'm not even sure how long we were in the cab but, eventually, it stopped - right in front of the Pudding Shop. I was shocked to see it. Shocked and relieved. I knew I could find my way back to my hotel from there. I knew I could get safe once I was out of the car.

As he let me out of the car, he said, "Don't you ever show your face at the Pudding Shop or I'll slap it again."

I ran back to my hotel as fast as I could and I cried myself to sleep.

The next morning, I felt completely lost. The Pudding Shop was the only place I knew in Istanbul and I was too scared to go there.

I began to wonder where the couple who drove me to Istanbul might have gone. They hadn't shown up in town as they'd promised. I had no idea where they might be at that point. I felt completely abandoned. I didn't know anyone. I didn't know the city. And no one knew where I was. No one.

I went downstairs to the lobby to figure out what to do next, and standing there was an unassuming, friendly looking gentleman, most likely Turkish, who asked me, "Were you the woman crying last night?"

"Yes," I said haltingly, "it was me." I replied with surprise.

He spoke English fairly well. "Why were you crying? What happened?"

I cautiously told him the story. I felt a sense of relief to tell someone what happened, and I was touched that someone cared enough to inquire about me.

He said, "I'm Frankie. I work at the Pudding Shop. I know this manager. This man, he's done this before. He never really hurts women, but he likes to scare them. That's not okay," he said. "Would you go to the police with me and tell them, because it's not okay what he's doing."

I thought, do I really want to go to the police? What have I gotten myself into?

He pushed further, "This guy needs to be stopped. He keeps doing this. You can stop him.

I'll go with you. I know them. We can go together."

Reluctantly, I agreed. We would meet later and go to the police.

The police station was more like a police office, and it was specifically for tourists. Inside the small square room there were two desks, two police officers, and much to my surprise - and concern - the manager of the Pudding Shop. He was in bad shape. He'd been beaten up and looked a mess.

In my head, I scrambled to figure out what was going on - Frankie must have called the police before we got there.

One of the policemen asked me, "Is this the man that hurt you yesterday?"

"Yes," I said, and apprehensively explained my experience to them. I told them that he slapped me in the face and that he threatened he would hit me again if I went back to the Pudding Shop. He really terrified me.

Mr. Pudding Shop cowered. I could see he was completely shattered.

The policeman asked, "What would you like us to do with him? If you want him to go to jail, we can put him in jail. If you want us to beat him up again, we can beat him up. If you want us to let him go, we can let him go. You choose."

As the police asked me to choose, the manager of the Pudding Shop got down on his knees, grabbed my legs and begged me, "Please. Please. Please. Don't have them put me in jail. Don't let them beat me up again. Please. Please. Please. I promise I won't touch you again. I promise, I promise. Please, let me go. Please, let me go. I promise I won't do this again."

I was stunned to have been given the power to choose the fate of Mr. Pudding Shop. How was I to know? Don't judges make those decisions? What was the right thing to do? I'd never had anyone's life in my hands before. And I didn't want to cause him any more harm.

And then, somehow, it struck me. I knew what to do, and it felt right. (At least, it was the best I could come up with.)

"I don't want him arrested this time," I nervously said to them. "But I want to be able to go to the Pudding Shop and to feel safe. I need him to stay away from me. So, I'd like you to give him this warning: If he even looks at me, I will ask you to put him in jail."

Without looking at me, Mr. Pudding Shop said, "I promise, I promise. I won't look at you. Thank you, thank you, thank you."

"OK, you are free to go," one of the policemen said. "But, if you look at her, we will come after you."

And he hobbled out.

(In retrospect, I can see how the power dynamic was confusing and complex, and there's a good chance that my white, Western identity played a part in why they gave me that power.)

I left shortly afterwards with Frankie, the kind man who came to my rescue at the hotel. He was an older man. Well, not that old. I was 19. So he was probably in his 40s, about the same age as the Pudding Shop manager. He walked me over to the Pudding Shop to make sure I was safe.

I felt pretty overwhelmed at that point. I'd only been in Istanbul for two days and I'd been smacked around, I'd been to the police, and I'd stood my ground with a physically abusive man in a city I'd barely heard of before.

The moment I walked into the shop, Mr. Pudding Shop wouldn't look at me. He'd simply walk away. He was clearly terrified. My threat worked, and I felt safe.

It was time to get down to basics. The couple driving the van were nowhere to be found. I was on my own and it was time to figure out for myself what I would do, and where I wanted to go.

I decided to settle into Istanbul for a few more days. I started making friends and I was actually enjoying myself. In fact, the two kind policemen had asked, "Please, would you come back tomorrow afternoon and help us learn English?" So I did. And I continued to visit each afternoon - to read their English books with them. We laughed, had coffee, and were even becoming friends.

Each night, Frankie would show up wherever I was, to walk me home and make sure I was safe. As grateful as I was to him, it was beginning to get on my nerves. He wasn't only there at night to walk me home, he seemed to be around a lot. And he'd taken to asking where I was going and who I was with.

I got to thinking, I've just left home, the last thing I need is someone acting like a father to me. I mean, I appreciated what he'd done for me, but he was just a bit too much in my face.

After being in Istanbul a week, I decided one day that I wasn't going to go to the Pudding Shop. I wanted to avoid Frankie. Instead, I decided to try a restaurant right beside the Pudding Shop. It was a typical Turkish place - mostly men, or all men in this case.

I sat down at a table and was waiting to order some food and tea when in walked my two cop friends. "What are you doing here?" they asked.

"Frankie's starting to bother me. I appreciate all that he's done. He's just around me all of the time, and I need a break from him."

"Oh, you shouldn't be here," they said.

"What do you mean?"

They leaned in closely and said, "This is slave trade headquarters."

I'd heard talk of the slave trade. I'd even seen little flyers posted here and there showing photographs of young women my age, asking, 'Have you seen...?' But, I assumed it was a thing of the past. I just didn't believe it was happening any more.

My two cop friends went on, "Here you are, by yourself, sitting in the middle of it, with all these men."

And all I could think was, how convenient, this place is right beside the Pudding Shop.

"You can't trust anybody," they implored. "There are cab drivers in the slave trade. There are police in the slave trade. There are lots of people in the slave trade. You need to leave."

Then they said, "One more thing: We saw you went to bed at 1:30 last night."

"What?" I was completely taken aback. "How do you know what time I went to bed? How do you know that?"

"Ever since Frankie brought you into the police station, we've been watching out for you."

"What?" I said, still in shock. My world was starting to collapse. I thought Frankie was a good guy.

"Frankie's in the slave trade, and he's setting you up to be taken."

All along, my protector - the nice man who had been walking me safely home at night, through the back lanes of Istanbul - was actually setting me up?

They said, "One of these nights, he's going to have men ready to take you away. We're worried for you. We like you."

"Where would they take me?"

They told me that young women who were kidnapped get taken to North Africa into the desert to harems, never to be seen again.

"There's no way you can leave," they said. "There are no phones. You are in the desert. Nowhere to run. No way to call."

Emphatically they added, "You need to leave Istanbul tomorrow. You need to get out of here! Would you like us to walk you home?"

I looked at them and thought, who can I trust? I had no idea if they were telling the truth. What if *they* were the kidnappers? What if they were going to abduct me? I realized I could trust no one.

"No thank you," I said. "Thank you for warning me!"

I said my goodbyes, and quickly went back to my hotel. I was petrified and I felt completely alone. No one knew where I was. The last my parents had heard, I was in Amsterdam heading to the Greek Islands. Instead, I was in Istanbul, and terrified. I cried myself to sleep. Again.

I woke up the next morning and straight away I heard some activity outside my window. I looked out and could see a mini-bus down by the back door of my hotel. A group of hippies was loading up the roof with their knapsacks. I thought, wherever they're going, I want to go with them.

I ran downstairs and asked who owned the bus. They pointed to a couple and their friend. I ran over to them and asked, "Where are you going? I need to get out of here. I need to leave now."

"We're going to Goa," they told me.

"Where is Goa?" I asked. "Is that the place in India?" I'd heard the name in the Pudding Shop, but I didn't know exactly where it was.

"Yeah. Goa is a beach area south of Bombay where hippies are living - it's like a festival there."

I had no idea how far away Istanbul was from India. But, it didn't matter. "Do you have room for me?" I asked.

"No, sorry. We're all full," they said. "We just have one seat, which we keep open for leg room."

I begged them. "I need to get out of here. I'm scared to be alone. Would you please, please, please sell me that spot?"

I don't know what changed their minds. I don't know if it was the money, or my desperation, or they just wanted the conversation to end and get their trip started. Whatever the reason, they relented and allowed me to ride with them.

I ran upstairs, grabbed my knapsack, ran downstairs, paid my bill, and that was that. Good-bye Istanbul.

It was clearly time for more change.

Part 2. Burkas, Barbers and Borders

When I jumped on that mini-bus, I truly had no idea where I was going. I had no clue I was about to embark on a journey that would take me through the rest of Turkey, Iran, Afghanistan, Pakistan and into southern India, and I certainly had no clue the journey would last a month.

Our bus was a 14-seater, and every seat was taken. Everyone knew somebody on that bus except for me. I was the only one travelling solo and I definitely felt like the odd one out.

The bus was owned by three Germans: a couple and the couple's best friend, a fellow. The three of them were in their mid-twenties and, like me, and everyone else on that bus, they were long-haired hippie 'freaks.' The three of them seemed like the leaders of the trip, by virtue, if nothing else, of owning the bus.

I thought, and hoped, they would take me under their wing, or help me get to know some of the others. But, no such luck. They made no effort to help me become part of the group.

Other than a couple from Quebec, my fellow travellers were all Europeans. I'm pretty sure everyone could speak English, at least a little bit. But no one did. German, Dutch, French and Italian were spoken, but no English. In fact, for most of the trip, no one talked to me. (Except for the driver's nightly instructions as to when to return to the bus.)

Every night I would fend for myself, first finding a place to eat, and then a place to stay. Sometimes we'd be in the same hostel together, but rarely did anyone ever ask me to join them. No one was even friendly towards me. Even though we were travelling as a group, I felt painfully alone. Yes, I was safe, and I was out of Istanbul, but I felt very much alone.

The trip through Turkey and Iran was smooth and without incident, just days and days of driving through desert. It was the first time I'd been in a desert, and found myself awestruck by its stark beauty. The highlight was arriving in Tehran and finding a grocery store where they sold halva, or in Persian, halvardeh, by the slab. Halva is a sweet dessert made of sesame seed paste and pistachios. There was a mound of it to the side of the counter, the size of a little Christmas tree. They scraped off a giant slice for me and placed it on my palm.

It wasn't just that it tasted divine - and it did - it's that it tasted like home. When I was growing up, my Bubbie and Zaydie would bring halva to the house whenever they'd come to visit. The sweet taste of halva shortened the distance from home and soothed the feeling of loneliness. I'll never forget it.

By the time we arrived at the Iran-Afghanistan border we had covered almost 35-hundred kilometres. We were just over half way through our journey to Goa.

We drove up to an area between Iran and Afghanistan which was locally called 'No Man's Land.' The border was closed for the night when we got there, 'there' being very much in the middle of nowhere. We slept on the tables of the lone restaurant.

When we woke up at daylight, our driver drove the bus to the border crossing while the rest of us walked over to the gate to enter Afghanistan.

We had been warned that the Afghan border police didn't approve of long hair on male travellers. Often, we were told, they wouldn't let the men enter the country until they'd cut their hair, and that's exactly what happened. The Afghan border police ordered all of the men on our bus to get their hair cut.

Conveniently, and by no coincidence, there was barber with a chair right there at the border, ready with scissors in hand. Once their hair was cut, there was a dealer nearby ready to sell us some hash. From the border to the barber to the hash dealer. It was one stop shopping as we crossed into Afghanistan.

A few hours after crossing the border, we arrived in Herat, Afghanistan. I was instantly drawn to the beauty and the slow-pace of the unfolding scene I witnessed along the wide main road. It was utterly stunning and mesmerizing.

Transportation along that one main street was mainly horse and buggy, with the occasional camel, donkey, and, most unusually, a car. The horses were adorned in ribbons, bows and bells. They looked and sounded beautiful as they trotted down the street.

The men of Herat walked along the sidewalks smoking hashish pipes. They wore their beards long and dyed red with henna, perhaps out of respect for the prophet Mohammed, believed by some to have had red hair. Their clothes were loose and light-coloured, and they wore the traditional turban, a lungee. Their shoes curled up at the toes.

The women, the few I saw, wore burkas with a lace screen across their eyes to see. Life in Herat felt like a dream to me. I was captivated and spellbound by it all. (A memory I treasure still.)

Our group stayed in Herat for a few days. Alone, as usual, I spent my time walking along the main road, going from one shop to the next. The shops were run by men, no women. Happily for me, they treated me like a queen. And I felt safe.

I'd walk in and the shopkeeper would offer me tea. Once I accepted, someone would bring in a tray of tea and candies, and we'd sip our tea and look at each other. We shared little language in common, but we would enjoy teatime together. I was never, ever pushed to buy anything. I would say thank you for the tea, and they would send me on my way.

On one particular afternoon, I visited a shop run by two brothers. One was a musician; he played the harmonium, an instrument that's a cross between an accordion and a piano. The other brother loved to dance, and asked me if I'd like to dance with him. (Yes, please!) I spent hours dancing and listening to music with them in the back of their store. It was all kindness, tea and dancing. I bowed in gratitude, and off I went.

Second Turn: Follow Your Impulse

Our next stop was Kandahar, and then Kabul. These places were nothing like what we hear and read about today. It was 1973. It was before Russia invaded Afghanistan and before the rise of the Islamic fundamentalist group, the Taliban. Afghanistan was a very different country from the one it's become today.

Kandahar was an oasis in the desert, filled with palm trees and fountains. It was the first time I ever saw peacocks. Kabul was not as beautiful, but had its own charm. It was more modern, and bustling with life - where old and new co-existed. It was also the place I'd become the most sick I'd ever been in my life. I didn't know what it was at the time (it turned out to be amoebic dysentery), but it made me painfully ill for a single night. Luckily, I recovered within a day, and we carried on.

Up next, Pakistan. Pakistan was the busiest country of all the places we'd seen, and when it came to driving, was the wildest. Vehicles of every description were piled high with passengers on the roofs and hanging off the sides. It was quite the spectacle and very unnerving.

Driving through the Khyber Pass was stunningly beautiful by day, but the night-driving was truly hair-raising. Every vehicle had different coloured headlights and backlights - purple and yellow in the front, green and orange in the back. No two cars were the same. You couldn't tell if cars were coming towards you or moving away. It didn't seem safe to me.

Then, it was time to prepare to cross the Indian border.

"When we get to the border," the owners of the bus told us, "you must make sure you don't have any hash on you. Not on you. Not on the bus. Not anywhere. This is not an easy border and we'll get into deep trouble. Dump your stash."

We'd been smoking hash the whole time during the trip. It was available everywhere, and, for practically nothing, you could buy a big chunk. Everyone promised to dump their hash.

When we pulled up to the border crossing, we got off the bus, and the border police got on to begin their search. I was confident that we'd get through no problem. We were all clean, right?

Well, we were clean until a border policeman picked up a magazine lying on one of the seats. Flat pancakes of hash tumbled out of its pages. Someone had hidden their stash in that magazine. They'd also stuffed tape-cassette covers with their hash, which were also easily found.

Seriously? Magazines and tape cassette covers in plain sight, what were they thinking? Good hiding, people!

It was not good news. One person's hash meant we were all guilty.

Each one of us was strip-searched. All of us were told over and over that we'd be thrown in jail. All of us were asked how much money we had, and were then instructed to count our paisa, the Pakistan coinage. Anyone whose paisa didn't add up would be thrown in prison.

'Oh, my god. I'm going to end up in jail.' I'd seen the movie *Midnight Express* and I thought I'm not going to come out alive. I was thinking rats and disease, starvation and beatings. I thought I'd never see my family again. There was no end to the nightmare I was imagining.

I was a goner. I sat down and cried, my head hung low and my hands wrapped around my face. Not guilty. Scared to death. Alone.

We weren't getting out of there until the border police knew whose hash it was. They wanted someone to confess. Finally, finally, finally! After nearly five hours of torment, the best friend of the owners of the van stepped up. Their best friend! It was his hash.

We were all flabbergasted. For hours, we didn't know if we were going to jail. We didn't know if we were going to get out of there alive. He'd put everyone at risk - all of us, and especially his best friends because, as the bus owners, they were the ones who would most likely be punished.

And, what did the police do? After all the strip searches and all the threats? The border police had him tear up all of his hash and flush it down the toilet, and they fined him a meager sum.

Then, cheerfully, as if nothing had happened, they served us chai. Chai! There we sat, at the Pakistan-India border, drinking delicious, sweet tea with the border police.

Six hours after they'd searched the bus, they sent us on our way, and we crossed the border into India, at last. Thank god I wasn't going to die in jail after all. We had escaped imprisonment, and I had survived. (That might have been the moment I began to believe in guardian angels.)

With a big deep sigh of relief for my life, and gigantic gratitude in my heart, my solo journey, full of twists and turns, highs and lows, continued.

Reflections

"No law can be sacred to me but that of my nature. Good and bad are but names very readily transferable to that or this. The only right is what is after my constitution; the only wrong is what is against it." Ralph Waldo Emerson

Have you heard of the acorn theory?

It's the idea that you are born with a soul that shapes your destiny - that your full potential already lives within you. It's a uniqueness that you carry into the world, particular to you. It's your inner voice, your emotions, your special genius.

This Second Turn is a solo journey into this theory.

In the First Turn, your task was to 'Listen.'

Now your task, and yours alone, is to tap into your 'acorn seed,' your unique potential - to discover it, re-connect to it, get to know it, and, ultimately, let it guide you. In essence, it's an act of self-love, self-exploration and self-understanding.

And the key is to be endlessly curious. Endlessly.

Be curious about yourself. Be curious about others. Be curious about life.

Your curiosity will lead you to source - into flow - into the divine dance where all life is ever changing, ever pulsing. Just like you! Your body, sensations, impulses, emotions and thoughts are just as fluid and changeable.

The best explanation I've found to describe this truth comes from the brilliant Neuroscientist, Candace B. Pert, in her book *Your Body Is Your Subconscious Mind*. She describes us as 'flickering flames,' fluid and shapeshifting, continuously changing through our thoughts and emotions. Our impulses, acting like an inner metronome, guide our way.

Our impulses guide our way.

Let me say it again.

Our impulses. Guide. Our way.

By paying attention to our inner impulses as they arise from moment to moment, we access our innate compass and personal genius. Our impulses inform who we are, what we want, and where we're going. Our soul path.

For me, my journey to Istanbul and India is a story of acting (and sometimes not acting) on impulse.

I could have said no to going to Europe on my own. That was an easier choice for sure. I could have said no to going to Istanbul, a safer choice, but I didn't. Because the stronger impulse was to say yes.

I could have chosen a number of other paths that fateful morning I impulsively begged for a seat on the mini-bus to India. I could have taken the train or a bus to Athens, or I could have headed back to Amsterdam, but I wasn't ready to turn back.

From my vantage point today, I can't imagine not having had those experiences, all of them. That trip from the suburbs of Toronto to Amsterdam, to Istanbul, through the Middle East to India, was one incredible blessing in my life. I am deeply grateful. And count my lucky stars to have received such life-long memories, lessons and gifts only following one's impulse can give.

At its core, following impulse truly is a solo practice, a solo journey of self-discovery. It's a life-long task to stay awake to what draws us in and what pushes us away... now. Not yesterday. Not tomorrow. Today.

Dear one, this is an act of devotion and it's your precious assignment to pay attention to what moves you.

If it nourishes you, follow that. If it strengthens you, follow that. If it releases you, follow that.

Go with what excites, what enriches, what grounds you.

Go with what intoxicates, what opens, what wholes you!

Follow THOSE impulses. Follow those.

Be curious.

Be MOVED.

Be *daring*.

Be Impulsive.

Practices for the Second Turn

- A Day of Curiosity
- Meander with a Pen
- Be Moved
- Become a Wanderer
- Dare to be Impulsive
- Divine with Oracle Decks

Playlist: Follow Your Impulse

"The especial genius of women I believe is to be electrical in movement, intuitive in function, spiritual in tendency." Margaret Fuller

A Day of Curiosity

"People travel to wonder at the height of the mountains, at the huge waves of the seas, at the long course of the rivers, at the vast compass of the ocean, at the circular motion of the stars, and yet they pass by themselves without wondering." St. Augustine

Yes! It is time to wonder about our own being. It's always time, but especially now, here, in the second turn of the personal dance. It's time to wonder about ourselves - our body, our divinity, our sovereignty, our wisdom.

Curiosity ignites wonder; at least, it does for me. It's one of my desired states of being. It makes me endlessly more…

Open
Soft
Joyful
Available
Alive
Creative
Loving
Present
Truthful
Authentic
Playful
Light
Shiny

It's utterly magical, and for that reason, I highly recommend, no, I insist you sidle up to curiosity, as soon as possible. Get up close and personal with it, as if your life depended on it, because it really does!

Be curious about curiosity, right this moment, because curiosity has its own unique wisdom, its own language, its own unique powers. It will change your life in ways you can't even imagine, and for the better. I know it has for mine. Because...

In my humble opinion...

Curiosity opens doors to limitless possibilities, breaking the spell of routine and the mundane. It necessitates new ideas, new creativity, new impulses. Like the infinity symbol, it keeps going, around and around - curiosity makes curiosity, making more curiosity.

Curiosity returns us to innocence, like the Buddhist 'Beginner's Mind.' It's a powerful place to be - to live without past assumptions or judgments - in pure joy, love and open presence. And, of course, more play!

Curiosity connects us to others (when practiced with a deep listening, mindfulness and respect for one-another's boundaries and privacy). As we become curious about the beautiful mystery of others, our impulses for judgment, pre-conceived ideas and prejudices melt away, leaving more space in our heart for compassion, connection and love.

Curiosity, when accompanying us into the unknown, leads us to being more courageous and trusting. It offers us the opportunity to flex our 'chutzpa,' giving our mind and our worries and fears permission to rest awhile.

Curiosity taps us into our wider truth. By expanding and clarifying our understanding and awareness of life and ourselves, we're uncovering the hidden wisdom below, so the real truth can shine through and be known.

And last, but not least...

Curiosity creates magic through the shifting of our perceptions. Simply asking, '**I wonder...**' can invite all kinds of shifts and changes to occur - in attitude, in belief, in wonderment.

Curiosity opens the door to magical outcomes.

Let's get curious...

Let's start with a few simple questions. These questions have the power to unlock wonder and open up possibility. They're a little bit of magic to keep in your pocket as you walk through your day.

What if ...?   What if I ...?   What if it ...?

What then?   Why not?   Who for?

Now, open the doors a little further. Put these questions to work. Invite curiosity to be your trusty companion for the day, from the moment you awaken to the moment you fall asleep.

Start your day with curiosity.

- As soon as you open your eyes, ask yourself the questions, '**I wonder what will happen today?**' Asking the question shifts our internal compass from 'I pretty much know what to expect' to 'What lovely surprises await me today?' - from assumption to openness. This simple question invokes a sense of adventure. It's truly magic-making, and one of my favourites!

- **Be curious about yourself and surroundings.** Ask yourself: 'How do I feel today? What do I need?' If there are others in your home, be curious about them too. See them, and yourself, as beautiful mysteries. Be fascinated. This will support a curiosity in the way you see the world when you go out into it.

- **Bring curiosity into your morning tasks.** Ask yourself: 'What will happen if I meditate instead of reading emails, or put music on and dance for ten minutes before breakfast, or have tea instead of coffee?' 'How can I bring more ease into my morning?' Break the spell of habits. Be flexible. See what happens.

- **What other ways can you bring curiosity into the start of your day?**

Fill your day with curiosity.

Carry the expansive openness and curiosity from the morning into your whole day. Keep the juices flowing with play and wonderment. Be endlessly curious with your whole being - mind, heart, body and soul.

- **Invite lightness.** A dose of levity can go a long way. As situations - especially those involving problem-solving and choice-making - arise in your day, ask yourself: 'Am I being too serious about this?' 'How can I bring more lightness and play in?' Be curious and open. See new possibilities emerge.

- **Be playful.** Play is another magical elixir. How can you be more playful with your spirituality, your relationships, your wellness? Play around, be frisky, wild and imaginative. No bounds, no rules. What would light up your playful Inner Child? Paint flower pots, skip down the sidewalk, or gaze at the stars? Pick one thing you can do today.

- **Adopt a Beginner's Mind.** Choose a task on your to-do list this week (or today) and approach it with a Beginner's Mind, the Zen Buddhist practice of observing everything as if for the first time, with no pre-conceived ideas or assumptions. Ask yourself: 'Who or what is this? How can I engage with it? Can I feel differently about it?' Return to innocence, to a state of soft, open presence.

- **Say, "I don't know!"** Say it often. Say it inwardly AND outwardly to keep your mind open wide, and to melt your ego, inspire limitless possibilities, and tap you into a wider truth and trust in mysteries. Let go of being the expert, and become more curious, receptive to new options, choices and potentials.

- **How else can you be curious throughout your day?**

End your day with curiosity.

- **Review your day with curiosity.** Think back to the flow of your day, to the people, activities and situations, and invite more curiosity into your thoughts, feelings and memories. Ask yourself questions like: 'What did I learn from ….? How do I feel about ….? What brought me joy? What needs tending?' Notice, feel, remember.

- **Witness your day as a Sacred Experiment.** Pause. Light a candle. Let the touch of gratitude and peace soften and fill your heart and mind for all that passed through your day - the difficult, the joyful, the easy, the disappointing. Trust that it all was perfect. When you see your life as a sacred experiment, no part of your day is out of alignment with source, with divine flow. Count your sacred blessings.

- **How else can you close your day with curiosity?**

+++

*"Once we believe in ourselves,
we can risk curiosity, wonder, spontaneous delight,
or any experience that reveals the human spirit."
e. e. cummings*

Meander with a Pen

"You can never enter the same river twice." Indian Proverb

Meandering is an art form in its own right. It's a form of wandering, usually aimlessly, without any particular destination or time-frame. It's a form of drifting, floating and traipsing, even dawdling and moseying. It's in the realms of trust, mystery and receptivity.

The mind wants to control - the pace, the direction, the outcome. Flow just wants to be. It doesn't want to go upstream, against the grain, or twist out of its natural shape. A leaf wants to be a leaf. An eagle wants to soar. Our impulses want to be set free to feel, to roam, to meander.

It's the unpredictable, changeable and fluid path that forms beneath your feet when you let impulse lead. It's the path of least resistance, the path of beauty, the path of creativity.

Meandering allows the unfoldment of life, unobstructed by pre-determined concepts and outcomes. It's where mind follows body, body follows impulse, and impulse follows soul. It's essentially divine flow; endlessly tapped into flow, and following where flow wishes to go. Meandering is an authentic path of no purposeful direction, particular plan, or straight line. And that's a gift and a teaching in itself.

If you don't want to bring magic and mystery into your life, please don't meander. Stick to the set or established course. Do not go off the beaten track. Stick to the familiar and habitual pathways. Be safe.

Because, truth be told… becoming a meanderer will incite, tempt and indulge your free spirit. It will stir your wild woman and invigorate the adventurer. Is that what you want? If so, by all means, go for it. Get meandering!

This practice is to meander with your pen, to follow your hand's impulse in the creation of a 'sacred doodle' using only <u>ONE line.</u> (See the example following the instructions.)

If you've ever done stream of consciousness writing it's like that, but instead of words flowing on the page, it's the dance of angles and shapes blossoming. This is following impulse in the subtlest of ways.

Set your Inner Artist free to roam like Diana in the woods. No plan other than where you start and end. Everything in between is the flow, the unfoldment, the art. It's an offering of your soul's expression, here and now, in the moment, arriving in its own way - as a wild map, an intricate weaving, or Zen garden. Who knows?

Be continually curious about its evolving form. It's all flow. It's all perfect. No two meanderings will be the same. No two hands can make the same creation. 'You can never enter the same river twice.' This is the beauty of artistic expression.

No one else can do what you do.

No one else can design, respond or initiate the same as you.

This practice may seem simple, and it is, in concept. But don't be fooled by its simplicity. It's more powerful than it appears. It has the potential to release creative-blocks, open your mind, and facilitate a letting go - of perfectionism and expectations.

Have fun. Be playful, spontaneous and curious. Let it be messy, flowing, wild or erratic. There's no right or wrong, only what feels right for you.

Here we go: Approx. 30 minutes

1. **Get out your journal or piece of paper, and pen, coloured pencil or marker.** You want to be committed to this, so NO pencil!

2. **Draw a spiral (like the one below) in the center of your page.** If you use the *She Reflects Journal & Colouring Book*, you'll find this spiral waiting for you.

3. **Place your pen on the outside end of the spiral.** This is the starting point for your sacred doodle. Once you start, keep the pen touching the paper until you reach the center.

4. **Go at your own pace.** Let the line dance around the page with its own rhythm and style, looking for empty spaces or crossing over itself.

5. **Don't stop and start.** Follow your hand's lead wherever it feels inspired to go. Let your pen meander as one continuous thread.

6. Keep flowing and meandering until you arrive at **the center point** of the spiral. Then the practice is done.

7. Once you've completed your doodle, feel free to **embellish it**.

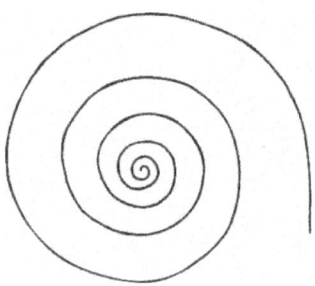

Here's an example:

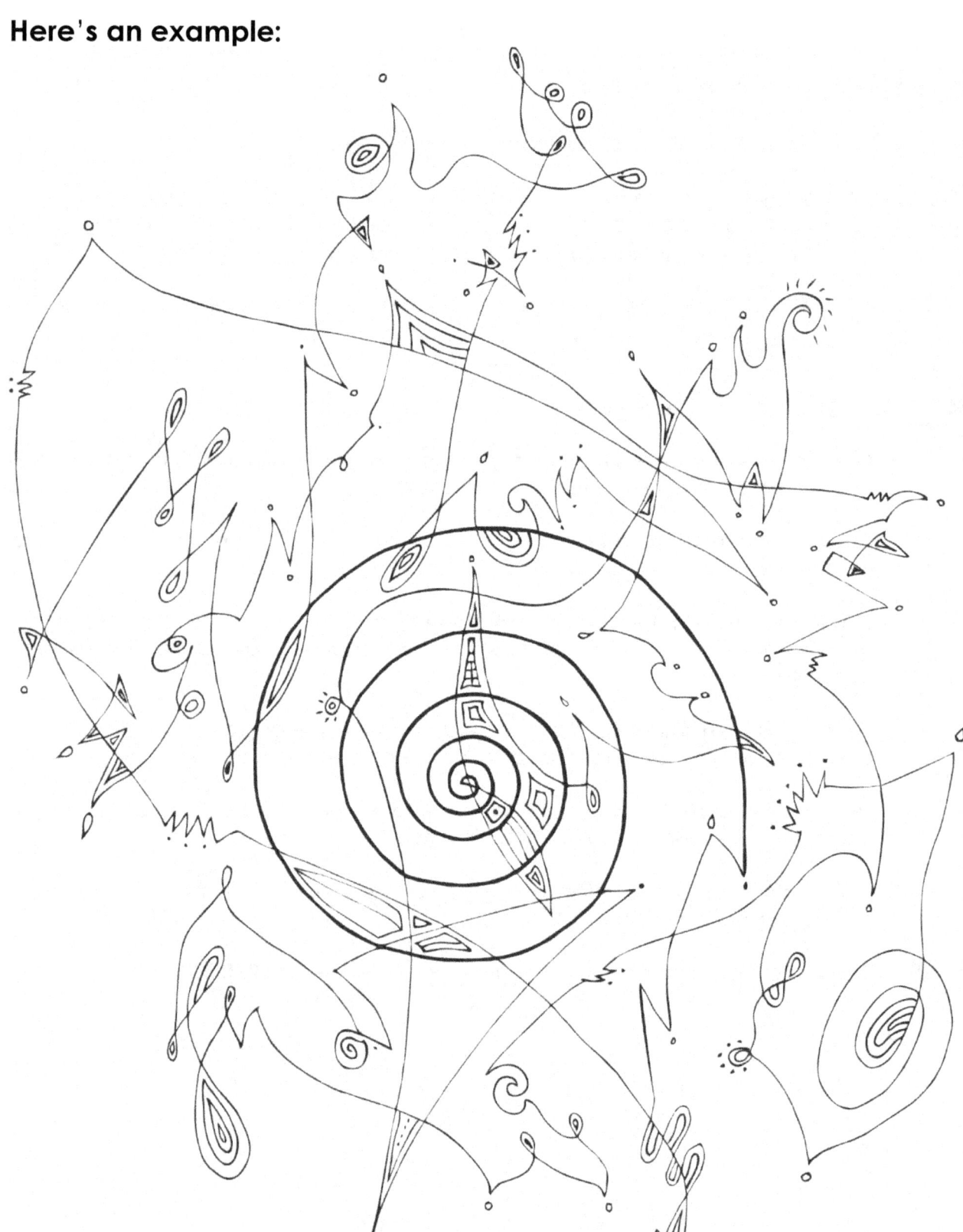

Be Moved

The Second Turn is a personal dance. It's an open-ended, sacred inquiry into the exquisite nature of your body, mind, heart and soul, in motion, in stillness, in life.

It's a deeply personal journey of allowing, engaging and bearing witness to your inner prompts and impulses wrapped around and carrying your desires, feelings and stories - the essence and truth of yourself - clear, unfiltered and unfettered.

This practice, 'Be Moved,' is a soft and beauty-filled path for this reveal. It's a permissive and responsive dance of inviting and welcoming impulse to come through. So you can be moved. So you can become moved.

It's not something you can force or will yourself into. It's not something you make happen. Rather, it's about allowing and yielding to the pulse of breath, of spirit, of presence, to move you. Not until then.

Breath will lead heart to move. Heart will lead belly to move. Belly will lead head to move. And so on. Each move a response to the softening, the listening, the responding. Each move, a declaration and vow to self, saying, 'Yes I am. Here I am. This is me.'

I know this to be healing, generative and transformative.

In life, it's about waiting for the cue that says NOW. It aligns you with divine timing, divine flow. Like when you respond to the impulse that says, 'Go now,' and you arrive at the perfect moment. Or when you follow the impulse that says, 'Speak now,' or 'Rest now.'

Looking back at the story of Amaterasu, I see this as a practice in, and a metaphor for, the holding up of our own individual shard of mirror - our body, our being - to hold it just so, in just the right position, to catch the light of our lives, to reflect and shine our own truth and beauty.

In other words... When we allow the mirror of our being to be moved, we'll naturally flow towards and face the light. We'll naturally find the truth of us.

The practice of "Be Moved" invites you to do just that: to follow the flow that leads you to your own exquisite light, truth and beauty. It's delicious in its simplicity. And challenging for the same reason.

When I first started practicing being moved, the ballerina in me needed to perform, as if on stage. I'd been wired and trained that way. It took time for me to let go and really BE. Through my 'undoing' also came sounds. Turns out, I have an active inner snake that loves to come out and 'hiss' when I'm dancing and moving. I used to suppress it (again, thanks to my ballet). Now I don't.

If sounds come through for you too, welcome them as part of the process, part of your truth. Above all else, be kind, permissive and compassionate towards yourself. You are already in divine flow. You are a brilliant moving goddess. Life is dancing with you, inside and out. And now...

It's your turn to Be Moved: 20 minutes or longer

Experiment with doing this without music and then with the **Follow Your Impulse Playlist**, and always where you feel comfortable and safe.

1. **Find a private space** where you will not be interrupted.

2. **Find a restful position.** Standing, sitting or lying down.

3. **Soften your gaze**, or close your eyes.

4. **Soften your breath and body.**

5. **Relax there for as long as it feels right and good.** There's nowhere to go, nowhere to be.

6. **Wait for an impulse to arrive.** Maybe it's to raise your hands up. Or to curl into a ball, or stretch a leg. Or maybe it's to make a sound, a sigh. Be with it. Trust it. Allow it to emerge and move you.

7. **Follow the impulse until it leads you to another** movement, another part of your body. See where the energy or feeling wants to move to. Be curious and fascinated by it.

8. **Notice and feel any body sensations or stories.** Allow them to guide you. You might find yourself becoming an animal, or a gardener planting seeds in the ground, or the holder of light. Without trying to make sense of it, follow it. Be moved by it.

9. **Move until you feel complete.** Trust your body's cues that tell you you're done. Let your body find its own completion, in its own way. Maybe it's to drop down to the floor, or to say a prayer, or to take a shape.

10. **Close your eyes** if they were open.

11. **Come into stillness.** Come back to your breath. Pause, relax and soften.

12. **Give thanks** for the experience. Feel free to just rest in the silence.

Become a Wanderer

"A subject to which few intellectuals ever give a thought is the right to be a vagrant, the freedom to wander. ... to take up the symbolic stick and bundle and get out." Isabelle Eberhardt

According to my mom, I've been a Solo Wanderer since I was two years old. I don't recall the first time, but I do remember the day after we moved to a new neighbourhood. I was five and spent the day wandering from house to house looking for new friends and exploring the greenbelt and nearby ravine alone.

Years later, when I was in my teens, I discovered the mythic character, 'The Fool,' in the tarot. I was instantly drawn to it. The image of him perched on the edge of a cliff, with a stick and bundle resting on one shoulder, about to step off the cliff, stirred something in me. It was a leap of faith. Innocent and ready to go, trusting in the landing. Well... that was essentially me! I happily consider myself a Wandering Fool, in the best possible way.

In the fantastic book *Nature and the Human Soul* by Bill Plotkin, he says the Wanderer embodies the essence of "the wild, the imaginable, the dream", and is a Visionary gathering information, "pieces of the unknown", whose "very existence inspires others to have faith in the unknown, to seek innovation and vision in hidden and unexpected places."

This totally speaks to me. It speaks to my soul. It speaks to the Wanderer in me.

Like the act of meandering, becoming a Wanderer has the potential to transform your world, both inner and outer. If you're feeling stuck, bored or tired, this will indeed defrost and release your creative juices. It will expand your mind and imagination, and will enliven and uplift your spirit.

You'll become more self-reliant, adaptable and resourceful. You'll become more comfortable with the unfamiliar, the unknown, and even with being lost.

Becoming a Wanderer, specifically in your own neighbourhood or town, will prepare you, at low risk, to hone the skills needed to be a Solo Wanderer out in the wider world, if that's a calling you've been afraid to answer in the past.

It's also the perfect antidote to alleviating the pain of the longing for travel, when travel isn't an option, by tapping you into a traveller's state of mind. (It's because of this practice I'm able to transform my pining for travel, into joy, the joy and acceptance of being exactly where I am.)

All this is to say... Being a Wanderer is a great thing. Being a Wanderer every day, at home and afar, is food for the soul. It will nourish and infuse you with delightful experiences, connections and possibilities.

Here we go. Take up the symbolic stick and bundle and get out.

Let the adventure begin: For as long as you like.

1. **Put on some comfy clothes and walking shoes** and head outside.

2. **Follow an impulse to go in a direction.** Move towards that direction, without second guessing or having attachment to where it will lead. Leave behind any expectations or compasses.

3. As you walk, **stay open and aware.** Open your mind, body and senses. Smell. Listen. Notice. Let your wanderings be a moving meditation, a mindfulness practice of being present with yourself and life around you.

4. **Wander** around, exploring up and down, noticing sky to earth, front, back and to the sides, **endlessly observing and flowing**, observing and flowing.

5. **Go beyond the familiar or known paths.** Allow your feet to go beyond the familiar, stopping when something catches your attention. Follow the impulses, the turns, around corners, behind trees, inside shops or parks. And if you get lost, even better!

6. **Be led by intuition and trust.** When you come to a crossroads or dead end, follow the next impulse that says straight ahead, or turn to the right. Let a foot, a hand, a curiosity, guide you. There's 'magic afoot.' Step into it!

7. **As always... be curious and kind.** Welcome encounters with people, with animals, nature, and whatever else is around you. Be interested, delighted and open. Be in wonderment. Let that be your compass.

8. **Be grateful** for whatever comes, whatever or whomever you see. Fill up with love and appreciation. Invite a sense of oneness. Expand your heart and mind to take it all in. Be touched. Be moved.

9. **Keep exploring until you feel ready to return home**, or to let go of this practice, and head somewhere specific in mind.

10. When you can, **record your experience**, and any new ideas, friends or experiences. Enjoy the rewards.

Bonus: When you feel ready, be a Wanderer in a less familiar part of town, city, or land, going further and further afield.

***Of course, always put your safety first. Please be mindful to not wander into unsafe spaces.**

Become the Wanderer.

*Go dancing into
the wilderness
of your own SOUL.*

*Inspire others
to have faith
in the unknown,*

*to seek vision
in hidden and
unexpected places.*

Dare to be Impulsive

Impulsive: acting without forethought, impetuous and hasty.

It's got a bad rap - it doesn't get much love. But, what about this?

Impulsive: acting on impulse - spontaneous, passionate and uninhibited.

Mmmmmm. Now that sounds good to me. Feels like my kind of freedom and bliss. I say, 'amen,' to that. 'More please!'

Sure, being impulsive can seem impetuous and hasty, and surely not from the realm of the rational, but so often it reveals parts of ourselves that have been hidden, neglected or need creative expression.

And quite mysteriously sometimes, being impulsive moves you along your path in just the right direction, in just the right way, for just the right reasons.

It carries you downstream with the rush and gush of life-force that flows from being spontaneous, daring and passionate. It gives you new wings and thrust. It frees your spirit and creative fire, and propels you forward.

In my world, impulses are not only welcome, but celebrated. These magical couriers of emotion, desire and inner truth are a very, very, good thing. Acting on impulse is essential to living a creative, joy-filled and expansive life of authorship, self-love and adventure. It's a form of soul-speak. And it's sexy.

Acting on impulse takes us down new avenues. Opens up possibilities. Catalyzes change.

You see an ad in the paper and suddenly you're booking flights for a trip you've actually been wanting to take forever. Spontaneously, you cut your hair off, or you put a pink streak in it. You see a sign on a telephone pole for guitar lessons and, much to your surprise, you make the call.

However, as others might say (or as we even might say to ourselves), 'Oh, you're just being impulsive' - you know, acting or doing something without (apparent) forethought. And, what I'm saying is, sometimes, and often enough, forethought is over-rated!

The risk and joys of going out on a limb, outweigh the need for comfort and security. I know this for a fact; it's a truth I've explored and experimented with for years. My trip to Europe, the Middle East and India, for example, was a kind of a dare to myself. It was a dare that I could trust in my own ability to navigate the world, and make it alone.

Heaven knows, I've fumbled and fallen, even broken, many times in my life, but I can honestly say I have few regrets. I don't wonder what I missed or wish I'd done it differently.

I made my choices, usually swiftly, with conviction, and I'm grateful for the ripple effects, the blessings, and the pain. I accept it all, and sleep well at night because of it.

What about you? How are you with being impulsive?

Do you over plan and over think, to the point you become stuck and unable to take action? Do you go around in circles trying to make decisions, out of the fear you'll make the wrong choice? Do you need to control, micro-manage and calculate every step you take?

Do you regret the many missed opportunities you were too afraid to say yes to? Do you never go beyond your comfort zone, take risks or go out on a limb?

If so, I've got good news! I've got a fix, an antidote for what ails you...

It's a dare... to be IMPULSIVE.

A dare to step out of your comfort zone and say yes without hesitation or doubt. A dare to make a decision on the fly without second guessing your natural instincts and impulses. A dare to dive in feet first, all the way submerged, to be unpredictable, exhilarated and surprised.

So, my love...

Are you ready to do something daring?

Are you ready to exercise your impulsive muscles?

Are you ready to go after your long-standing dream, your heart's desire?

Are you ready to TRUST that the universe has your back?

Test the waters. Dare yourself to:

- **Go solo.** Are you nervous to experience life by yourself? Do you feel uncomfortable going to the movies or a restaurant, or attending a course or retreat on your own? Is there a festival in the next town you'd love to go to, but no one's available to go with you? Would you love to take a road trip but have no one to join you?

    Dare yourself to go and do that by yourself. Feel the freedom of acting on your own behalf... a woman unto herself!

- **Do something that scares you.** Being scared, when it comes to doing something you dream to do, isn't a bad thing. I'm scared often, but I still go for it. What will you regret not doing that you're afraid to do? Do you have a bucket list destination you're scared to visit? Are you afraid to talk in front of people, but know in your heart of hearts that you're a storyteller? Are you afraid to leave a job or relationship that's sucking the life out of you?

Dare yourself to step out on a limb today. Take a chance. Dip into the stream of your life and say YES! *Your safety is essential, so use some discernment, of course.

- **Try something new** that's beyond your normal comfort zone. What's new in your 'hood that you could explore that you normally wouldn't ever step your foot into? A new art gallery, a new park, a new cafe? What pulls at your heart strings but is too wild, 'off the charts,' or hands-off for you? A book of erotica, a sailing expedition, dying your hair rainbow colours?

Dare yourself to make that call, begin that course, book that trip. Start. NOW.

And afterwards, CELEBRATE your courage. You are awesome!

So, the question is...

What do you **DARE** to do TODAY that you've never done before, that moves and excites you?

Divine with Oracle Decks

We bring the practice of 'Following Impulse' full circle - from the Curious One to the Meanderer to the Wanderer to the Daring to be Impulsive One - to return back home, to the third eye, to intuition, to the Visionary.

Just as the Wanderer follows her impulse, out into the world to lands near and far, so too does the Visionary, but her journey is an inward one. Her terrain is the landscape of inner vision, prophecy, and of soul and spirit.

I truly believe we all have prophetic abilities within us. We are all Visionaries, Seeresses and Prophetesses in our own right. (Side note: I've heard that the word "mense" is a name for Prophetic Priestesses, and is the root word for menstruation, mind, meaning, moon.)

If this is your calling, to activate or expand your visionary abilities and gifts, beautiful. There are many soul-centric tools, teachings and initiations to support you. Look for practices that evoke in you a wider, deeper or altered state of consciousness, such as: dream-work, vision quests, or shamanic journeying and drumming. Magnify your insight and imagination with sacred and visionary art, films and music.

Or… 'Divine with Oracle Decks'… one of my personal favourites.

Divining with cards isn't only inspiring, transformative and informative, it's accessible. With your own deck, or even online, you can be the Visionary in your own home. You can follow your own impulses through the asking, listening and responding to what's alive within, and paying attention to the signs and symbols that show up, to see what speaks to you. *The word 'oracle' means 'to speak.'

I've been playing with cards for decades now. I even became a certified tarot reader years ago, but rarely read for others, and no longer use the traditional tarot. Instead, over the years, I've fallen in love with other, non-traditional decks, mostly related to the Divine Feminine.

I use the cards as **inspiration** when I feel blocked or in need of fresh ideas, as well as to beautify and adorn my home altar, desk, or my hotel room when I travel.

I use the cards as **council** when I'm at a crossroads and need some additional insight to help me make a decision (thank you, Hekate), or when I'm entering a new chapter of my life or a new year.

I also use the cards as a **sacred tool** and doorway, for myself and my clients, to access new insights and messages. I'm always amazed at how perfect every reading is - each card holding and revealing the mysterious language of the psyche, the deeper realms of soul, of the Visionary; each card wrapped in divine beauty and wisdom.

To ground this in history (herstory), the tradition of female Oracles and Visionaries has existed for millennia. You'll find examples of how women practiced and empowered their visioning, intuitive and dreaming skills.

For instance, in the book *The Sibyls: The First Prophetess' of Mami (Wata): The Theft of African Prophecy by the Catholic Church* by author Mama Zogbé, it shines a light on a powerful order of **Sibyl** matriarchs who ruled Africa for 6,000 years. They created the world's first prophetesses and oracles known as "Pythonesses." They were also found working in ancient Babylon, Greece, Israel, Rome, Syria and Turkey.

In ancient Greece, there were sleep sanctuaries, 'incubares,' where women slept to witness, share and interpret their dreams. The Celts slept in oak groves, and on sacred stones and burial 'cairns' - memorial stones for the dead. They also made dream pouches and put patchouli oil, lemon balm, or lavender in them to amplify and activate their dreaming.

They knew something we've forgotten - our ability to see, divine, know, and dream. Goddess mythology reminds us of our own potency and magic, that we are powerful beyond measure, and wise beyond our own belief or understanding.

Just look at the Navajo weaver **Spider Woman**, the Brazilian Prophetess **Iemanja**, still honoured annually, and **Miriam** from the Old Testament. There were **Sybils** in ancient Persia too, the name given to women who spoke divine poetics, where in trance they would write poetry and prophesies on leaves for others to find. And **Saga**, the Scandinavian Goddess of Inspiration, Artistic Expression and Psychic Abilities, and of course... none other than our beloved **Uzume** from Japan.

YOU, my love, like them, are a Visionary. You belong amongst the Goddesses and Prophetesses. Believe me! You are a seer in the dark, and a beacon of light and a light worker. It's time to step into your sovereignty and intrinsic power.

What message is waiting for you today?

Here's a simple guide to how I divine: 30 minutes or longer
Use this as a guide or follow your own heart/path/process.

1. **Set the stage.** Find a time when you won't be disturbed. Turn off the phone and create a sacred space for yourself - on your bed, pillows on the floor, at a table or altar. I like to put out a beautiful piece of fabric and light a candle.

2. **Choose your deck.** If you have more than one deck, even choosing which deck to use is a divining process, of trusting your instincts. (I sometimes pull out a few decks to multiply the possibilities. For me, there are no rules about this.) Take the cards and **lay them face down**, ready to be divined.

3. **Get comfortable.** Find a comfy position to be with the cards and to relax into the 'ask.' Soften your critical mind. Soften your heart and body. This is a soul practice, a creative process, a magical moment.

Second Turn: Follow Your Impulse 91

4 **Find a question**, not as a tool for predicting the future, but rather for deeper and wider insight into your life. For example, your question can be specific, "Am I ready for this new job?", or general, "What do I need to know today?" **Trust** in whatever you feel called to ask. The cards will be the messengers.

5 **Begin to shuffle.** You can shuffle them like playing cards. You can keep them face down and fan them out (one of my personal favourites). You can divide them into different piles. You can choose to use a 'layout' suggested by the deck's guide book. Some love to clap three times before they shuffle. Do as you like.

6 **Tune in.** As you shuffle, stay connected to your question and close your eyes. Invite your hands to flow with the cards. Keep asking and opening to receive, until you feel ready to pick a card or cards. Follow the yes. **Follow the impulse.** Your hand will land on it. Trust your inner Prophetess as she aligns with divine knowing.

7 **Be with the card/s.** Once you've picked your card or cards, move the rest of the deck aside. One at a time, or as a grouping, turn the cards face up, spend time connecting and listening to them. Allow any words or sensations to inform you. Turn it into a meditation.

8 **Wait before reading the interpretation.** If there's an accompanying book, which there usually is, notice how the card/s make you feel first. Allow your own Inner Visionary to speak to you. In time, when you're ready, open the book and see what it has to say. (The book's message may be completely different, and that's okay.) Whatever messages you receive, written or from within, are worthy of investigation and reflection.

9 **Give thanks.** Complete the process by giving thanks for any messages received. (By the way, you may not like what you received, or feel it wasn't what you were asking for, but trust me here, it's perfect. You'll see!) Keep your card/s out and place them on an altar or by your desk, or put them back in the deck.

For the next few days stay curious and softly observant. Notice anyone or anything that resonates with the messages you received. Often, the messengers appear later. *Go to 'Listen for Signs and Synchronicities' in the First Turn for more thoughts about that.

If you don't have a deck yet, I hope you'll be inspired to get one, and come back to this practice for when you do. I highly recommend putting a deck on your 'birthday, anniversary or holiday wish list.' Receiving one as a gift is a really special thing. Check out my list or ask friends for recommendations. (There must be at least a hundred other decks to choose from so enjoy the possibilities.)

*And remember, your cards are sacred tools. Keep them clean and clear energetically. If they're newly bought (new or second hand), touched by others, exposed to a lot of negative energy, or haven't been used in a while, bathe them with sun or moonlight, or bless them with a visualization or prayer. And if you love beauty like I do, wrap your decks in gorgeous cloths or bags, and keep them in a special place.

Here are some of my favourite Oracle Decks:

- **Black Angel Cards**, by Zenju Earthlyn Manuel
- **Daughters of the Moon Tarot**, by Ffiona Morgan
- **Dust II Onyx: A Melanated Tarot,** by Courtney Alexander
- **Kuan Yin Oracle**, by Alana Fairchild, Art by Zeng Hao
- **Medicine Cards**, by Jamie Sams & David Carson, Art by Angela C. Werneke
- **Medicine Song Oracle Cards & Music**, by Brenda MacIntyre
- **Motherpeace Round Tarot**, by Karen Vogel & Vicki Noble
- **Sacred Rebels Oracle**, by Alana Fairchild, Art by Autumn Skye Morrison
- **Sacred Creators Oracle**, by Chris-Anne Donnelly
- **Soulcards I & II**, by Deborah Koff-Chapin
- **The Goddess Oracle**, by Amy Marashinski, Art by Hrana Janto
- **The Mayan Oracle**, by Ariel Spilsbury & Michael Bryner, Art by Donna Kiddie
- **The Triple Goddess Tarot**, by Isha Lerner, Art by Mara Friedman

Plus, I have my own laminated deck, created with collages on one side and affirmations on the other. You, too, can create your own deck.

I ACT ON MY OWN BEHALF

I AM A FLICKERING FLAME

I AM CURIOUS

I AM DARING

I AM BEING MOVED

I AM WONDER-FILLED

I FOLLOW MY IMPULSES

I HONOUR MY RHYTHMS

I TRUST MYSELF

I WANDER WITH DELIGHT

Follow Your Impulse Playlist

Be curious. Trust your inner beat. Follow your inner dancer.

1. **Staraja Ladoga**, Yoga Moods, by Achillea
2. **Dreamcatcher**, Call of the Mystic, by Bahramji & Maneesh De Moor
3. **Rhythm of Life**, Amen, by Paula Cole
4. **Soul's Journey**, Bar de Lune Presents Egyptian Beats, by Leila
5. **Shake it Loose**, Gateaux Youth, by Dolphin Boy
6. **All I Need** (Air & Beth Hirsch), Moon Safari, by Air
7. **Porto De Partida**, Pyramid In Your Backyard, by Praful
8. **Flow**, Lovers Rock, by Sade
9. **Angels** (feat. Norah Jones), Nublu Sessions, by Wax Poetic
10. **Bandy Bandy** (feat. Erykah Badu), Ancestry In Progress, by Zap Mama
11. **Namadjidja**, Mali Koura, by Issa Bagayogo
12. **Cha Cha Cha**, Remember Tomorrow, by Mo' Horizons
13. **Face A La Mer** (Massive Attack Remix), Compilation Remixes, by Les Negresses Vertes
14. **Sidudla** (Gus Gus Remix), Music With No Name, Vol. 2, by Mabi Thobejane
15. **Outro Lado**, Chill Top 50 - Armada Music, by Zuco 103
16. **In the Music**, Wonder Woman, by Omawumi
17. **A Night In Lenasia**, Flute for Thought, by Deepak Ram
18. **Tamly Maak**, Tamally Maak, by Amr Diab
19. **Mariposa** (Praful's Lovebug Remix), Remixes, Vol. 1 - EP, by Bardo State
20. **My Love - My Song** (feat. Sonya Sohn), A Gift of Love, Vol. 2 - Oceans of Ecstasy, by Deepak Chopra
21. **Ancient Lullaby**, Praying to different Gods (feat. Sandhya Sanjana) by Ikarus
22. **Illumination**, Resurrection of the Divine Feminine, by Jehan

Go to: www.EricaRoss.com/playlists

Third Turn

The Partner Dance

"The river that flows in you also flows in me." Kabir

Part 1. The Set Up

"You've got to meet him. I think he's your soulmate!" Nori said for the hundredth time.

Nori was assistant director at the Spring Street Enamels Gallery in Soho, New York. She kept telling me about her friend James, an art student who was studying at her university in Arizona.

Nori was relatively new to the gallery but I'd already been there awhile; first as an apprentice to Joan, the owner and director of the gallery, and then as Joan's assistant teacher in the studio.

I'd absolutely lucked out. I had studied enamelling, jewelry-making and silver-smithing at OCA, the Ontario College of Art (now called OCAD U) in Toronto, but my favourite was enamelling - painting glass on metal and firing it in a kiln. There I was working at a beautiful enamel gallery in New York City.

I found the gallery just days after arriving in NYC and was right around the corner from my flat. In the beginning, I just helped around the gallery - selling, wrapping and shipping glassware and enamels. In return, Joan let me use the large studio in the back for free. She and I hit it off immediately.

Soon after we began our work exchange she offered me an apprenticeship position and got me an apprenticeship visa. Then she offered me an assistant teaching job as well. It all fell into place quite quickly.

Really, I couldn't believe my luck. I was living in an amazing apartment, in Soho, doing what I loved, at an enamel gallery in Soho. The angels were surely smiling down on me.

The Spring Street Enamels Gallery became my second home. It was beautiful. The space was divided in two - in the front there was glassware and enamel work on display, and in the back there was a large studio space with two big kilns, a variety of smaller portable ones, and lots of table space for students to create on. I was selling art, making my own enamels, and I'd become the in-house artist.

Plus, I also did repairs. In fact, I even repaired a large enamel made by the legendary American pop artist Roy Lichtenstein, whose work has sold for over 95 million dollars. Working there was an amazing experience and it was, literally, right around the corner from where I lived.

Along the way, as it got busier and busier, Joan hired an assistant director. Her name was Nori, and Nori, it turned out, would change my life.

Almost immediately upon meeting her she started telling me how I reminded her of this man she knew from university, an art student originally from Philadelphia. At lunch together I'd share a quote I loved and Nori would say, "Oh, my goodness Erica, I just got a letter from James and he said exactly the same thing you just said."

"Really?" I'd say. "That's bizarre."

Then, while I was working on my art she'd say, "Oh, my goodness, your art reminds me of James's art."

It became an on-going thing. 'You remind me of James.' 'You're just like James.' 'You've got to meet James. I think he's your soul mate.'

One day I had to ask, "You're talking about this guy, telling me he's my soul mate. It might be time to find out what he looks like."

Nori smiled. "He's beautiful. He's short and super fit. He's artsy-looking. You'll love him."

'Oh. Wow.' I'm thinking. 'He sounds perfect: He's short, I'm 5'2". He's fit, I'm a dancer. He's artsy-looking, I am too. Oh my... maybe Nori was right. Maybe he truly IS my soul-mate!'

At the same time as I was hearing all about James, I had met a man from just outside San Francisco. He'd been in town visiting and before he went back he invited me to visit him. We'd had a brief affair and I liked him. I said yes.

About a week before I was to leave for California, Nori said, "Guess what? James's coming. James's coming to visit."

"What do you mean he's coming? When?"

"He's coming to the gallery. Today."

"What? Not now. To the gallery? Oh, no!"

It was so unexpected, not to mention poorly timed. I was leaving for California in just a week. What if James really was my soul mate? I was not ready to meet him.

"Oh, and he thinks he's coming to be with me," Nori went on, "but really, I'm setting him up to be with *you*."

What? James didn't know the first thing about me. But it was too late and I had no idea what to do.

Within the hour the doorbell rang. Actually, it was a security buzzer. The way the entrance to the gallery was set up, I could see James at the door, but he couldn't see me. I peeked to have a look and my heart leapt out of my skin. He was so gorgeous!

I nervously went to the door to let him in. He asked for Nori right away. Clearly, he didn't know a thing about what was going on. I quickly got Nori.

"James!" Nori exclaimed, wrapping her arms around him.

I was standing off to the side, just trying to stay relaxed, pretending I knew nothing. On the inside? Well, let me give you a sense of the very reasonable, calm, cool, and collected thing that was going on inside my head: 'He's beautiful. He's BEAUTIFUL! Oh, my god! He's so BEAUTIFUL!' Ahem. Yes, very, very calm.

Nori turned to me and said, "James, I'd like you to meet Erica."

I said, you know, "Hello."

"James is my friend from university," Nori said as though she was telling me for the first time.

"Hi, James," I said, and I noticed he was wearing an earring in the shape of a scorpion. "I'm a Scorpio. Are you?"

"No, no. I'm a Leo/Virgo."

"Oh, that's cool," I responded, but to myself I said, 'It's got to be a sign. He's wearing my sign. He's wearing a scorpion. He must be my guy!'

Now in his mind, James had come from Philadelphia to spend the weekend with Nori. He had to be expecting to leave the gallery with her, but Nori lived in Brooklyn with her family. They're religious Jews, and it was Friday afternoon. Soon the sun would set and the Sabbath would begin.

Nori said to him without even checking with me, "James, I know you've come for the weekend, but what I didn't tell you is that I live with my parents. So, we're going to have to stay at Erica's place."

He looked at me and he looked at her, and I could tell he was wondering what the heck was going on. I could also tell that there was an immediate vibe between us, a kind of instant 'zzzzap' when we met. It wasn't just me.

"Okay, right," I said, a bit baffled and taken off guard.

"I have to go back to Brooklyn first," Nori said, "to do Shabbat with my family. So, if you don't mind, will you both go back to Erica's apartment together and wait for me? I'll join you afterwards."

"Sure," James said.

And I said, "Fine," thinking to myself, 'sneaky girl.' This is the first I'm hearing about this arrangement. Luckily, I had no plans, so it was a green light on my end.

A bit awkwardly, James and I headed off to my apartment just around the corner. As we were walking over, James with his suitcase in hand, I was thinking how innocent he was. He had no idea what was going on!

When we got to my apartment I offered him a glass of wine and we waited for Nori. And we waited. And we waited.

Finally, the phone rang. "You know what," Nori said, "I'm actually feeling sick. Would you mind if I don't make it tonight? Will you two be okay on your own?"

Honestly, I had no clue what Nori was going to do next - she didn't plan any of it with me, but I went along with her every step of the way!

By the time she had called, James and I were really connecting. I checked with James, and we agreed it was no problem. I told her we'd see her the next day.

At some point that evening I noticed he was looking at me and I was looking at him. I wondered what he was thinking. I assumed his intentions were to be with Nori, even though I knew they were never lovers, they were friends. But now, how did I fit in to this equation? Did he still want to be with her, or did he want to connect with me? And, did I want to be with him?

And, then, well, the answer became crystal clear. We surrendered to the chemistry and wound up in bed together. We made love and fell asleep wrapped in each other's arms. It felt like a home-coming.

I had a dream that night, and when I woke up in the morning I told James all about it.

He said, "I've got to show you something." He grabbed his sketch book where he'd written a poem on the train ride from Philly to New York. What he'd written was my dream.

It was just as Nori kept saying, 'You and James are connected, connected, connected!' It seemed like living proof.

All I could think was, 'Who are you?!'

I confessed in the morning to what had been going on behind the scenes. "You need to know something. I didn't know it at the time, but this was a set up. Nori told me about you a while ago, and wanted us to meet. She repeatedly noticed us sharing the same information at the same time, through our art and our words, and she believes we're meant to be together.

I knew I wanted to meet you, but I had no idea you were coming this weekend. She didn't tell me a thing about it until an hour before you arrived. And she certainly didn't tell me that she was actually setting us up to meet!"

James's response? He didn't even blink an eye. He wasn't the least bit upset with her. We were so connected, so fast. It all seemed to be right.

Not surprisingly, Nori never showed up that entire weekend. Just as Nori might have predicted, James and I were just fine. More than fine. For three days we were inseparable. I'd never felt that intensity, that oneness with another person. It was an incredible feeling of, well, I couldn't call it love at that point. A soul connection? A sense of destiny? Whatever it was, it was a powerful feeling. It was like we'd known each other forever.

Just before he was to leave New York I took him over to visit my best friend, to introduce him to her and to explain my disappearance all weekend. He then caught the train back to his parents', and onwards to university. His Christmas break was coming to an end.

Within ten minutes of his departure - no exaggeration - ten minutes, I came down with a huge fever and flu symptoms. I felt awful and I knew it was because he'd left. I spent the next five days in bed, sick with a fever, trying to figure out what to do about California because it was obvious that, yes, James was already under my skin.

Before James had left, he asked me, "Can I write you when I get back to school?"

I said, "Of course. That would be wonderful, but ... guess what, I'm on my way to be with a guy in California for a month. I don't think it's a good idea for you to write me while I'm with this other man."

I had to tell James the truth. I mean, it occurred to me to cancel my trip but I wasn't totally sure of the impact James had really had on me. I thought it was possible the intensity and beauty of the experience would kind of float away. Little did I expect that I would fall so ill when James left me. I had definitely fallen HARD for him. And fast.

Still, I chose to go. I never told my Californian friend that there was another man in my life, but I'm certain he must have felt my distance and disconnection. I cut the trip short. I knew that what had happened with James was something special.

For the next five months, James and I were on fire; completely inspired by love and tapped into our creative juices. We sent dozens of love letters, and paintings and collages, back and forth to each other. It was a time of great heart-expansion and bliss.

James had told me when he left that he would write me using a pseudonym. "I'm going to write as Marie Antoinette. I'm going to sign my letters as Marie." So, he did. All of James's beautiful love poems to me were signed, 'Marie.' He even sent me a ring as 'Marie.'

The same kinds of synchronistic things that happened before James and I met continued to happen afterwards, only now Nori wasn't the go-between. It was a direct connection between James and me. I'd think of James and the phone would ring. He'd make a painting for me, and I'd make one for him, and sure enough they were the same. It was uncanny. It was clear to me we just had to be together.

Around April, out of the blue, I received a short card in the mail from my friend whose apartment I was subletting. All it said was, 'Did you know you and Marie Antoinette have the same birthday?' That's it. A card, out of the blue, passing along that little tidbit of information. What? I called James and asked, "James, how did you even think of Marie Antoinette?"

He shrugged, "I don't know."

"That is so bizarre. You've been writing to me as Marie Antoinette for four months and I just got a message from the woman who sublet this apartment to me saying, essentially, if you're Marie Antoinette, you and I have the same birthday!" You can't make this stuff up!

By May, nearly five months after we'd met, James was moving in with me. He finished the term, and decided to come straight back to New York to be with me.

But our time together in NYC would be short-lived.

In September I got notice from immigration that my apprenticeship visa was expiring. I had to leave the country. I was in tears, heart-broken. It was devastating news. "I don't want to go," I cried to James.

He just looked at me, and without skipping a beat he said, "Let's get married."

"Really?"

"Yeah, really! I love you," he said. "And I don't want you to leave. I want to be with you."

And so it was. Just weeks later, on September 18, 1981, we were married. My parents and sister flew down from Toronto, James's parents drove in from Philly. It was a chaotic, last minute affair at city hall with a cranky justice of the peace and a flock of friends and family, many meeting for the first time - including my family meeting James and his family. (My poor parents. They'd never even seen a photo of him until then!)

With the marriage, I could stay in the US, but staying in New York City was not in the cards.

Shortly after we were married, I received word that my friends who had sublet the apartment to me were coming home. James and I needed to find a place to live, fast.

New York was really expensive. I was paying only $250 a month. Anything more than that was beyond our means. Manhattan became out of the question. Brooklyn might have been an option but James had a better idea: Winter was on its way, and according to James, for the same price as a small space in Brooklyn, we could find a house in Arizona - with a pool! That sounded good to me.

We packed up and headed out. Our first stop was Philadelphia, but our hearts were set on Arizona, and the next chapter of our lives.

Part 2. The Dance

My soul mate, it turned out - my beloved, creative and brilliant James - wasn't the easiest housemate.

When James suggested he'd fix up his old car, a '67 Firebird, and we'd drive to Arizona, it seemed like a good plan, although he did mention the car may not be a quick fix. That, it turned out, was an understatement. I don't know if the issue was really the car or James, but weeks and weeks and weeks went by and we weren't any closer to leaving for Arizona.

During that time we stayed with his parents, sister and her beautiful new baby. Not only was this a big change from having our own place and living in Manhattan, but we were newlyweds and we were living in his old bedroom at his parents' home, with no privacy.

I mean, the house itself was beautiful. We were living in a nice neighbourhood and his family was the sweetest, but I felt like a fish out of water. I'd traded the life I loved for a life that didn't even feel like mine any more.

Months went by. The repairs were endless and the car never worked. Any excitement I had about moving to Arizona was eroding with each passing month. We were definitely stuck and I was definitely itching for my own home.

"Look," I said, "if we're not leaving for Arizona, we need our own place. Maybe it's time we find a home in Philadelphia." I had resigned myself to the fact that we weren't going anywhere. Philly was going to be our home.

We found a three-story, four-bedroom brick row house across the street from a small church. We used the house as both our home and studio. I had a jewelry studio on the top floor, and on the ground floor, instead of living and dining rooms, James had his art studio. We settled in and made a life for ourselves: We had lots of good friends and his family couldn't have been more supportive or more welcoming and generous.

But as I mentioned, James was challenging to live with. He was very, very smart, spontaneous and funny, *and* he had his own unique and particular way about doing almost everything; he fully embodied the expression 'marching to the beat of your own drum.'

A pattern emerged a little too quickly where I'd give in to his needs because he was so particular about things. Here's a classic example: James only liked to listen to punk, rock and some reggae. Me, I loved most kinds of music. So, we listened to his music.

"Since you can listen to anything, and I can only listen to some things, we should listen to my music because you won't mind because you like it all." I couldn't dispute his logic.

Or he would say, "I can't sell myself as an artist. I need to do my work and not worry about making money." I didn't know how to argue that. According to him, I was 'able' to make jewelry commercially, to make money, so I wasn't really 'the artist.' He was the artist. He, who rarely finished a single piece. He, who never held an exhibition of his work. He was 'the artist,' not me.

As it turned out, the man I'd met and married - the creative genius, the incredible poet, the beautiful artist - had a hard time being in and of this world.

So, what did I do? I became his patron. I became a go-go dancer to support us, and I made a number of different lines of jewelry, from paper to plastic, to silver and gold-plated with semi-precious stones. I was doing art shows and fairs in Philly and NYC to sell my wares. I was dancing afternoons or evenings, and making jewelry between midnight and four in the morning.

I took care of the rent. I took care of the home. I took care of him.

While I was busy, I held the dream that one day he'd get serious about his art and have an exhibition to showcase his work - his vibrant, magical and powerfully evocative paintings - but that dream never realized.

I was crazy madly in love with him (and he with me), no question; but slowly, despite the love and the good moments we shared, I was losing my sense of self. I began to come undone, and so did our marriage.

One of the issues that really wore me down was jealousy. James was constantly making me feel jealous and insecure. I know, I know. No one can make someone feel jealous, you're thinking. But, seriously, he had a way of provoking me, of conjuring up the worst insecurity in me.

Take dancing. James and I both loved going to clubs and we both loved to dance, but James was spectacular to watch.

Picture him. He had a body like a ballet dancer. He wore psychedelic tights as pants, adorned himself with earrings and bracelets, rings, nail polish and makeup, and his hair was shaved on the sides of his head with dreads on top; Jimmy Hendrix meets Bob Marley meets the Clash.

He was unique and he was wild! I don't know if it was because he wanted to be taller, but when James entered a room, he walked like a peacock - he literally walked on his toes. In his psychedelic tights, with his jewelry and his hair, we would walk into a club together and the crowd would take notice. James was in the house.

But, after the grand entrance he would leave me. James would head over to the bar to buy himself a drink. If there was a woman at the bar beside him, he'd buy her a drink too. Did he buy me a drink? Nope. And what money did he use? Mine.

I'd shrivel up just watching him, and instead of calling him on it or going off on my own, I would sit and watch what he'd do next. By the time he hit the dance floor (often with other women) I'd usually had enough.

"I'm going home," I'd yell at him over the music. "I don't even know what I'm doing here."

"Why are you leaving?"

"I don't want to be here watching you dance with other women."

"What is wrong with you? You're the one that I married! How can you be so insecure? Do you think I'm fucking them in the bathroom or something? I'm just dancing for god's sake. Relax. You're the one I married."

And that was supposed to be enough.

I would end up leaving, and he'd come running after me, and we'd have a big fight. Club nights out often ended that way, and each time he'd use that line, "But you're the one I married. I chose you!"

All I could think was, 'Then, why aren't you dancing with me?'

The marriage itself was dancing a slow death. Fights about money. Fights about other women. We stopped having sex. Eventually I said, "Let's go to therapy together because I can't cope anymore."

He said, "I'll go because you need help." There was nothing wrong with James, at least from his perspective. The marriage problems were because of me, because I was insecure. "Let's go and sort *you* out," he said.

I turned to Kim, my best friend back in New York City, and one of my closest confidants. I told her we weren't having sex anymore, that I didn't know what to do, and I told her we were in therapy. I was incredibly sad. My love for James was huge, but I was heartbroken and confused. She listened, as best friends do, and she commiserated.

In the middle of all this, I told James to get a job. "You need to make money. You've got to contribute here. You've got to!"

Suddenly, he had a job interview. I don't know how the interview came up, but I was thrilled to learn he was, at least, in the running for a job. The interview was in New York City, and the one person we knew there was Kim, whom he'd come to know over the years. I suggested, "Why don't you stay with Kim." And, so, he did.

He made the trip. He didn't get the job. Life carried on.

A couple of months later, James suggested we visit Kim for New Year's Eve. "Oh, that's a great idea! I miss her. Let's do it!"

When we got to New York something felt off. I felt like he was giving her too much attention. But, I thought, no, it's just my insecurity kicking in. I tried to get over it, but I never did and at a certain point I simply said to them both, "I don't want to stay. I need to go home."

James was upset, but I told him that the situation didn't feel right to me, and we left. Once we got home I felt relieved, but still worried about the future of my marriage.

A week or two later, James told me he was going to take a trip to visit his cousin who lived just outside Philly, who, coincidentally, didn't have a phone. James said he was missing his cousin.

"So, I won't be able to get a hold of you while you're there?" I asked. (This was before cell phones.)

"Yeah. But I won't be gone long, just for the weekend. It shouldn't be a problem," he said. As I watched him pack his bag, I couldn't help but notice he packed his dance tights, which was odd because his cousin lived in the country. I didn't say anything. I just watched, feeling down and lonely.

I knew our marriage was falling apart. I could feel I was losing him. He said goodbye, and that he'd be back on Sunday. As soon as he left, I got a strange, sick feeling, and I thought to myself, he's going to New York.

Then, I did something that I never do: I started going through his stuff. I needed a sign, I needed to know what was going on. I went through his clothes in the dresser, and sure enough, at the bottom of the drawer I found some computer paper, the old kind of computer paper that had holes in the sides. The only person I knew who had a computer using that kind of paper was Kim. Could this be Kim's paper?

And then, it happened again, that sick feeling. I started reading the pages. It was love poetry. It didn't say who they were to, or who they were from, and I didn't really know if it was her paper. I just knew they were love poems on computer paper just like Kim's.

I got to thinking about our New Year's Eve trip to New York, how something felt off. And as I stood there with the love poems in my hand, that's when I realized for sure that he was not going to his cousin's house.

I called Kim. Right away. I needed to know. I needed to know immediately. But the call went right to the answering machine. She didn't pick up.

My friendship with Kim was the kind of friendship where she would pick up or call me right back if she knew I was calling. She didn't call me back that night. She didn't call me back the next day, nor the next night. And she didn't respond all day Sunday. I must have left three or four messages over that weekend, never saying anything specific, just asking her to call me because I needed her... and I did!

If I'd had any doubts, by Sunday they were gone. I knew he was with her. I knew. I knew. I knew it in my bones. There was no way she wouldn't have responded to me unless he was there. I felt sick to my stomach at even the thought of it.

Then, Sunday night came and she returned my call. He must have left by that point, I figured. He was probably on the train heading home. "What's the matter?" Kim asked. "You seemed really upset. What's going on?"

"Kim, I can't even believe I'm going to ask you this, but was James with you this weekend?"

"What? No!! Why would you even think that?"

I said, and I'll never forget it, "I am standing naked here in front of you. I'm asking you this question. You are my best friend. We swore that no man would ever come between us. Please, tell me the truth. Can you imagine what it must feel like for me to even be asking you this? I need you to tell me the truth. Was James with you this weekend?"

She broke down. "Yes," she cried.

"Do you love him?"

"Yes."

"Does he love you?"

"I think so."

And in that moment, my world fell apart. I felt like I had two knives in my heart. The woman whom I would've run to for solace was now the other woman, my rival. She was, up until that moment, my best friend. I loved her. And I could even understand why she would love him and why he would love her, because we love each other and she's like me. But, what the fuck!

"Please Kim. He's my husband and I'm still trying to work this out with him. Please give us some space to do this. I need you to back off. I still love him."

And she said, "No, I can't do that. I'm not going to let him go. I love him too."

And just as she said that, James walked in the door.

"Kim, I gotta go. James is here." And I hung up on her.

James casually sauntered in as if he'd been at his cousin's.

"Don't even," I say. "Don't even. I know. I just got off the phone with Kim."

And his face just dropped. (As in, 'Shit, I just got caught. I'm screwed.')

As I was trying to talk to him, the phone kept ringing and ringing. Kim was calling to plead, "Don't be mad at him. Please, don't be mad at him."

"Fuck off! Don't call me. What the fuck! This is my husband! I'm sorry, I love you, but..." And I hung up the phone on her again.

The issues in the marriage were reaching a peak, but James and I still didn't know if it was over. We hadn't given up on therapy. In fact, once I knew about the affair, the therapists convinced me to stay in therapy with him. "Most love affairs don't last," they told us. "Usually, favour is on the side of the wife. So why not let this play out?"

With the support of the therapists, I said to James, "Go see Kim. Figure this out. You have to decide."

The therapy was kind of interesting. Our therapists were a couple. James and I would go to therapy together, but we would start off individually. Each of us with one of them; I was with her and James was with him. Then, we would all come back together to discuss what had come up in our individual sessions. It seemed effective.

For seven months we went to therapy together, and, once every month, James would head to New York City for a weekend with Kim, supposedly to help him decide if he wanted to be with me or with Kim. Every month.

Every time he went away I would cry myself to sleep, picturing them in my mind. I cried in the rain. I cried with friends and family (including James's). I cried everywhere, it seemed.

And every time he came back, I would ask, "Have you decided?"

He would answer, every single time, "I love you. And I love her. I don't know. I love you both."

At a certain point, James stopped going to therapy, but I decided to continue. Once he was out of the picture, both therapists started to say things to me like, "We never wanted to say this in front of James, but there's nothing wrong with you. You just lost your sense of self. You need to recalibrate, and you need to come back into your own power. You lost your power in this relationship. You became the 'Yes' person."

"At this point," they said, "you just need to get strong. There is nothing wrong with you. In fact, you are an amazing woman."

Finally, after eight months knowing about James and Kim's affair, I went to James and said, "I'm not waiting for you to decide anymore. I'm leaving."

I wanted someone who just wanted me and no one else. I had to ask myself, (which I hadn't done up to that point because I hadn't been strong enough), 'Why am I waiting for him to decide? I can decide, and I say no more.'

I walked out, suitcases in hand, with only my personal belongings and my art. Everything else, I left behind. I left behind everything James and I created for the house. I left everything we'd bought for the house. I even left behind most of my jewelry-making supplies and equipment, which were worth thousands of dollars.

*A couple months later I discovered that James had sold my big ticket jewelry-making items including a kiln and torch to a local jeweller, and I bought them back!

I found a new place to live in Philadelphia, a wonderful loft in an old armory building, and started my new life.

After I left, James came to see me, "I've left her. I want you back."

"No. I can't go back," I said. "I waited eight months for you to decide, and you didn't. I'm taking my life back."

Once I'd made the decision that I was done, I was done. "If you'd told me a month ago that you'd leave her, I wouldn't have left you. But for me to have to walk out that door, there's no walking back in. I can't. I won't."

Leaving James was the hardest thing I'd ever done. He was my soulmate. I'd never loved like that before. I thought we'd be together forever, but going back was not an option.

The whole experience, from finding out about the affair to leaving him, had been devastating, emotionally and physically. I'd lost thirty pounds. I'd stopped eating. My mother came to visit me and I remember I weighed about 95 pounds. The best I could do was eat half a bowl of soup a day; it was all I could get down.

But things started to turn around for me.

A friend in New York who owned a clothing boutique came to visit, and she said, "Come and stay with me in the back of my boutique."

I jumped at the chance to visit the city I loved. Once I was there, I asked her, "Do you want a partner in this boutique?"

And, she said, "Yes!"

Part 3. The Healing

There was no question about it, I was ecstatic to be back. I had pined for the New York I left behind. Philadelphia might have been only 90 minutes away but it felt a world apart. Philly represented an unravelling of my life, and New York had been a flourishing. When I returned, I felt like - I'm back, I'm back!

New York was just the remedy I needed. It was a beautiful distraction, a place to heal my broken heart and find myself again. Life unfolded in wonderful ways during that time. Our boutique was doing well, and after a year working together we started designing our own clothing line: a rock 'n roll meets boho style. We established a home and business in Bali to print and batik our fabrics and make the clothes.

Being back in NYC also meant I'd inevitably see Kim again. For the eight months of therapy, while James was continuing to visit Kim, the one boundary I maintained was that she was never to call me or my house, and he was never to call her from our home.

I told him, "If you want to talk to her, you have to go to a payphone! No way. It's enough that you're going there to see her. You're not talking to her from our home!" I had completely "'X'ed" her out of my life. But when I returned to NYC, I saw her a couple of times on the street. Each time, I turned my head. I couldn't even look at her. It felt awful. She had been my best friend, and I couldn't look at her.

Our business required that we spend more time in Bali. My partner and I started taking turns living in Bali for months at a time to oversee our clothing production. I loved it. Two countries. Two diverse life-styles. I was living the dream, the best of both worlds - the vibrant urban scene of Manhattan, and the beautiful, spiritual life of Bali.

It was an amazing time, but I was beginning to feel a pull to put down roots and have a baby. With ample notice to my boutique partner and friend, I decided to leave the business. And with her blessing, I packed up all of my things in Bali and put them into storage in the basement of the boutique.

I'd met a man from Wales in Bali and decided to follow him to Australia for a few months before going on a solo journey to find land somewhere in S. E. Asia to build a home to dance and make art in. But once I got to Australia my life would change forever.

I was given the best gift of all - I became pregnant! It was a dream come true!

When morning sickness set in, we decided to go to Bali together first to rest for a few months, and then we returned temporarily to Toronto where I gave birth to a beautiful daughter by candlelight in our apartment bedroom with my boyfriend, my mom, my sister (who caught her) and my dear maternal Bubbie Mary sitting with a front row seat!

My daughter was born in September, and I remember thinking how I'd love to introduce her to James one day. We had ended so badly, that when I left I couldn't imagine ever going back to Philly to see him.

He came to visit me once in New York, and a few times he asked me to come back, but, again, I just couldn't. And sadly, I'd been hearing stories about him struggling with substance abuse.

My life was rising and his seemed to be sinking. It was heartbreaking for me, but I needed to keep moving forward with my life. I needed to keep feeling joy - something I'd found again. I felt that leaving him had saved my life, and staying away did the same.

Four years after leaving James, my life in Toronto with my beautiful baby daughter felt like a new beginning. My hope was that I'd see him again. I'd heard that he was cleaning up his life. Maybe, just maybe, we could reconnect one day.

Only a few months after the birth of my daughter, I got a phone call from James's family with the tragic news that he had died. Possibly of a drug overdose, they just didn't know. I was in shock and disbelief. I felt numb and deeply saddened by the news. My love for him was still deep in my bones.

Not surprisingly I thought of Kim, and I had a decision to make. Did she know? Did she even have a connection to him? I had no idea - I had moved on. But, I felt I had to tell her because I knew how much she loved him. Quite remarkably, I still had a number for her. I dialed it not knowing if I'd reach her, and she picked up.

"Kim," I said. "Hi, it's me, Erica." She was surprised to hear from me, no doubt. "Kim, I have some very sad news about James. I don't know if you're still in contact with him, but I've just learned that he's died. I'm so sorry to tell you this. I'm so sad and heartbroken."

She hadn't been in touch with him for a while, but she did have an altar for him, she told me, of dried flowers and fresh fruit. She was always praying for him and hoping he was okay. Her world had fallen apart after he left her. She lost him, and she'd lost me.

She felt really alone, she said, and then she asked if she could come see me in Toronto. I couldn't answer her at first. I needed time to think. It was one thing just to call her and tell her about James, but I wasn't sure if I wanted her back in my life.

Less than 24 hours I knew what to do. I wanted her to come visit - I missed her. She was the best friend I'd ever had (besides my best friend in elementary school.)

We had two and a half years together in New York City that were just incredible. We were so close. We never fought. We were so in sync. We were like two peas in a pod. We danced. We laughed. We played. We were inseparable. It was pure magic and joy. And I missed that, and I hadn't had it since. I told her to come on up.

She came to Toronto and stayed for a few days with my partner and me, and our baby. That's when the stories came out. A lot of things started to make sense. Through pain, courage and vulnerability we pieced the truth together.

Kim thought that James had chosen her; that he'd made his decision when I was still in Philly. She thought James and I had stopped being lovers, but that wasn't the case. We were still together at that point. Then, out of the blue, he broke it off with her, which was just after I left him. We realized that James had been playing us both. He was saying things that weren't true in order to keep us both. *"I love you. I love her. I don't know. I love you both."*

There was a whole lot of healing during Kim's visit. I was so happy to have her back in my life, and I really understood that she had paid a price. Losing him was one thing, and losing me was another. She had suffered enough and I didn't need to hold it against her anymore. I needed to let it go. I needed to forgive her, to forgive him, to move on.

And I did.

It's been more than twenty-five years since that Toronto visit and Kim and I remain very close. We've travelled together. We've visited at each other's homes more than once. I went to her wedding. And maybe best of all... We've had the chance to rendezvous a few times in NYC, spiralling us back to where we met, and even back to our favourite dance party, The Loft, just like the good old days!

I never did go to James's funeral, and I'm sorry I didn't.

I was overwhelmed with a four-month-old baby, and the thought of returning to Philly was just too hard and painful. I regret not finding the strength to be there to support his family, a family who claimed me as theirs, who only showed me love and support, always.

I know they understood why I didn't join them. And I know that any weight I feel in my heart about that decision is mine to carry, and mine alone. And that's okay. This is how we learn and practice self-forgiveness and compassion, right?

On a happy note, I did return to Philly, many years later, with my teen daughter in tow. James's parents welcomed us both with open arms to stay for a couple nights in their home. It was an emotional and love-filled reunion with stories and shared memories over meals and photo albums, joined by the extended family. And I finally got to mourn James's death with them in person. It was deeply healing. I was grateful to be back in their lives.

It's an unexpected ending to a story of love and betrayal, but forgiveness is powerful. And so is love. Kim will be in my life until the day I die, and so will James's family - my extended family.

I continue to hold James close. (David Bowie's 'Wild is the Wind,' "our" song, never fails to bring him even closer.) Like so many beautiful and gifted souls, he left far too soon. I truly believe the world lost a good and bright one the day he passed, and I gained another guardian angel.

Here's to love and all that it brings!

Reflections

"When we choose to love, we choose to move against fear, against alienation and separation. The choice to love is a choice to connect, to find ourselves in the other." bell hooks

From the Personal Dance of the Second Turn, we flow into the dance of Partnership. We move the focus from self to the focus on being with another; continuing the practice of following impulse, of showing up as ourselves, fully.

And when we do come face to face with another, it becomes crystal clear where the work is to be done. We quickly discover how easy it is to be pulled out of our center; the center we so diligently work at having when we're on our own. It's so easy to forget who we were a moment before the other showed up. What happened to us?

What happened was a shift away from our own needs and desires and knowing. Our attention becomes about the other. We find ourselves being drawn in by an attraction, or pushed away by an instantaneous rub or dissonance. Or, we come upon a fresh fear of being seen or being too much, or an envy, a judgment, or even a delicious inspiration.

If we choose to stay there in that powerful force called 'partnership,' we need skills to navigate the twists and turns, to not forget who we are, to not be pulled off center and knocked off our path. Otherwise we'll surely find our natural radiance and confidence diminish, slowly but surely.

So, the questions become...

How can you stay in your truth, in your own dance, just as you are, and at the same time stay open and available to another and in a co-creative space?

In other words, how do you honour yourself, the other, and the co-creation of you both, all at the same time? How do you not lose your power or center in the partnership?

How do you want to be met? How do you hold yourself back from meeting another, or from being met?

There's something so delicious when we drop into listening to ourselves, and seeing the other and allowing the co-creation to unfold without attachment.

This can be the hardest thing to navigate in life. That's why whoever shows up to be in a relationship with us becomes our greatest teacher. It's about navigating boundaries, and the flow of giving and receiving and continually returning to the softening, listening and responding from a place of loving kindness, as a loving witness.

When we hold the belief that it's all perfect, that we're perfect and divine mirrors for each other, we become a healing ally for the other. Open-hearted, open-minded, open-bodied, we hold space for the other to be themselves, to follow their own impulses. We're witnessing and being witnessed.

But sometimes the mirror of love becomes distorted, cloudy and dusty. Sometimes the light itself grows dim. With the loss of light comes the loss of the dream which was wrapped around our partner.

And when and if the time comes where we need to part, the practice of compassion and forgiveness is vital. Compassion for all concerned. And after all is said and done, in time, we realize that our hearts are amazingly resilient. They can and will break open again and again.

Because we need love. We're born to love, and we need each other.

In fact, the "Stone Center for Women's Research" at Wellesley College is discovering that females, and those with a strong feminine essence, are wired from day one to be relational. Men are as well, but not to the degree women are. It's important for women to have 'relationship authenticity,' to feel emotionally connected and purposeful in relationships.

Like Uzume did for Amaterasu, we can help each other recognize the beauty and light we each possess. Each one of us is a mirror reflecting the light of each other. Yes, we are sacred. And yes, we can hold our piece of mirror up, especially for those around us who are still in their caves for whatever reasons, and practice showing up fully, in our own center and power, and let go as needed.

Let the Partner Dance begin...

May you dance into deeper and wider LOVE and compassion.

May you dance into and from your center.

May you dance yourself home.

Practices for the Third Turn

Opening to Love Practices:

- Create an Altar for Aphrodite
- Design Vows of Self Devotion
- Dance with Love, AKA 'Love Comes Dancing'

Partnering Practices:

- Listen Compassionately to Another
- Consciously Collaborate
- Nourish your Relationship

Moving On Practices:

- Boast Your Way Out
- Let Go with De-Cording
- Forgive with Metta (Loving Kindness)

Playlists: Opening to Love
Partner Dance
Moving On

Opening to Love Practices

*"Your task is not to seek for love,
but merely to seek and find all the barriers
within yourself that you have built against it."* Rumi

Create an Altar for Aphrodite

Oh, how I adore the Greek Love Goddess, Aphrodite - 'The one who emerges,' 'The Golden One,' the 'Virgin* of the Sea.' She's the lover and the Goddess of Light - the 'Shining Star of Heaven,' and in Sumerian mythology, 'She Who Shows the Way to the Stars,' expressing the divine nature of love and light within us. Her sacred symbols include the swan, the dolphin, the rose and the dove.

*The term 'virgin' in this instance is from the original definition as I understand it; 'a woman unto herself,' meaning a woman who is self-reliant, independent and strong.

I see Aphrodite as the glistening and glowing one, stunningly radiant, life and love-giving, and the perfect goddess to evoke when we wish to open further to love - to call in the one, to dance with heart in partnerships and relationships. She offers us endlessly flowing divine love, ecstatic joy and radiant light.

By the way... If you prefer to create an altar for a 'Love Goddess' from a different culture, please do (and replace Aphrodite's name with your own goddess's name). For example, there's Oshun, Radha, Branwen and Milda - each one a love goddess in their own right, and whose essence is fundamentally the same.

Aphrodite teaches us to love fully; to love and be loving in all forms and expressions. She reminds us that love is our birthright, and that being female is a sacred blessing. Her presence invites us to see beauty and divinity in everything and everyone (including ourselves).

When we deny her presence in our life it's easy to become vulnerable to and overpowered by the ornery inner judge who thrives on criticizing, shaming and censoring our innate radiance, as well as others. We lose our ability to see, sense and feel the beauty, light and love in the world, within and without.

But it's never too late. When we invite Aphrodite in and ask for her guidance, we reorder our world, revise our vision, and restore our original radiance.

When we embody her and her teachings, we become shiny magnets electrified with pure love-light. We become attractive, compassionate and remember our wholeness. We become powerful beyond measure, a force for good, for all.

In honour of opening to love, the invitation is to create a beautiful altar for Aphrodite, YOUR Aphrodite, to activate and align with her power, her beauty, and her teachings.

The magic and transformative powers of your altar begin the moment you set your intention for it. Once complete, it becomes a beating heart or hearth, calling you home to your true nature - the divine lover. It's here at the altar where you can commune with your Inner Aphrodite, to be blessed by her, and remember you *are* love.

Third Turn: The Partner Dance

By opening to love you open to healing, magic and grace, which reciprocates in kind, creating more love. The love spiral turns and expands inwardly and outwardly. There's no end to where it will flow, or how it will move and touch your life. Its power is beyond our understanding. It's mysterious, magnificent and beautiful.

And there's no wrong way to do this. It doesn't matter if you've ever created an altar or not, whether you're meeting Aphrodite for the first time, or you're a life-long devotee. Your altar is unique to you.

This is your personal expression. Your relationship with Aphrodite. Your sacred art-making.

Trust and be guided by your inner impulse, your Inner Aphrodite's impulse, and stay in the mystery and curiosity of your creation. Ask Aphrodite for help in the creation. It might be simple, it might be complex. You might want to keep it up for a day, a week, or a month. Do as you please. Do as *She* pleases.

Love is opening the way.

Beauty is on your side.

Magic is in the making.

And so it is!

Create your Altar for Aphrodite: 1 hour or longer

1. **Relax and set your intention.** In your own way and time, tune into the qualities, healing and teachings you'd like to receive and embody from Aphrodite's presence and essence. Ask yourself: How do I wish to be touched by her? What do I need: more self-love, more joy, renewed partnerships? Am I missing beauty in my life?

   Or… choose to stay in the mystery and set an intention for Aphrodite to come to you as she wishes. Whatever the intention – specific or open - relax and open into it as an act of love.

2. **Find a spot for your altar.** Now, with the clarity of your intention, scout your space for a corner, a bedside table, a nook, a shelf, or an already designated altar space. Keep in mind that you want to be able to see it often or do activities near it, so don't hide it away in a hard to reach spot. Roam your space, listening within. Wait for the impulse that says YES! You'll know when it's right.

3. **Gather and place your altar items.** Now that you know where your altar will live, begin to look around your space and ask yourself questions like, "What feels like love? What feels beautiful and heart opening to me? What would Aphrodite like to see? What images, words, objects and/or colours evoke love?"

Invite Aphrodite to guide you. Perhaps she'd love a beautiful piece of fabric for the base adorned by a special photo, sculpture, or hand-written poem or affirmation. Maybe she'd love oracle cards, feathers and crystals. Or some fresh flowers (Aphrodite loves flowers).

Arrange everything until it feels just right. This is a fluid, living creation, so feel free to move things around, and to add or subtract as days go by. Stay true to your needs.

4 **Use it.** Now that you have your altar, use it as often as possible. Your altar is a sacred space for you to meet and be blessed by Aphrodite's beauty, grace and light. She asks nothing more from you than that - to join her in any way, at any time. Love is all that exists for her.

Spend an hour divining cards, meditating or writing love poetry, or ten minutes chanting her name or dancing her dance. Say love prayers or count your blessings by it.

No matter what, keep returning to this sacred space. Keep inviting the embodiment and remembrance of your 'divine lover' self as you need. Only you will know what that is, what it will look and feel like, what makes your Aphrodite smile.

5 **Take care of it.** Keep it clean. Keep it alive and energized with your loving care. Give it your utmost love, attention and devotion. Exchange dead flowers for fresh ones. Treasure it as long as it feels right. Let it go when it's time.

Design Vows of Self-Devotion

We all long for deep heart-centered connections where we can relax and be fully met, seen and heard just as we are. We long to be honoured as the Divine, the Beloved One.

Our longing comes from a profound desire and knowing deep in our bones and blood that it's our birthright to love, and be loved. And this knowing needs to be met by our own consciousness, within the altar of our own sacred heart and temple of our being. No exception on both accounts.

This practice to 'Design Vows of Self-Devotion,' inspired by a piece called, 'Me Wed,' from Rob Brezsny's book *Pronoia*, is offered to you now as a sacred exploration and container to align with your Beloved Within as you open into the dance of partnership.

These vows and promises of self-love are your soul songs to embody and commit to, to remind you of who you are and how you wish to live in the world, and most of all, to support you in staying true to course - to remain faithful to yourself, regardless of what happens.

When you let your vows sink into you, soaking deep into your marrow and tasting of the sweetest kiss on your lips, then, no matter what happens, or with whom or where, you'll be okay. More than okay.

You'll become an ever-flowing wellspring of delight, love and kindness. Your partnerships and relationships will flourish because of it.

You'll become an irresistible gift, radiant with beauty and joy; unstoppable in devotion not just to yourself but to all life. And all the ways you've betrayed, hurt or starved yourself - self-doubt, ridicule, shame, denial - will diminish with every vow made, every promise honoured, every contract kept. You'll be cleansed and re-polished.

It's never too late. It's a matter of re-assessing, re-orienting, and re-membering.

Even past heart-breaks, wounds and loss will melt under the warmth of your softer heart and mind. They'll no longer hold power over you or weigh you down, but rather, they'll merge with you, finding their place in the shape of you now. A part of your love dance. A part of you.

With courage, compassion and care, love will thrive. Life will mirror your rising up, your blossoming, and meet you right where you are. You'll be seen, felt and honoured just as you are. That's how it flows. Life's good that way. With these seeds of inspiration...

May this process, and your vows, be deeply personal, meaningful and important to you. Your Beloved One Within depends on it. She's waiting for you. This may seem cliché, but truly...

You are the one you've been waiting for.

Are you ready to step into this sacred path of self-love, self-remembrance and self-flowering?

Here's the process: 30 minutes or longer

1. **Find a sacred space and time** where you can be alone and undisturbed. (By your altar to Aphrodite would be perfect.)

2. **Get comfortable** and begin to relax, perhaps with conscious breathing, or soft music, or dancing. Whatever will connect you to yourself.

3. **Come into a softening** and tenderness towards yourself. Take your time. Take as long as you need.

4. As you feel into your heart and listen with compassion and quiet curiosity, **ask yourself, 'What do I need to be The Beloved One in my life?** How might I have betrayed myself or let myself down in the past?' Your answers hold the keys to the vows you're about to make.

5. **Let the tears flow.** Let any emotions come. This is part of the process. Feel the purging of old habits, ways of thinking and acting on your behalf. Be kind and compassionate to your tender heart, to the wounds and aches of not being fully met by your own self. Give yourself permission to listen deeply, and hold your truth with soft gloves.

6. With your heart's truth **ask yourself, 'What am I willing to promise myself today?'**

   Design your vows as the antidote and cure for your aching heart. For example: You let others control and dictate your life choices. Your vow: 'I vow to listen and follow my own truth.' Let your vows come from your needs. (Take inspiration from the vows offered on the next page.)

7. **Write your vows down** in your journal. Choose one, two or a few. Perhaps, write down a handful, and then come back to them and edit it down.

8. **Be blessed by them.** Bless your body, your mind, your heart and your soul, your rhythms and cycles, your vulnerabilities and strengths. Let their magic touch you. Dance, make art or meditate with them. Align with these new promises, this new pact.

9. **Remind yourself of them.** Keep returning to your words. Say them out loud, make a mantra, chant or sing them. Write them on a small piece of paper and put it in your purse or by your bedside table. Use them.

I am **devoted** to my wellbeing.

I am in love with all of me.

I am the one I've been waiting for.

I love myself.

I **promise** I will never betray myself.

I promise to treasure myself.

I **vow** I will be faithful to myself, regardless.

I will always treat myself with compassion.

Dance with Love, AKA 'Love Comes Dancing'

"You only have to let the soft animal of your body love what it loves." Mary Oliver

Love Comes Dancing is an open love letter to your soul; an invitation to soften and imagine, feel and sense yourself as a breathing, moving, living heart.

I truly believe with my whole being that LOVE is what we are made of, and what flows through us. Love makes no exceptions and is omnipresent. It's the greatest gift we can receive and give. It's the greatest power in the universe.

Call it as you wish - The Beloved, God, Goddess, Divine Light, Allah, Krishna, All That Is, The Beauty Path.

Love is the way, the Tao, the One. And it's our responsibility, task and privilege to BE love; to be a loving witness to ourselves, to our own beautiful heart, and allow the flow of love to live and dance in every cell of our being.

Regardless of past experiences, your state of mind right now, or future fears, YOU have the right to feel the pulse of love, to dance as love would dance. You have the right to reorder your world, to self-blossom in love, and realize your magnificence.

In this practice, 'Love Comes Dancing,' the invitation is to invite love in, and dance with love as your dance partner. Yes, your dance partner.

One small detail... Guess who gets to lead?

Love leads, my friend. Love wants to take you in its arms and rock you, sweetly, wildly, peacefully. Who knows how else? Love asks only one thing - for your hand. Where it will lead you is hard to say.

That's the magic of letting go to love's dance. That's the beauty of love coming to dance... for you, towards you, around you, and within you. **Let love in. Let love guide you. Let love rule.**

Love Comes Dancing: 20-30 minutes

*Regardless of physical abilities or limitations, love can come dancing - on your feet, in a chair or lying down; with one arm, half a body or just your face moving. And if moving isn't an option at all, no problem! Draw on the power of your imagination - your subconscious mind can't tell the difference between what's 'real' and imagined.

1. **Find 20-30 minutes of flowing music,** or play the **Opening to Love Playlist.**
2. **Make some space** where you can dance freely and won't be disturbed.

3   **Begin the music.**

4   Wherever you are - lying, seated or standing - **grow roots from the soles of your feet or base of your spine, down into the earth**, to ground and support your dance. (Gaia is always there to support us!)

5   **Imagine, sense and feel yourself dancing under a waterfall of love.**

6   **Relax your face and eyes,** softening to receive and be touched by love.

7   **Slowly move, feeling love** flowing all through you.

8   **Breathe in love. Breathe out love.**

9   **Fall in love with yourself** as you dance in this shower of love, allowing every cell of your body to be touched by love and love's light.

10 **Become a moving embodiment of love.** Wherever you move, love is there.

11 **Bless yourself**, loving up each body part, bringing more fluidity and love, especially into your pelvis, head and heart.

12 **Expand and shine your love.** Dance with and for love. Smile, move, glow. Radiate love's light beyond your skin, beyond the room. Let your love light shine up into the stars, down into the Earth, and to everyone and everything. Nothing is untouched by it.

13 **Stay in the dance as long as you like.** Keep flowing and glowing as long as it feels good, as long as you can.

14 **When you feel satiated and complete, slowly come into stillness.**

15 **Find and hold a shape that feels like the shape of love.** Hold love there for a moment. Breathe into it. Sink in, and see what you notice. What and how do you feel?

16 **Slowly open your eyes, release the shape and give thanks.**

After the dance, see how long you can maintain the feeling of love flowing. See how long you can keep shining, to continue to embody love and light in the world.

Keep glowing and flowing. You ARE love.

*If you feel vulnerable, extra sensitive or raw (this can happen), please be gentle with yourself. Take time to ground if you can, especially if you need to leave your safe space and go out into the world.

Partnering Practices

"Each friend represents a world in us,
a world possibly not born until they arrive,
and it is only by this meeting that a new world is born." Anaïs Nin

Listen Compassionately to Another

"An enemy is one whose story we have not heard." Gene Knudsen Hoffman

The word compassion means literally 'to suffer with.' It's the ability to *attend* to, and have concern for, suffering.

Compassion is the loving practice of being with another unconditionally, of allowing others and ourselves the space to go through what needs to be experienced and to feel what needs to be felt. Loving kindness, acceptance and forgiveness are aspects of compassion. Our capacity to care and empathize, and to experience intimacy, expands with compassionate practices.

One of the ways we can practice offering compassion is in how we listen, specifically compassionate listening. Compassionate listening is the art of being a silent witness, holding a safe and non-judgmental space for another to express their heart, their truth.

Buddhist monk and writer Thich Nhat Hanh speaks often about compassionate listening. He says that even one hour of compassionate listening can relieve the suffering of an individual. It can initiate transformation and healing.

He takes it further: Compassionate listening, he believes, has ripple effects that could ultimately put an end to war and change the world for the better. I believe him. I believe it's that powerful a practice.

So, how do we do this?

By sitting, listening, and being with another, holding safe space so they can express what is alive in them - in their truth and heart. We offer our undivided attention, concern, love and compassion without giving advice or counsel unless asked. We're there to understand more, and judge less. And ultimately, to find connection and union where your heart and theirs can become one.

As I reflect on compassion, I can't help but think about one of the dearest goddesses in my life - my beloved **Kuan Yin** (pronounced kwan yin); 'Regarder of Sounds,' 'She Who Hears Our Cries,' the Chinese Goddess of Compassion.

Kuan Yin was a young woman who reached enlightenment in her lifetime, despite, or maybe because of, the hardships she endured. She didn't have to come back after death but chose to stay on Earth as her sacred duty to relieve the suffering and encourage the enlightenment of everyone.

Like Buddha, she's a *Bodhisattva. *Bodhisattva comes from the Sanskrit words 'bodhi,' meaning enlightenment or awakening, and 'sattva,' meaning sentient being.

Kuan Yin is so powerful, as the story goes, that simply saying her name relieves suffering. She appears often as a temple guardian with 1000 arms or 1000 eyes always alert.

Tara from Tibet and India, **Mary** from Christianity, the **Virgin of Guadalupe** from Mexico and **Isis** from Egypt are also 'Compassionate Ones,' reminding us to touch and be touched by the world around us, and that our tears connect us with all beings.

The next time a loved one, friend, colleague or neighbour asks for support, or you sense needs support, lean in, reach out, and invite them to join you in this powerful space of compassionate listening.

Practice being loving and kind. Practice being Kuan Yin, a Compassionate One, for others.

Compassionate Listening: 30 minutes or longer

1. Invite your loved one, friend, sister, or whomever it is, to **sit with you**.

2. Tell them you wish to be **a compassionate listener**, to practice being fully present in love and compassion.

3. **Invite them to share** as they wish, to take their time.

4. **Soften** your heart, your mind, and the gaze of your eyes. Allow your body posture to open and relax, to reflect the soft and available nature of your presence.

5. **Listen with your whole being** when they speak, as they speak.

6. **Stay present with them.** Keep your gaze gently on them, letting them know you are fully there with them; fully listening.

7. **Give time and space** for their unfoldment, in their own way and at their own pace.

8. **Allow their feelings to come** - to vent, purge, cry or be in silence for as long as they need.

9. **Do not give advice or counsel unless they ask.** You're there to be an ear, a confidante and a friend.

10. **Check in with them from time to time** to see if they need anything - more time, silence, loving touch, to close their eyes, to sit closer or farther away.

11. Tune in to sense when they may be ready to end their sharing. **Ask them if they feel complete.** Stay with them until they say they are.

12. When they are complete, **thank them for their beautiful and courageous heart.** Thank them for sharing and that you'll hold their words in confidence, protected in your heart. (And mean it.)

Third Turn: The Partner Dance   127

13 If it feels right, you can ask them if they'd like to hear what your experience of compassionate listening was like. If not, let it go. If so, share from your heart, as they have done. This is healing for everyone.

*A wonderful resource: The Compassionate Listening Project is a non-profit organization dedicated to empowering individuals and communities to transform conflict and strengthen cultures of peace.

Consciously Collaborate

Have you ever danced the tango, or seen really good, mature and seasoned tango dancers?

I've only danced it once (with a master dancer), but I've been blessed to have seen great tangos from Argentina a few times. I'm always blown away by the grace, the passion, and the strength. It's so powerful in its essence, and complicated in its technique. It takes great skill to navigate, to lead and be led, to integrate and syncopate arms and legs crisscrossing and moving together precisely.

The tango, in my humble opinion, exemplifies and embodies the beauty and power of a shared experience, a shared creation. A shared love.

I offer it here as an example of a 'Conscious Collaboration,' literally and metaphorically, to inspire your own tango dance, so to speak.

The collaboration: the dance itself that can't be done without both partners. The consciousness: the utter focus and attention that's required to be present with and sensitive to the other.

This invitation to Consciously Collaborate is a sacred playground for practicing all the skills you've explored in the first two Turns, but now, in partnership with another; to co-create a path of mutuality, a dance, like the tango, of reciprocal love and respect.

Because here's the thing... we're collaborating in partnership all the time, anyway. EVERY time you engage with another, one-on-one, you're consciously or unconsciously co-creating. You, plus another, can't help but generate something that wasn't there before. That's the truth of it.

Wouldn't it be a wiser and sweeter choice to engage consciously? Wouldn't it be wonderful to know and feel that your encounters were a meaningful part of your life path and sacred dance? With eyes and heart open. Mindful and present.

It can be that way. But it takes practice. All mastery takes commitment and practice. Conscious collaboration is no exception.

This means practicing being awake and mindful through it all, from the conception, seed or vision of your collaboration, to the saying YES to it, to the implementation and then completion, and if not completion, its ending.

No matter what size, shape, duration, meaning or depth the conscious collaboration holds. Be aware, responsive, and sensitive - to both you and your partner's needs and truth, like a tango dancer offering herself to the dance. The dance of reciprocity.

Personally, I've been blessed and am grateful for the opportunities I've had to practice collaborating consciously. Regardless of the outcome, they've taught me about myself, and I've grown exponentially because of them. With each new collaboration, my capacity to stay awake, responsive and sensitive to my collaborator, myself, and the co-creation expands. (This book is a perfect example.)

Even though there surely are challenges, obstacles and risks in collaborating consciously, such as navigating power dynamics and boundaries, being triggered emotionally when there are clashes, and being brave enough to speak up and stand in your truth and integrity, it's worth it for the chance of co-creating something you couldn't possibly birth on your own.

So, my lovely...

Are you ready to get co-creative?

Are you ready to step out of the lone-wolf syndrome that many of us have?

Do you have a big idea you need a second set of eyes, ears and hands for? Have past experiences with collaborating left you hesitant to trust a partnership again? Are you new to the idea of consciously collaborating?

Wherever you are on the spectrum of collaborative experiences - from beginner to master - let these suggestions nudge you. (Sacred experiment.)

Remember, it's a practice. Start with the smaller ideas and work up. Enjoy the process, my love.

Expand.
Grow.
Blossom.

Let the tango begin...

*When I say 'someone,' I'm referring to a friend, a family member, a spouse, a lover, a colleague, a kindred spirit, a neighbour. It could be someone you know well, or someone you'd like to get to know better. You choose.

- **Co-create an art piece.** Get a large piece of paper and coloured markers. With your partner, take turns laying down one line, shape or colour at a time. One draws while the other watches, consciously engaged with an open heart and mind. Keep going back and forth until it feels complete by both of you.

    When it's done, flip it over and cut the paper in two, or in smaller pieces, not influenced by the drawing on the top-side. You'll both have an original piece of art and a piece of your partner's genius! This would be especially delicious to do with a child. Just sayin'.

- ◎ **Write a collective poem.** Using the same technique as above, take turns writing a line of a poem. Watch how it unfolds. Try doing this without editing. Riff off of the other's previous line. Co-create a beautiful thread, story, rhythm or rhyme. Stay consciously connected and sensitive to your partner's words. Pause as you need, giving each other space for their muse to flow.

  When it feels complete, read it out loud from top to bottom, and then bottom to top. Photo copy it so you both have a copy, or take a pic with your phone. Take it further and turn it into a song or a chant. Or take one line of it and turn it into an affirmation or mantra. Ah, the possibilities are endless!

- ◎ **Co-create a delicious meal.** Invite someone to make a meal with you, someone you've *never* made a meal with before. Enjoy the whole process together - from deciding on the time and place, the menu (pick some recipes neither one of you has done before to add to the fun), to shopping for groceries, prepping the food, setting the table (and ambiance and esthetics of the space), to enjoying your delicious collaboration. Have fun, and be adventurous and creative.

- ◎ **Find a collaborator for a business venture.** Do you have an idea for a new business or organization - profit or non-profit - or you already have an existing one, but you know it's just too much for you to do yourself? Look around and see who might be a candidate for a shared, conscious collaboration with you. And if not them, then ask if they might know someone. Network in and outside of your community.

  Set your intention to find the perfect collaborator, and see what magic arises. There are so many benefits to having a partner in business. The key is to stay 'conscious,' aware and sensitive to the other, and stay in your heart. Anything is possible when you flow and work in that sentient space.

- ◎ **Take tango classes.** How can I talk about the tango and not suggest you do it? And if tango isn't your thing, how about salsa, swing, hustle or any other form of partner or ballroom dancing? Find a local dance teacher or studio and sign up for a trial session with a friend or partner. If you love it, sign up for a series of classes and dive in. If there are no classes near you, look online. YouTube is filled with dance instruction videos. Get movin' and groovin' with a partner, and have fun!

- ◎ **What else would be wonderful for you to do with another?** Co-create a two-person theatre piece? Co-write a book? Co-create a retreat? Co-facilitate a workshop? Whatever you do, do it consciously, creatively and courageously. Go for it! There's a whole lot of joy and limitless possibilities waiting for you there.

Nourish Your Relationship

If you are in a romantic relationship - married, living together, dating, or coupling in any sense of the word - then this section is for you!

And just like Conscious Collaboration, this is a dance of one-on-one. Your heart, their heart. Your feelings, their feelings. Your dreams, their dreams. One with one.

Out of this mutual desire to be together, to co-create and interweave your lives, is the birth of the relationship itself - a living, breathing tapestry housed in the sacred temple of your hearts and minds.

Regardless of proximity, duration or arrangement, all relationships have the same nature, the same natural structure, and that is fluidity. They are flickering flames, just as you both are. As you ebb and flow, so does your connection. As you grow and change, so does your relationship. As it changes, you change. Fluid, shapeshifting and alive.

Which means… we need to practice, consciously, our own ability to be flexible, aware and relevant to its shapeshifting nature. In order to feed it - and it does need sustenance and nourishment - we need to get creative, and be more playful and less attached to the outcome. We need to mindfully and compassionately balance the give and take, the rhythms and pulse.

Otherwise… well… you know the result of malnourishment and neglect. Let's not go there.

Instead, let's go to where the joy, the heart and the delight live.

The invitation is to find ways you can feed and nourish your partnership, your romance, your love and lover, from the smallest activities like doing crossword puzzles together, to the most extravagant, like travelling the world together. The possibilities are endless. The map is mysterious and promising.

May these suggestions below inspire you to get more creative and excited about your relationship, and invent ways to connect more deeply and deliciously.

May they bring more meaning, enchantment, gratitude and fulfilment into your lives.

May you both become the brightest partners you each can be.

And so it is…

Nourishment for your Relationship:

- **Find simple things to do together.** Sometimes it's all about the simple things, activities we take for granted or overlook as options for a sweet shared experience. What simple things are right there, right now, that you can enjoy with your partner? Just the two of you. How about: Taking turns reading a book out loud to each other, gardening, or playing Scrabble? Or, finding faces in clouds, singing a song, or sitting in silence together? Enjoy the small moments of delight, wonder and union.

- **Have a romantic night.** Set aside time to be alone for a night. Turn off the phones, turn down the lights, and turn up the Barry White. Light some candles and get close and cuddly. Dance together. Pamper each other with sensual experiences - massage with essential oils, delicious food, bathing or showering together. And make love. (Which can be interpreted however you like. Remember, your sexuality is as fluid as your relationship, so honour where you both are at.)

  Oh, and one last thing… slow down your pace with it all. There's something deliciously healing and pleasurable about slowing down with another. It feeds the soul of the relationship. Slow eating. Slow dancing. Slow touching. Slow kissing. Yummmmmm.

- **Explore together.** Put curiosity in your pockets and head off together, exploring the great outdoors regardless of whether you're urban or rural. Take a stroll in your neighbourhood, meandering hand in hand. Go on a picnic in a local park. Find a new coffee shop to have an afternoon tea and a chat. Go to a museum or art gallery and discuss what you find. Go camping or canoeing, and discover new landscapes. Take a road trip, taking turns driving and navigating as a team. Invest in your relationship this way.

- **Learn your love language.** According to Dr. Gary Chapman, pastor, marriage counselor and author, there are five emotional communication preferences or Love Languages - Words of Affirmation, Acts of Service, Receiving Gifts, Quality Time and Physical Touch. Knowing each other's primary love language is a revelation in understanding how each other loves and longs to be loved, and shines the light on how we can best communicate and create meaningful and touching acts of love.

  Take the quiz separately and then share your findings. And then, practice using their love language and level up the love vibe, the love quotient. For example: If Words of Affirmation are your partner's love language, tell them how much you appreciate them, or write a love poem to them. If your love language is Receiving Gifts, that's your partner's cue to get creative and thoughtful in their gifting. You can find his quiz here: www.5lovelanguages.com.

- **Do something you normally don't do together.** What might that be for you? What do you do independently that you'd both be willing to share? Take your partner to a yoga class? Divine cards or meditate together? Go to each other's offices? This is an opportunity to push the envelope a bit, to stretch yourself as a couple, to learn something new about each other. Open up the possibilities of new co-creations, adventures and mergers.

- **Create a 'sacred inquiry' night.** (I don't suggest you do this as a surprise for your partner. Ask them first if this is something they'd be down with, and have a pre-arranged time.)

    This night is for bringing more curiosity into the relationship. Think of some really juicy questions you can ask each other to deepen your understanding of where and who you are now.

    Write down your questions on little slips of paper, fold them up and put them in a hat. Set the stage for an intimate evening, perhaps with a bottle of wine, candles and some soft music. When you're ready, take turns pulling one question at a time out of the hat, answering the question picked as truthfully as you can. Take your time. Have fun, share deeply, and listen compassionately. End with gratitude. Share your appreciation for each other's honesty, transparency and courage. Express your love.

- **Go on a couples' retreat.** Find somewhere near or far where you can spend a weekend, a week or longer, where you can be alone together. Set the intention, talk to your partner and start investigating. Depending on your budget, financially and time wise, Google and explore your options. Get creative, especially if money and time are tight. There's always a way.

    Once you're away the key is to stay engaged as a couple. There may be others around you but be sure to BE with your lover. This retreat is for your relationship - for the wellbeing, renewal and upliftment of your sacred love and connection.

- **Design a ceremony** in honour of your relationship as a couple. This is a private affair, something just for the two of you, something you'll design together to acknowledge and bless your chosen intertwined path - a version of a wedding, a second wedding, or a renewal of vows.

    As you design it, think about and feel into what would reflect who you both are, what you love. If you both love to play music, include music-making in your ceremony. If you both love nature, design your ceremony to either be in nature or bring nature into your setting.

    Think about what emotions, qualities or desires you wish to evoke, or re-create together. Get creative. Think spoken word, song, divination, writing, movement, singing, art or altar making. The possibilities are limitless. Think about the flow of the ceremony from beginning to end. Decide how long, and where and when it will be. Decide together. Prepare it together. Do it together. And enjoy!

    Suggestion: Create a buffer before and after the ceremony so you can really revel in the experience. In other words, don't plan to do anything prior or after it. Trust me on this. By the way, don't forget to **take pics or video**.

Moving On Practices

*"When I let go of what I am, I become what I might be.
When I let go of what I have, I receive what I need."* Lao Tzu

Boast Your Way Out

There comes a time - unless you're so evolved you have transcended the teachings of partnership - where the shit hits the fan. Your beloved, a friend, a business partner or creative collaborator no longer feels harmonious, connected or good. The sacred bond is unravelling. The cherished dream is dissolving into a puddle, unrecognizable. The partner dance is tearing up from the storm of loss and confusion.

You feel deep disconnection, with yourself and with the other, and with your passion, creativity, joy and power. It happens! I know. It's destabilizing. It's core shattering. Heart breaking. Devastating. Been there. Done that.

But here's the thing… You are amazing. You truly are. Remember?!

You are courageous. Exquisite. Creative, resilient and powerful beyond measure.

You can and will dance yourself out of the storm because it's part of your journey of curiosity, courage, compassion and creativity. Believe it!

Remembering this is the way through to healing and freedom. It's the wild heart ride beyond the safety of knowing. The trick here is to listen in, trust the impulses, ride the waves of emotion, and be swept clean. Let the storm move you to take action on your own behalf, to get real and vulnerable and strong.

Laugh. Cry. Don't hold back. Become familiar with your fierce-loving self. Ground in the truth of your strength and divinity. And trust, trust, trust.

Re-member your holiness. Your brilliance. Your original radiance.

Be full of yourself. I mean really full!

Here's a favourite way to fill up…

Get BOASTFUL.

Yeah! Pump up the volume of life-affirming memories of who you are, what you've done, where you've been, and the countless ways you've showed up to dance in and with the world. Celebrate.

After all, **YOU ARE A QUEEN.** A goddess. A force of love.

Regardless if you stay in the partnership as is, make big changes within it, or leave, you'll be just fine. More than fine.

Now, it's time to…

Remember how magnificent you are!

<u>Make a juicy list</u> of attributes, talents and traits you love about yourself - acts of courage and kindness, obstacles you've overcome and anything else that reflects your shiny self. Get pumped. Get full of yourself. (One of my beloved teachers, Elizabeth Purvis, calls this the "Goddess State of Mind Exercise".)

Fill it with all the juice you've got. I mean, really get braggadocious on yourself. No one's watching, so go ahead, wrap your arms around and give yourself the biggest hug. Then let your arms relax, take a deep breath in, and on your exhale give your best Lioness roar!

Tell the world you are HERE!

Make the gods and goddesses rise up in wonderment and awe. See, hear and feel their celebratory and resounding howls and standing ovation.

Use this list to ROAR.

May you know how magnificent you are.

May you trust in this very moment.

May you feel strong, whole and beautiful.

May you find your way home.

May it be so.

Let Go with De-Cording

We truly are interconnected. I believe that to my core. One web of life. One beautiful tapestry. And within this web are energetic threads or cords which tie us together.

The most basic form of cording is between a newborn child and its mother. But temporary cords connecting us to others are created all through our lifetime. These cords are usually found by any or all of our seven chakras (energy centers), where we receive, assimilate and give energy.

It's natural to make these cords of connection, however, we can end up with cords from so many people that we overload our energy centers, causing us to feel tired, confused and drained. We become overburdened by other people's energies.

And, sometimes, these cords prevent us from letting go. Like when we've broken up with a lover months ago and yet we can't stop thinking about them. We can't move on. What's happening on an energetic level is that our invisible cords are filled with energy still actively attached to the ex.

Many will advise you to 'cut the cord,' to release it. But I've got another idea. It's called de-cording.

This practice, inspired by a technique called "Chakra Cording", taught to me by Debbie Papadakis after receiving my Hypnotherapy Certification at her "Hypno Healing Institute" in Toronto, is a cleansing process of completing and transforming the energy found in these cords, and redirecting it towards yourself for liberation, empowerment and self-healing.

I recommend adding this practice to your self-care plan from time to time.

And this is not just for clearing the energetic cords you have with people you wish to release from your life, but also for the health and wellness of the relationships you cherish and wish to keep. It's like hitting the reset button.

Why? Because it clears out grudges, hurts and disappointments. It releases expectations and over-attachment. In its place, we find freedom, acceptance, love and peace. We are all set free, you and the other. Mother, sister, lover, daughter. Free to be. Unconditional love. Unity. Oneness. Then, we can bring our best selves to the relationships we wish to nourish and feed. That's a great gift to give.

Knowing how powerful, deep and soul-stirring this process is…

PLEASE do not do this alone. Have a close friend guide you through the instructions so you can close your eyes and drop in. Let them hold a safe space for you, especially if you've never done this before or if you feel at all vulnerable, weak or emotional.

As you go through the process, share your experience out loud, from time to time as you feel appropriate, so they can be with you and track where you're at.

If you are proficient in shadow, soul or trauma work, then go for it, but call in your angels, guides and deities - your spiritual support team - to be with you as you journey.

Also, as you do this de-cording you will be drawing on the skills of visualization and imagination, but don't worry if you aren't visually inclined. Trust in the power of your intention and your personal experience, even if you see nothing or feel very little. Believe me, this is energetic work and is often invisible to our physical senses.

Lastly, I'm immensely grateful to Debbie for inspiring me to 'de-cord' as it's helped me and many others. May it serve you too.

Here's my de-cording practice: 30 minutes – 1 hour or more

1. **Find a time and place where you will be undisturbed.** Turn your phone off, shut the door.

2. **The first step is to close your eyes and relax**, using any technique you prefer. You want to be in a state where your body is relaxed and your mind is still alert. Ensure that you feel a sense of protection and grounding. Let the first thing to come to mind be without any judgment or censorship. Here's where you need to trust in the process and let whatever happens, happen.

3. Once you're in this deeply relaxing place, **state an intention**. For example: "I am ready to let go of the cords that bind me to my ex-partner."

4. **Imagine that person** and begin to sense where in your body you are holding energy when you think of them.

5. **Mentally scan your body** to find those places (often there are several cords, in different locations). Go to the place that stands out as the strongest connection.

6. **See or feel what the cord looks like.**

7. **Follow it** to see where it connects on the other person's body. Remember, this is energetic, not physical, but your mind can imagine it in a tangible way.

8. Once you feel, see or sense this cord, **begin to explore it**. Notice what colour it is and how large or thick it is. Sense the texture of it (smooth, shiny, rough like rope, silky).

9. Now, **imagine yourself shrinking** small enough to go into the cord. **Go inside it.** What does it feel like inside? What's the temperature, colour, smell, texture, etc.? Observe without judgment.

10 **Notice the quality of the energy** and emotion running through the cord.

11 Begin to connect with your sense of hearing. **Listen for messages** flowing from you to the other and from them to you. Relax into this.

12 **Start a conversation.** Perhaps ask yourself, *'What do I need to say? What are they saying to me?'* Take your time to listen and to be with this dialogue back and forth.

13 When you feel the conversation is complete, explain to them that you'll soon draw back your cord from them. Tell them what you need to say to **bring closure to this cord** now.

14 Then, ask them what **they need from you** and what they need to say to you **so they too may have closure**. Listen.

15 **Allow all feelings to be felt**, honouring each other's words and feelings.

16 **Give thanks to them** for being a teacher, or whatever way you choose to honour who they've been for you.

17 **Tell them your next intention** - to have a clear and fresh connection with them in the future, or to end it completely, or something else.

18 **Step out of the cord** now and come back to yourself, to your normal size, and once again observe the cord.

19 **Begin to transform it.** Imagine the cord slowly becoming vaporous and light-filled. See the colour getting lighter and lighter, less and less opaque. The size and texture changes too.

20 Once you see or feel the cord as light, **gently disconnect** the end of the cord where it's connected to the other person, slowly drawing the cord back to yourself.

21 Take this beautiful and powerful light from your transformed cord and flood the spot where it was connected to your body. **Use it** to mend, so as to leave no energetic scar. Radiate light to the whole area around that chakra.

22 **See and feel the other in white light**. Wish them love, and set them free. Feel the freedom in your own body. (I love to imagine both of us naked, floating freely in the sky.)

23 Now, **scan your body again** and see if there are any other cords connecting you to that same person. **If so, do the same procedure as before:** See the cord, shrink into it, receive and give messages, bring to closure, come out of the cord, begin changing the quality of the cord until it is pure light, then bring it home to yourself for healing.

24 Keep doing this until your **body is clear of cords.** (I've done numerous de-cordings in a row, and from more than one person in a session.)

25 **Give thanks**, as always. Take a few breaths, and **take your time** before opening your eyes. Ground yourself.

When the process is complete, check in to see how you feel. **Be gentle with yourself.** This is courageous work. Allow your friend to hold you, be with you, whatever it is you need. You may need to sleep and dream, or have a bath to ground. Or perhaps you feel like writing down positive affirmations, or capturing your experience in your journal. Go with what feels nourishing and good. You deserve it.

In the days that follow, pay attention. Notice the potential of the magical ripple effects. In fact, it's common for the person you've de-corded from to respond to you in new ways. See what happens. Use this healing practice as often as you need.

Forgive with Metta (Loving Kindness)

"One kind word can warm three winter months." Japanese Proverb

I first came across this Metta practice back in the early 90s when I was a new mother living in Swansea, Wales. After finding a group of practitioners who met every Friday night, I became a faithful member. Since then, it's been great support on my heart path.

The practice of Metta, meaning **loving kindness** in Sanskrit, was created by Tibetan Buddhist monks many years ago. The practice inspires forgiveness and compassion first towards ourselves, then to a loved one, to someone we have neutral feelings towards (acquaintance), to someone we have difficult relations with, and lastly to all sentient beings.

Through the power of this practice we cultivate forgiveness, kindness and equanimity. It softens our hearts, and untethers us from the shadow of grief, anger, separation and guilt. Conditional love unfolds into unconditional love. This love is truly boundless and unifying.

I, personally, have experienced the most incredible expansion of love in my entire being. It's part of my path of 'keeping my heart open, regardless,' my daily practice of remaining faithful to love in every circumstance, with everyone. (To the best of my ability, of course.) It's one of my favourite tools of all!

My wish is for you to be inspired to try this out for yourself.

<u>The best scenario is to have a friend guide you through it at first.</u> Otherwise, you'll need one eye seeing outwardly to follow the steps and recite the mantras, and the other eye looking inwards to access your imagination and visioning.

As you move through the practice, take your time connecting with each person, welcoming them with a hug, or holding their hands. You can recite the four blessings silently or out loud. Whatever feels right.

And if you want to add another dimension to this: Imagine you're sitting in a circle with people you love. (I love imagining I'm in a clearing in a forest with a ring of trees around me.) Ground in the sensation and amplification of doing this practice with others. Imagine each new person arriving to receive Metta entering the circle to stand before you. After the practice is complete, look around the circle and see it glowing like a ring of light and love.

However you do this… be kind to yourself. Trust the process. Whatever happens or whomever shows up is perfect. You may not see anything. You may just feel and sense.

It's all good. This is all part of the practice of loving kindness!

Here's my version of the Metta Practice: Approx. 20 minutes

1. **Sit in a comfortable position** in a quiet space. **Take a pulse on how you're feeling.** Give yourself a number on a scale of 1-10, 1 being very stressed, 10 being blissed and in complete joy.

   Relax and ground. Find your breath. Invite the flow of universal love to enter your heart and mind. Allow your breath to soothe and relax you. Once you have a sense of relaxation, draw on the power of your imagination with these next steps.

2. **Imagine, sense or see your own self arrive.** Embrace yourself as a beloved. After connecting heart to heart, look into your own eyes and recite:

   "May I be safe and protected.
   May I be peaceful and happy.
   May I be healthy and strong.
   May I have ease of well-being."

   See yourself smile and shine with love. Then slowly see them disappear in your mind's eye - walk away or dissolve into the ethers. Let yourself go with love.

3. **Next, imagine, sense or see a loved one arrive.** Embrace them. After connecting heart to heart, look into their eyes and recite:

   "May you be safe and protected.
   May you be peaceful and happy.
   May you be healthy and strong.
   May you have ease of well-being."

   See them smile and shine. Then slowly see them disappear in your mind's eye - walk away or dissolve into the ethers. Let them go with love.

4. **Next, imagine, sense or see a neutral person arrive.** (Someone you neither like nor dislike.) Embrace them. After connecting heart to heart, look into their eyes and recite:

   "May you be safe and protected.
   May you be peaceful and happy.
   May you be healthy and strong.
   May you have ease of well-being."

   See them smile and shine. Then slowly see them disappear in your mind's eye - walk away or dissolve into the ethers. Let them go with love.

5. **Next, imagine, sense or see a difficult person arrive.** (If you're new to this practice, don't choose the most difficult person you know, as it can be more challenging to do.) Embrace them. After connecting heart to heart, look into their eyes and recite:

   "May you be safe and protected.
   May you be peaceful and happy.

May you be healthy and strong.
May you have ease of well-being."

See them smile and shine. Then slowly disappear in your mind's eye - walk away or dissolve into the ethers. Let them go with love.

6   **Next, imagine, sense or see all sentient beings arrive.** (People and creatures.) After connecting to their hearts, look into their eyes and recite:

"May you be safe and protected.
May you be peaceful and happy.
May you be healthy and strong.
May you have ease of well-being."

See them all smile and shine. Then slowly see them disappear in your mind's eye - walk away or dissolve into the ethers. Let them go with love.

7   **Take a few minutes to sit and bask in this love.** Feel and shine your light. Ground yourself in love and forgiveness. You are love. And the practice is complete!

8   **Check in and see where you are now on your stress scale.** Having done this for myself and facilitated this for others for years, I'm confident you'll feel more soft, open, loving and peaceful.

9   **Lastly, keep this practice alive.** As you go about your day, remember Metta. Shower each new person you see or meet with love and light. Silently wish them a blessing. And do it for yourself. When you become hard on yourself, bestow a blessing, and wrap yourself in love.

144   She Reflects: A Spiral Journey for the Feminine Soul

Opening to Love Playlist

Open your heart to love. Become the lover.
Do your love dance, in celebration of heart and romance.

1 **Kinder**, The Right To Be Here, by Copper Wimmin
2 **Heart of Gaia**, Jewels of Silence: Meditations On the Chakras for Voice and Crystal Singing Bowls, by Ashana
3 **Ready for Love**, Acoustic Soul, by India.Arie
4 **I'm Not Afraid**, Beautifully Human - Words and Sounds, Vol. 2, by Jill Scott
5 **Love and Affection**, Track Record, by Joan Armatrading
6 **Money Can't Buy It**, Diva, by Annie Lennox
7 **Ready for Love**, Bad Company (Deluxe Edition), by Bad Company
8 **I Open My Arms to Love/Jai Radhe**, My Heart Bows Down To You, by Brenda McMorrow
9 **Soldier of Love**, Soldier of Love, by Sade
10 **Come On Now** (Set It Off), Come On Now (Set It Off) (Remixes) - EP, by Juliet Sikora & Tube & Berger
11 **Love Is My Religion**, Kraak & Smaak: The Remix Sessions, by Kraak & Smaak vs. Karl Moestl
12 **Inside**, Inside - EP, by The Funky Lowlives
13 **Love Honey**, Beach Disco Sessions Vol. 1, by Sugardaddy
14 **You Got It, Baby!**, Passions, by Weathertunes
15 **Rhythm of Love**, Rhythm of Love, by Anita Baker
16 **The Love In Me**, Something About Faith (Deluxe Edition), by Faith Evans
17 **Ascension** (Don't Ever Wonder), Maxwell's Urban Hang Suite, by Maxwell
18 **Love Goddess**, Essence of Balance, by Cane Garden Quartet
19 **Eastern Sun** (Ryan Herr Remix), Hollow Bone (Remixes), by Ayla Nereo
20 **Love Complicated**, Love Feelings, by Sambox
21 **Preparation Pulse**, The Shaman's Heart, by Steve Roach & Byron Metcalf
22 **Opening**, To Love, by Essie Jain

Go to: www.EricaRoss.com/playlists

Partner Dance Playlist

Dance with a partner. Allow all feelings to move you. How do you wish to meet and be met, see and be seen, feel and be felt?

1. **The First Time Ever I Saw Your Face**, First Take, by Roberta Flack
2. **Protection**, Protection, by Massive Attack
3. **Sunrise** (feat. Rachel Lloyd), Speck of Gold, by Afterlife
4. **I Belong to You**, 5, by Lenny Kravitz
5. **Massage My Mind** (feat. Marti Nikko) (DJ Drez Remix), Expanding: EarthRise SoundSystem Remixed, by EarthRise SoundSystem
6. **I Feel It Coming** (feat. Daft Punk), Starboy, by The Weeknd
7. **I Care** (12" Master), The Club Mix Hits, by Soul II Soul
8. **(We Got) Telepathy**, L Is for Lover, by Al Jarreau
9. **Got to Be Real**, Cheryl Lynn (Expanded Edition), by Cheryl Lynn
10. **Love Injection**, Love Injection, by Trussel
11. **How Deep Is Your Love**, How Deep Is Your Love - Single, by Clavin Harris & Disciples
12. **Groove Is In the Heart**, Groove Is In the Heart - EP, by Deee-lite
13. **Really Love Ya**, Really Love Ya, by Siopis
14. **Big Love** (Album Mix), Big Love the Album, by Low Deep T
15. **Crazy** (Nôze Remix - Extended Club Version), Crazy (Remixes) - EP, by Ornette
16. **You Stepped into My Life**, Children of the World, by Bee Gees
17. **Touch My Soul**, Reflections, by Lounge Groove Avenue
18. **Make Me Stay**, Not So Soft, by Ani DiFranco
19. **De Cara a la Pared**, La Llorona, by Lhasa de Sela
20. **Ocean Pearl**, Resurrected, by Jacksoul
21. **Freak**, Honeymoon, by Lana Del Rey
22. **Tempest**, Tremors, by Sohn

Go to: www.EricaRoss.com/playlists

Moving On Playlist

After the storm. Dance with forgiveness, renewal and joy.
Move on. Feel good.

1 **Falling Out of Love**, Mercy Now, by Mary Gauthier
2 **Don't Come Around**, Do Something (The Remixes) - EP, by Macy Gray
3 **She** (Robin Hannibal (Quadron/Rhye) Rework), She (Remixes) - EP, by Laura Mvula
4 **Patience**, Patience, by Layah Jane
5 **If I Rise**, 127 Hours, by Dido & A. R. Rahman
6 **Unbreakable**, Wonderland, by Coco Love Alcorn
7 **Away Away**, Away Away - Single, by Ibeyi
8 **Bruised But Not Broken**, Introducing Joss Stone, by Joss Stone
9 **The Uncomfortable Truth**, Victim of Truth, by Nneka
10 **Gentle Healing** (Trust), Natural Selection, by Sounds From The Ground
11 **Count To Ten** (Acoustic), Count to Ten (Special Edition), by Tina Dico
12 **Finally Moving**, Taking Up Your Precious Time, by Pretty Lights
13 **Reborn**, Indian Electronica, Vol. 1, by Akshai Sarin
14 **Hey Lion**, Soft Animals - EP, by Sofi Tukker
15 **Kwanele**, Zabalaza, by Thandiswa Mazwai
16 **Dreams** (Surfers Mix) (feat. Stevie Nicks), Say Hello / Flashing for Money / Dreams - EP, by Deep Dish
17 **Be Strong,** Chill House, by Pound Boys
18 **And the Beat Goes On**, Greatest Hits, by The Whispers
19 **Get Lucky** (feat. Pharrell Williams & Nile Rodgers), Random Access Memories, by Daft Punk
20 **Sunset**, Onezero, by Nitin Sawhney
21 **Brand New Day**, Brand New Day, by Sting
22 **Feelin' Good** (Joe Claussell Remix), Verve Remixed, by Nina Simone

Go to: www.EricaRoss.com/playlists

Fourth Turn

Collective Joy

"Unshared joy is an unlit candle." Spanish Proverb

Saturday Night Fever

The first time I experienced my wild soul was in India. I was 19 and living on the beach in Goa with hundreds of other travellers from around the world, also seeking liberation and freedom of expression. And we found it, together, as we danced around camp fires, and danced in the ocean and danced under the stars. We danced with abandon and joy.

It was a powerful experience to be able to express myself so freely, without inhibition, especially through dance. It was also a powerful and liberating experience to bear witness to others doing the same.

When I got home to Toronto, the physical and emotional experience of liberation in my being shifted from sensing it under the stars to discovering it under the strobe lights of dance clubs. By day, I was studying at the Ontario College of Art, and at night, I was dancing - and feeling free - at the clubs.

I loved it. Hours of dancing on packed dance floors, moving to the beat, letting go, feeling alive and unrestricted. There were a handful of hot clubs in the city at the time. My friends and I would pick one and dance the night away.

I remember one night, I arrived alone at one of the clubs. It was early in the evening and not many people had arrived yet, including my friends. The dance floor was pretty empty, but the music was on and sounded good.

The DJ started playing a song I loved and I jumped onto the dance floor. I was boogying alone, with almost the whole dance floor to myself. I was a young, classically-trained dancer, with a body that could do almost anything I wanted it to do: If I wanted to leap, my body would leap. If I wanted to spin, I would spin. I had technique, vitality, and endless passion for it. And I also had immense joy.

This was my bliss, before I even really knew what bliss meant. Before I'd ever heard of Joseph Campbell and his coined phrase 'Follow Your Bliss,' I was following my bliss through dance, and it felt so good! And this night was no exception. I was on!

After a while, the music and tempo changed to something less pleasing to me, and I took it as a cue to take a break. As I turned around to leave the floor there was a group of women about my age staring, well actually, more like glaring, at me. They were standing all huddled together with their arms crossed, and with a look on their faces of, 'Who the hell do you think you are?'

I was completely taken aback. I was shocked, really. The moment I saw their faces, I felt my entire system collapse. I went from this giant high - of feeling so good, of being in my element, of feeling my bliss - to 'What have I done?'

I shriveled up inside and slunk off that dance floor feeling decimated. The look on their faces said, 'You're a show-off. Who do you think you are? And, what the hell was that?' They looked at me like I was some kind of an ego-tripper - conceited and self-absorbed. It was a terrible experience for me. Their message, the one I absorbed was, 'Don't you dare shine brighter than the rest of us.' (The same message Amaterasu received from her brother Susanoo.)

All these decades later, I still remember so vividly how it felt. I was humiliated. I couldn't go back on the dance floor that night and I wouldn't, I decided, let myself be seen that way again. Ever.

As a young twenty-something at the time, I just wasn't experienced or wise enough to be able to say to them, "What's your problem? Get a grip!", and to say to myself, 'Who cares what they think! I'm not holding back.'

In fact, sadly, it was quite the opposite. I was deeply soul-crushed by it. Their look was a smack in the face that said, 'Get in line. What you're doing is not okay. You should never be so bold, so magnificent.'

Whenever I went dancing after that, I kept it simple. I'd find the beat and get in the groove, but I would never, ever let my spirit soar. I didn't want people to think I was being a show-off. I wanted to feel a sense of belonging, and to not have anyone look at me that way. I knew it wasn't safe to stand out.

And then, I moved to New York City.

I had a friend in NYC named Elke. She had written to say come visit, and the timing was perfect. My job as art director at Uproar, a new and soon-to-be Toronto publication, evaporated when the magazine went under. My boyfriend and I had split up after two-and-half years, and I'd just finished art college. No job. No boyfriend. No school. New York City? It was a big 'Yes!'

While I was there, I visited an acquaintance, an astrologer from Toronto, who was living in Soho with her husband, a musician from New York. While we were chatting, she happened to ask if I knew anyone who would like to sublet their apartment. Her husband, a sax player (he used to play with Chaka Khan, among others), had picked up a gig in St. Thomas, the British Virgin Islands.

"We're going to be away for three months and need someone to sublet our apartment. Do you know anyone who could help us out?" she asked.

I looked at them and without hesitation said, "Yeah, me! I'll take it."

"Deal," they said.

And, then, I asked, "How much is it?'

"$150 a month," they said.

$150! A month! I was in!

I would stay in their fully furnished, fourth floor walk-up on Sixth Avenue between Prince and Spring Street, for the meager sum of $150 a month while taking care of their two cats.

I hurried back to Toronto and broke the lease on an apartment. I sold what I could and stored the rest. I packed up two suitcases and moved to New York for three months.

I was super excited. I was just 24 years old, living in New York City. I was over the moon!

I hadn't been there a week when my friend Elke took me to a private dance party at "The Loft", where the late legendary David Mancuso lived, partied and DJ-ed. Conveniently, it was just three blocks from where I was living.

Little did I know, David was a pioneer. His DJ-ing, and the concept of The Loft, was at the forefront of the private dance club scene, influencing DJs Larry Levan of NYC's Paradise Garage and Franky Knuckles of Chicago's Warehouse. All three were the godfathers of house music and the DJs of their time.

David would host his invitation-only parties every Saturday night. And thanks to Elke who was already a member, I was able to score my own membership card, and I was in.

Suddenly, I felt like I'd really arrived, both in NYC *and* in my own soul - I knew I was home. The freedom of movement on the dance floor was contagious. I knew I no longer needed to hold back my light, and instead, I was inspired to shine my brightest. I'd found my bliss again, and I was hooked. Every Saturday night after that, I was at The Loft.

The Loft became my weekly taste of heaven, and the place where I met most of my friends and lovers. First, I met Kim, a university student originally from California, who would fast become my best friend. Kim and I would arrange our entire week around going dancing together at The Loft. I'd even go to bed early Saturday night so I could get up and meet her there around 4:00 a.m. Kim loved to dance and so did I. And so did everyone else we met there.

It's hard to put it into words, but here's what a Saturday night at The Loft was like for me:

At 4:00 a.m. (doors opened at midnight), Kim and I would arrive at the front door of a large, two-story warehouse in Soho. Friendly faces would greet us as we showed our Loft membership cards with a picture of Spanky and His Gang, and the words 'Love Saves the Day' written on it. We'd pay our nominal admission fee and head in.

Inside, dozens of friends would be milling about, chatting and hugging. Bowls of fruit and water were laid out on the counter. (No alcohol was served.) Wafting from the second floor were the rhythmic beats of tunes like 'Get Ready For The Future' by The Winners, 'Soul Makossa' by Manu Dibango, or 'House Party' by Fred Wesley.

We'd run into the washroom, change into our dance outfits, and check our street wear into a locker. (You know there's some serious dancing going on when lockers are needed.)

Wearing our beautiful, soft leathered Capezio jazz shoes, tight stretchy Lycra pants and colourful tops, we'd spring up the stairs into heaven - a huge room alive and throbbing with the pulse of a few hundred dancers - a beautiful, mixed (sexually, racially, economically), inclusive 'family.' Many were from Queens, the Bronx and Brooklyn.

The lights were dimmed. The high ceilings were filled with multi-coloured balloons, and the dancers - men and women alike - wore sexy, fluid and vibrant dance clothes. The beauty, love and collective joy was palpable, infectious and hypnotizing. It was the most inclusive, sexy and welcoming space I'd ever experienced.

David, our fabulous DJ, stood near the back watching over the scene, spinning vinyl, one full song at a time. No mixing, but seamless none the less. He played for literally hours, non-stop. He'd play anything he believed was danceable, uplifting and pride-inducing - African, disco, funk, reggae, jazz, blues, rock and early dubstep and house; a diversity of tunes virtually unheard of in the clubs across North America at that time.

We'd dance until we couldn't dance any more. Then we'd take a nap on pillows on the soft wooden floor, wake up from time to time, refreshed and ready to dance again. Often my friends and I were amongst the last to leave, 2 p.m. most Sundays. We'd then hit the streets of Manhattan and dance our way home, or in good weather, head to Washington Square Park with a boom box to keep dancing until sunset.

We were sweaty and disheveled. Exhausted and make-up-less. But we were on such a high! Sunday nights I'd have the best sleep of the week, and I couldn't wait until the next weekend.

Looking back at it now, I can honestly say that it was one of the best times of my life, and if there was a time machine I'd dial 1979, NYC, The Loft. With the deepest gratitude, I'd hug David, Kim, and all my friends because there, at The Loft, I found my light and my bliss again.

I found freedom. I found healing. I found belonging. I found collective joy.

May this be for you!

May you find freedom.
May you find healing.
May you find belonging.
May you find your light and bliss.

May you find collective joy.

Reflections

"I am convinced that life in a physical body is meant to be an ecstatic experience." Shakti Gawain

We are inherently joyful by nature, don't you agree? Regardless of our past experiences or present emotional state, joy is always pulsing below. At our core. In our soul. Part of our essential self. It's there to return to. Through worry. Joy. Through grief. Joy. Through confusion. Joy.

And so it is, as the spiral turns once again, it's time to get up close and personal with joy. It's time to grow beyond the solo dance of self-discovery and beyond the partner dance of conscious collaboration, and engage in the collective dance of life, of COLLECTIVE JOY.

At this Fourth Turn we expand our reach, our sphere of influence, our breadth of connection. This is where we share who we are with others and the world. We arrive at the delicious experience of community and belonging. The oneness of the circle. The empowerment and healing of collective celebration and acceptance.

We come to a sacred gathering space, a healing ground where shared laughter heals us, where inclusion mends us, and where collective joy wholes us.

Whatever it is you do, when shared with others - friends and strangers alike - it will be amplified. Intentional or not, the experience expands, the sum being greater than the parts.

If you share love, love will magnify. If you share peace, peace will deepen. Happiness will become revelry. Pleasure will become bliss. Gratitude will grow.

I'm sure you know the feeling, yes? That night you laughed out loud with a bunch of strangers at a comedy club. That afternoon when you witnessed your child's graduation and you along with the others rose to your feet in a standing ovation of pride and satisfaction. That night you attended a dance party when everyone was wildly pulsing and flowing together, in sync and in celebration.

That's collective joy!

It's found anytime we come together to unite and devote ourselves to a common cause, goal or desire; in business, pleasure, study and life. It's found in peaceful demonstrations, world prayers and grassroots activism. It's found in civic choirs, community kitchens, citywide carnivals and pride parades.

It's about alignment. Connection. Belonging. Harmony. And it's mighty powerful. We can move mountains together. Its ripples are strong and far-reaching. Who knows how it will change us, or how it will change the world? But one thing is for sure - we do know it will! I believe collective joy can heal beyond our own comprehension. I truly believe.

In the story of Amaterasu, it was the power of her brother's rage (a collective shadow) that caused her to withdraw into her cave, but it was the force of <u>collective joy</u> that coaxed her out, restoring the light back to the land.

It was all the mirrors together - the collective - that created the reflection for Amaterasu to shine.

Humanity needs us to do the same. To show up, like Uzume and all the gods and goddesses, laughing and dancing with our mirrors in hand. Joy and healing combined.

Yes, bring on the mirrors!

Bring on collective Joy. Collective Love. Collective Healing. Collective Power. Let there be collective intentions for light, kindness, compassion and unity. The world has always needed that. We are the gift. The light. The joy.

And, know this, my lovely…

Not all groups of people are created equal. Not all groups are YOUR people. Like that night in the disco when I felt stung and dismantled by that small group of young women staring at me with their faces full of disdain and disgust. They weren't my people! They didn't understand my joy.

You have to find those who are, and take the risk inherent in being seen, heard and known. It's a risk because there's always the potential of a critic being out there. We've all had the experience of looking over and seeing somebody not approving of us, somebody judging us. How we respond to it makes all the difference, and that's the dance of life.

Yes it sucks. But, it doesn't have to shut us down, or, at least, not for long. We may recoil for a moment, but we can come back to our own truth and move on. (It's also a reflection of our own inner judge and how we respond to her.)

As you know… I experienced first-hand 'shrinking so that other people wouldn't feel insecure.' I dimmed my own light to avoid the judgment of others. I made myself small. I didn't have the inner skills and agency back then to know how to navigate that painful situation.

I realize now that those young women, all those years ago, felt threatened by my sense of freedom. Their response was harsh and I responded in kind by dousing my own light. We were both so wrong.

If that same thing happened to me today, well, first I'd be shocked. I'm used to being with people who celebrate each other. But, if it did happen, I'm not gonna lie, it would still sting. I would be thrown off. But, this time, I'd respond with, inside myself if not out loud, 'What? Really? Oh not that shit again.'

I'd feel sadness. Sad for them, for me, and saddened by the fact that women are still bashing women, that it's still a thing. So much work is still left to be done there.

But after all that, I'd keep dancing. I'd be aware, but I would choose to still SHINE and be in my JOY! I'd feel compassion because I know now that we are *one* - if they're hurting, I'm also hurting. The healer in me would want healing.

A big part of the work I do is inspired by the lessons I learned from both that group of young women at the Toronto dance club and the freedom seekers at The Loft.

I believe in sisterhood. I believe in the power of women coming together in community. Complexities, diversities and all.

I believe we need more spaces where we can practice being kind. Where we can hold space for, and be receptive and responsive to, each other's needs, differences (race, religion, gender orientation, ability) and wellbeing. We need to celebrate each other more and to not hold ourselves back from doing what brings us JOY. Collectively.

So, go ahead...

Find new or ancient ways of gathering. Tell your stories around a camp fire. Unite for causes of peace. Join a prayer group. Join a sisterhood of authentic and loving women who are shiny mirrors for each other, reflecting the wonderful diversity of women's lived experiences, or start one yourself.

Find your peeps. Light up the sky with your passion and compassion. Find the places or create the spaces where we can heal, celebrate and flourish together. Dance, sing, play and rejoice together.

One heart.

One love.

Together.

United.

Radiant.

JOY, JOY, JOY!

Fourth Turn: Collective Joy 155

Practices for the Fourth Turn

- ◎ Find Your People
- ◎ Be a Mirror
- ◎ Get Playful / Laugh Together
- ◎ Throw a Dance Party
- ◎ Form a Healing Circle
- ◎ Know Your 'Group' Self

Playlist: Collective Joy

*"Individually, we are one drop.
Together, we are an ocean."* Ryunosuke Satoro

Find Your People

I'm all about bringing Heaven down to Earth. The practices offered in this book, *She Reflects*, are designed for that.

These experiential practices support your being fully here and now, so you may find heaven within and around you - practices ranging from very specific actions and prompts, to more general yet intentional teachings and lenses. From the micro to the macro, from the focused to the broad, from the inner to the outer. From the practical to the spiritual.

This practice, in particular, is about setting an intention to find the path of belonging - to find YOUR people.

When I discovered The Loft in NYC back in the late 70s, I had found my people. There was immense healing for me there. I experienced feelings of belonging and acceptance. I found a great sense of Collective Joy.

After my Loft days I longed for that feeling of belonging again; that visceral experience of interweaving the invisible web between myself and the other dancers, and to all of life. It was intoxicating and life-giving, and I wanted - no needed - to feel that 'high' again. And again.

That longing gave birth to my ecstatic dance practice, Dance Our Way Home. That longing sparked me to say yes to co-creating The Move, a weekly ecstatic dance event and community in Toronto.

What about you?

Have YOU ever longed for that deep sense of belonging? Where you feel safe enough to let your guard down? Where you can practice being fully YOU?

I pray your answer is a resounding YES, and if not, that's okay. Just know that it's in the realm of possibilities.

The thing is... when we find *our* people, we find home. That's just the way it goes. When we do, the world becomes a very different place, a friendlier, warmer place. We experience what it is to be held just as we are.

We become both mirror and mirrored, personally and collectively, for each one of us to shine.

Regardless if we're at the dinner table eating with loved ones or in a huge night club dancing, it's there in the state of belonging where we can practice showing up courageously, compassionately, curiously and creatively.

And sometimes it turns out that our sense of home and belonging was never quite on, never quite there. Perhaps it was due to growing up in a family who didn't understand you, and you felt like a fish out of water. And you were! You didn't belong. You weren't meant to belong there at all.

The truth is... there was nothing wrong with you. You just weren't with the right people, like the story of The Ugly Duckling. They weren't and aren't your people. You need to find *your* people.

*I acknowledge that the word '*home*' may bring up a spectrum of painful emotions - from sadness and anger, to profound grief and loss - especially if you've been physically displaced from your homeland or have been rejected or estranged from your family or community (like the example above). If that is your lived experience, I honour and celebrate your resilience, and invite you to gently feel into your inner soul-home and heart with self-compassion.

Regardless if you know what belonging feels like or not, we've all learned to censor ourselves. From small to vast degrees we've learned to adjust ourselves to be accepted. We all lose connection to our true expression after years of reshaping and rejecting parts of us so we can fit in. We tell ourselves 'That's not acceptable,' and we hide our true self.

The antidote is to do our own solo work and practice falling in love with our whole self, AND find our people: our allies and cheerleaders ready and waiting to love us, and remind us of the truth about ourselves when we forget. **Our people help us relax into ourselves so our natural expressions can shine through.** So we can return to our original radiance and joy. So we can become like Amaterasu. So we can belong.

In my ecstatic dance practice we dance together as a group in many different ways - in circles, in line formations, and in waves across the floor. They're all delicious, but for me there's nothing like dancing in a circle to feel that deep sense of belonging.

There's something stunningly beautiful, powerful and ancient about it. There's something about the shape, a sacred symbol of inclusivity. Oneness. Where everyone is seen. (There's nowhere to hide.) Everyone is valued and necessary to the whole. Everyone is included. Everyone belongs.

Whether you dance in a circle of women, belong to a local chess club or hold quilting bees in your home, it's your right to bond and belong. It's your right to find a sense of home. It's your right to find your people. Treasure them when you do.

You no longer need to be the lone wolf. Go ahead...

Howl to find your pack!

The universe is listening, and it longs to shower you with possibilities for that realization, that home-coming.

Below is an exercise to help you get clear on where you belong, and who your people are. Follow the steps to help you find your truth, your home, your howl. It's time to gather, contribute and co-create. It's time to expand the collective joy quotient! Here we go...

Find your people:

1. **Get clear.** Create a list of your favourite activities, passions and desires, including hobbies, callings and causes that speak to you - anything and everything that lights you up and feels good and right and juicy.

    Find a comfy spot and have a piece of paper and pen on hand, along with a nice cup of tea or glass of wine. (Enjoy the process!)

    Ask yourself, '**What do I love and love to do above all else?** What is deeply meaningful to me? What lifts my spirit? What do I long to do with others?'

    Without editing or judging, write down your responses in point form. Is it dance, travel, social justice, animals, wellness, fashion, sisterhood? (No answer is beyond reason, and no answer is too big or too small.) Within this list lies the key to finding your people. You're ready to move on to the next step.

2. **Drill it down.** Get focused. Now that you have your list, give yourself time to be with it. Circle the most important ones and focus on those. Imagine you're engaged with those activities or desired experiences. Get into the feeling of it.

    Put your list on your altar, keep it by your bed, or **create an affirmation** from it: Use present tense and stay away from phrases like 'I long' or 'I want.' Write it as if it's already here: 'I belong with people who care for animals.' 'I am with women devoted to the Goddess.' 'My people love and live to travel.' Say it out loud often as part of your 'howl.'

3. **Take action.** You've got your list, and your affirmations and musings. Beautiful. You're already on your way. But, it's not enough to give it up to spirit, to mystery, alone. The law of attraction works best when dreaming and action come together; when both are activated and entwined. Below are ways to take your intention further, into actionable steps.

4. **Pay attention.** Listen and watch for signs, signposts and synchronicities that point you in the direction of others. Follow the trail of breadcrumbs. Look around. Trust in the impulses that say, 'YES, this feels good, this feels right. I want to know these people. I want them to know me.'

5. **Look around.** Do your research. With a clear intention of what you wish to experience and with who, get busy searching. Look for local clubs, community events, potlucks, or whatever or wherever your possible people will gather in your area.

    Or, perhaps your people are spread out around the world and connecting globally lights you up. Make friends with Google and social media. Look for retreats and events you could travel to or find groups that are virtual.

6. **Join in.** Test the waters. Once you've found something locally or virtually, ask to join. Find a way in. Take a chance. When you show up, regardless if it's in person

or online, bring your best self. Be courageous and immensely curious. Ask questions. Stay open.

Get to know some people. What are their personalities and their collective principles and protocols? Do they feel to be in integrity? Share as much as it feels right. Keep checking in with yourself: 'How do I feel?' You may need to assess your feelings afterwards: 'Was this a safe space for me to be myself?' Trust your body and heart wisdom as to whether you'll return.

If the first group or event doesn't feel like YOUR place, your people, don't be disheartened. Maybe you were meant to meet ONE of your people, and that's a big blessing in itself. Take it as an opportunity to discover what and who feels right. (Kind of like dating!) Keep looking and keep going.

7   **Start your own group.** Call in your people. If all else fails and nothing feels like a fit, create your own event or group. Send out your howl. Get creative. Be courageous, open and curious. Stay strong in your intention. You WILL find your people, no doubt.

Be a Mirror

"Without a mirror, you can't see the back of your head or neck or upper back. And so, it's up to the community to see the rest of you. If you don't have a community, you're left to twist yourself into contortions to get some perspective on yourself or to walk around believing only in the parts of you that you can see." Tad Hargrave

Imagine you are Uzume or one of the gods and goddesses who came together with their shard of mirror to save the day, to remind Amaterasu of her beauty, power and radiance. Imagine yourself as one of those Divine Beings because you ARE! You have the power to reflect light, love, truth and wisdom for your community, family and work.

The practice of being a mirror is being offered to you now to explore and play with. It's a reminder of your innate ability to, well, REFLECT. Ahem… **She Reflects!**

And there's no right or wrong way to be and do this. It's all in the intention of being of service, a positive role-model, a great listener, a holder of safe and inclusive space for others to unfold while holding space for your own true self.

Why practice this? Because you are needed, my friend. Your unique shape and shard of mirror is your exquisite gift to us, all of us. Your reflection can't be duplicated or copied. Your reflection is needed.

Being a mirror, a clear and polished mirror, means rising up in order to raise others. It means practicing self-care and self-love so you can show up with more tenderness, to be a nurturing and positive role-model.

Being a mirror, a smooth and shiny mirror, means working on and healing your own shadow and wounds so you can sit with the pain or silence of another, even when their stories, identities or experiences are not what we want to see or are not what we know. It means leaving no one behind.

It's an opportunity for unlearning as well as learning.

The questions become…

'**How can I best show up?**

How can I be the clearest and most polished mirror, without distortion, without tarnish, and without losing myself?'

Through the work of polishing our own mirror, we find ourselves. We find our wholeness. We find acceptance. We find joy. We find…

In the end, the mirror finds itself.

Be a mirror: There are endless ways to be a mirror, physically, emotionally, mentally and spiritually. Here's what popped up for me.

- **Be a friend, neighbour, sister.** A sister to her sisters. A neighbour keeping watch. A friend through thick and thin. A companion of play. A cheerleader raising up and celebrating others. A confidante. An ally for the cause.

    Who needs you to be there, to walk beside them? Be their mirror.

- **Be a teacher, facilitator, leader.** A positive role-model. A teacher stirring the imagination. A facilitator of wild circles. A leader leading from the heart. A guru for the weary. A coach for rising stars. A muse. An inspiration for deeper learning.

    Who needs you to teach, inspire and be a positive role-model? Be their mirror.

- **Be a priestess, lover, healer.** A holder of sacred space. A lover embracing the beloved in another. A doctor of broken hearts and wings. A healer of tired bodies and souls. A spiritual advisor. A wisdom keeper. A guide embodying the sacred.

    Who needs you to hold sacred and loving space? Be their mirror.

- **Be a visionary, creatrix, storyteller.** A dreamer of magnificent dreams (and shares them). A weaver of stories for the disenchanted. A visionary igniting the possible. A map-maker for the lost. A creatrix of magic. A mother of wondrous inventions.

    Who needs you to spark their creativity and hope? Be their mirror.

- **Be a peacemaker, advocate, activist.** A protectress for the weak and vulnerable. A beacon of light and peace. A breaker of rules. A catalyst for change. A balm for our collective angst and fear. An advocate for the disenfranchised, disadvantaged and marginalized.

    Who needs you to stand up for and with them? Be their mirror.

May whatever goodness you mirror for others <u>reflect</u> back to you a thousand-fold!

Get Playful / Laugh Together

*"Knock Knock! Who's there?
Norma Lee. Norma Lee who?
Norma Lee I have my key, can you let me in?"*

*"A Zen student asked his master, 'Is it OK to use email?'"
"Yes," replied the master, "But no attachments.""*

*"A Zen master once said to me,
'Do the opposite of whatever I tell you.' So I didn't."*

*"Before you criticize someone, you should walk a mile in their shoes.
That way, when you criticize them, you're a mile away
and you have their shoes."*

Did you know humans are one of the only species who laugh? (No, laughing hyenas don't count. They aren't really laughing. They just give out a sound similar to it.)

We take laughing for granted, but think about that. I mean, isn't it a wonderful blessing to be able to respond to life that way - with delicious, spontaneous sounds and movements of joy and laughter, warming our hearts and feeding our souls?

And why be so serious, anyway? Just because you're a fully formed adult with big responsibilities and daily struggles and challenges doesn't mean you need to leave behind your playful self, at least from time to time. You know how good laughter feels, and especially when we laugh with others.

Laughter is one of the best remedies around. It's free to all, and it's deliciously contagious. Just hearing it can cause us to soften our hearts and break out into our own full-blown laughter, without even knowing the reason for the laughter in the first place.

Laughter not only awakens and uplifts our tired bodies, minds, hearts and souls, it also boosts our immune system, oxygenates our blood, and helps us release blocked emotions, stress, pain and anxiety.

Laughter is a natural and potent painkiller and opiate, breaking the spell of negative thought patterns and emotions into positive feelings and outlooks. It supports connection, bonding and a sense of belonging in our families and communities.

Our shared laughter amplifies love and the lightness of our being. Our shared joy is life-giving. Yes... I'll take *that* prescription any day.

I'd even go so far as to say here, in my humble opinion, that laughter is one of the highest forms of offerings we can give, to ourselves and to others.

So don't hold back. Laugh more often and more fully, right down to your toes and into the Earth. And then, pass it on; give it away as a sacred gift.

This invitation is for you to do SOMETHING to get you laughing and increase the collective joy factor in your life, this week! Yes, this week. Or even today. Or right NOW. It's time to get playful and silly. It's time to laugh. With others. A lot!

(And don't worry: your problems, concerns and responsibilities will still be there for you to return to, if need be, so please don't feel guilty about giving yourself this time of levity.)

Get playful. Laugh together:

- Throw a party!
- Watch a comedy, at home or in a cinema.
- Go to a comedy club.
- Try a Laughter Yoga session.
- Read a funny book out loud.
- Watch funny videos online.
- Have a games night: Charades, cards, board games, twister.
- Listen to a comedian on TV, a radio show or a podcast.
- Learn and memorize some jokes and share them.
- Get your toddler on: Talk gibberish, and make funny faces and gestures.
- Dance in different styles or eras. Have fun. Improvise.
- Have a pillow fight or snowball fight.
- Try different forms of laughter in unison. Ha ha. Hee hee. Ho ho.

"Time spent laughing is time spent with the gods." Japanese Proverb

Throw a Dance Party

Humanity has united in dance for as far back as we can trace.

It's a world-wide story. Starting on the oldest continent of Africa and spreading around the globe, we've gathered to celebrate the turn of the seasons, the harvests, the hunts, and all significant moments and passages collectively through dance.

Today, whether it's the whirling dervishes of Turkey, break-dancers on the streets of Los Angeles, or Canada's First Nations' Pow Wow dancers, rhythmic movement, together, creates a deep source of collective joy and healing.

In his book *Keeping Together in Time*, respected American historian William Hardy McNeill shares these sentiments and reveals the possibility that coordinated rhythmic movement, and the shared feelings it elicits, has been a powerful force in holding human groups together.

I couldn't agree more.

McNeill focuses on the instinctive and emotional sensations that group movement stirs, especially in the elated feeling he calls 'muscular bonding.' He suggests these sensations inspire co-operation within groups, which in turn improves their chance of survival.

This really speaks to me. It affirms what I've always known in my bones, that the collective experience in dance can be downright powerful, downright blissful. I get what McNeill means by elated feelings. It's what I feel when I dance with others. **Elation. Ecstasy. Joy.**

I've felt it in The Loft days of NYC, the beaches and clubs of India and Bali, the countless music festivals, concerts, street and house parties, ecstatic dances and retreats in Canada and around the world. The people, times and settings may vary, but the desire for personal and collective love, freedom and joy remain the same.

There's something about it: Good tunes plus good people equals good times.

So, my lovely, this invitation is to Throw a Dance Party, to gather your favourite people together to experience your own 'muscular bonding,' and more than anything... to raise the roof with collective JOY!

I'm sure you don't need instructions on how to throw a dance party, but I do have some suggestions to help raise the joy factor - having learned a thing or two from all the ecstatic dance parties I've thrown and DJ-ed over the past 20 years.

And if you need to enlist others to help you throw it, do it. In fact, I highly recommend you do; at least one other person, if not more. Do whatever it takes.

Ok. Let's get this party started: 2 hours or longer

1. **Decide when and where you'll have your dance -** In your home, in someone else's home, in a park, in a studio, or on the street. And decide if it'll be at night or during the day. Consider this... Dance parties in the day can be really delicious (some of my favourite parties were Sunday 'tea' parties in the afternoon). Throw your party where there's lots of room to move and the floor is easy on the body - no carpet, linoleum or ceramic tiles. Invite your favourite people.

2. Decide if it's adults only or kids are welcome too. Oh, and ask everyone to dress up for the occasion. Festive, bright, flowy and shiny. Or create a themed party - roaring 20s, disco, you name it. Have fun with it. (Please note: Using another person's culture as a costume is cultural appropriation.)

3. **Prepare a playlist of dance tunes** or use the **Collective Joy Playlist**. It's filled with up-tempo and happy tunes. (Some are from my Loft days.)

   If you create your own, decide how long your dance will be, and plan your playlist accordingly. For the structure of your set, I suggest having music with a slower tempo to start, building up to higher energy in the middle (or for most of the set), and then slowing it back down towards the end.

   I prefer to use iTunes or Spotify on a laptop, crossfading at maximum length so each song blends into the next. If you decide to have someone else DJ, have them use the Collective Joy Playlist or your own.

4. **Use a good sound system.** What I mean by 'good' is to have decent speakers where you can turn up the volume without causing cracking and squeaking. If you have a mixer that plugs into speakers, turn the volume up on your laptop and play with the volume controls on the mixer. I find that gives a better sound.

5. **Create an ambiance.** If your party's at night, dim the lights just enough to create a soft and sexy vibe. If you're dancing in the daytime, enjoy the sun! Have lots of water or suggest everyone bring their own water bottle. Have bowls of fresh fruit like bananas or apples, and any other snacks you love.

   Fill the space with colour: coloured balloons, lights, flowers or streamers. Keep the space ventilated, with fans if necessary, but never have the space too cold. Dancing bodies don't do well when they're cold.

6. **Most of all... Enjoy yourself!** Be a shiny mirror for everyone attending. Wear your party gear. Put flowers in your hair, bangles and bells on your ankles (you get the picture). Get onto the dance floor as much as you can. Create circles of dancers or start a bunny hop line dance. Catalyze the collective joy experience. Be spontaneous. Be playful. (*Dance for those who cannot dance.*)

Form a Healing Circle

Dear healing circle. Oh how I love you.

*Thank you for gathering us together in your ancient container,
wrapping us up in your warm and loving embrace.*

*Your sacred shape of inclusivity,
of unity and oneness, heals us into wholeness.*

*Thank you for holding and loving us
while we lay down our burdens and wash away our tears.*

*Thank you for granting us permission to release what wishes to fly,
and root what needs to be planted.*

I sing your praises. I bow at your feet.

I wish for every living soul to know you.

And may it be so.

Because we all need to be held. We all need to be loved. We all need to heal. Truth!

So why not do it with others; within a safe and sacred space of heart-centered friends and beloveds? In a place of comfort, belonging, acceptance and compassion.

Through history and around the world, circles have been held, just for that. Healing circles, talking circles, peacemaking circles; they are ancient forms of gathering, portals for healing, for reconciliation, for transformation.

Women have reigned in the rich history of these healing circles. I think it's in our DNA to create healing spaces for each other. Our ancestors did it. You may even be one of the lucky ones to have been raised by women who sit in healing circles still today. If so, you are truly blessed, my friend.

The healing circle is needed today as much as it was in the past. We all surely could use its grounding and nourishing support - to bring heaven down to earth - to tap us into the collective power and unifying field of love, and to heal into wholeness, radiance and joy.

This invitation and instruction to Form a Healing Circle is based on my own experience of holding circles both professionally and personally, in studio with clients and in my living room with dear and trusted friends. I don't in any way believe this is the only way. It's just my way. It's what I know.

As you go through the instructions, know you can improvise and change it as you feel fit. I suggest, especially if you've never done this before, to mostly keep to the script, only for the purpose of supporting you in keeping the experience safe and grounded.

If you have your own way, by all means, disregard what I'm suggesting. The prompt is to have a healing circle, however you wish. (Although, perhaps there's a piece in what I've shared that can be sweetly woven in to what you already do and know. If so, yay! I love being a muse.)

Also…

If you've never attended a healing circle, and you're thinking this is out of your comfort zone, or that you can't do this, let me just say this…

In all my years of holding circles, I've found that **EVERY woman has an Inner Healer inside**. Every woman is a Healing Woman. She lives in us all. She just needs a safe space to beckon her, and initiate her presence. In other words, you *can* do this! I believe in you.

So go ahead. Decide on a date and time. Invite some friends and family to join you. I love the number <u>eight</u> as a circle size, including yourself. I always invite more than that, because some will not be able to attend, or will cancel at the last minute. (That's life.)

Form your healing circle: **Approx. 6-8 minutes per person, plus 2-3 minutes** for the transitions of swapping people in the center. Adjust according to how much time you've allotted for the full experience.

Pre-circle:

- **Set up the space.** Create a comfortable spot for the circle with chairs or pillows. I prefer to create a bed on the floor with cushions or a yoga mat with soft fabric over it, and then place pillows around it for the circle of friends to sit on. Scatter shakers and rattles around the pillows if you have them. Crystals are also wonderful to place around. You may also love to create a beautiful altar nearby, to infuse the space with your sacred intention for healing and relaxation.

After their arrival:

1 **Invite everyone to sit in the circle** of pillows or chairs.

2 **Read the instructions below.** (I'm going to call the one in the center Amaterasu, and the others Mirrors.)

3 **Tell them how long each one will have in the center** as 'Amaterasu,' and that you'll have a timer.

4 **After** the instructions below have been read, **ask someone to come into the center** of the circle to be the first Amaterasu.

The circle begins:

For Amaterasu: Once you've arrived in the center...

1. **Share out loud what needs healing.** Heart, body, creativity, pain? A release, a support, a rest. Or share no specific need, other than to open up and trust in the mystery of healing possibilities.

2. **Express how you'd like to receive the healing.** This is important. For example, "I love having my head and feet massaged." "I'd love for you to sing or sound or use shakers." "I'd love for you to do whatever comes to you intuitively... sound, touch, words. All are welcomed." "I'd love anything *but* physical touch."

   *There's something magical about the act of ASKING for what you need. There are healing ripples from that act alone.

3. **Then**, the best part... **Lie back and let the magic begin.** You may wish to call in your angels or guides as everyone is settling in around you. Relax and RECEIVE! Experience the power of the circle, the healing of community. Drop into yourself and feel what you feel. If tears come, let them flow. Whatever is felt, it's good for your healing. You can't get this wrong. Trust. It.

4. **After** you hear the timer and the healing session ends, take your time before sitting up. **Give a gesture of thanks to everyone.** Ask who'd like to go next and swap places with them.

5. **Keep going until everyone has had a turn.** Complete the experience with some kind of closure. A group hug, a cup of tea, a meal.

For the Mirrors: (Mirrors are working together, simultaneously.)

1. **Move closer.** Find a spot to start off in - by the feet, the hands, the head, etc. (or slightly behind others if space is an issue). **Set the timer.**

2. With Amaterasu's request in mind and in your heart, respecting their requests, begin to **ground and relax** into your deeper knowing, your intuition, your Inner Healer.

3. Close your eyes or keep them open, **listen in and trust your impulses.** You never know what will be medicinal for them. If you feel a desire to sing, sing. If you feel compelled to whisper sweet words in their ear, do that. **Feel free to move around** and swap places.

4. Besides following your own Inner Healer, take cues from others also. For example, if one person is massaging a hand, join in by taking the other hand and doing the same. If someone starts to sing, sing with them. **Stay fluid and present** in the healing web you're creating.

5. And lastly, **don't hold back.** This isn't the time to be shy or to overthink. This is an

incredible gift you're giving, so give it. (Staying mindful of boundaries that have already been expressed.)

6 **Keep going until you hear the timer.** That's your cue to slowly bring whatever you were doing to a close. Bring yourself back to a pillow, giving space and time for Amaterasu to open their eyes and come back to the room.

7 After you've been thanked, it's time for someone new to enter the circle.

*Oh, and don't forget. **Take a pee break** if you go over an hour.

After the circle:

- Stretch, mingle and offer some tea or snacks. Depending on how much time you have allotted, and it's important to honour that time-frame, you could come back together in the circle to share the experiences as both Mirror and Amaterasu, or keep the sharing informal until you need to wrap it up.

- Afterwards, and into the next few days, gently notice how you feel. Check in with your friends too. And if they loved the experience, start a monthly Healing Circle, taking turns in each other's homes.

Know Your 'Group' Self

We are all so unique. Different personalities, attractions, desires, preferences, skills, abilities and experiences. Some situations just naturally suit us, and some don't. Group situations in particular can be exhilarating or inhibiting depending on the setting, the day, the person. And that's okay.

The main thing is to take the time to know what's right for you. You hold the key to your own joy and peace. It's up to you to show up and participate in group situations - from the close intimacy of a circle of friends, to the coolness of the boardroom or the anonymity of a large party filled with strangers. It's up to you to find your way. Right?

Every situation, whether it's how you are on your own, in a partnership or in a group, offers an opportunity for self-discovery and positive change. The first step is to bring awareness.

Understanding how you are in a group setting is powerful, life-affirming information. You learn where you have work to do, when you're triggered and what feels safe(r). Then you can create a plan, a new map that includes the remembrance that some groups are not for you, that you're doing the best you can, and that you're perfect just as you are.

(A side note: If you're a creator of groups, consider how you can make them more inclusive, welcoming and safe. Too often groups feel exclusive or inaccessible. Just sayin'.)

And as you know, there will be times when you can't avoid a group situation you'd rather not attend, but through self-awareness you'll be better prepared to navigate more easily, by knowing your natural impulses - the where, what, when and why of how you feel, where you thrive, when you get stirred, and when you're in flow.

With it comes compassion, patience and love. Self-knowledge will always lead you to new healing and growth, and ultimately to the liberation of your natural radiance lying under the fear, doubt, shame and wounds, regardless of circumstances.

To help you get to know yourself...

On the next page you'll find some questions, musings and prompts to inspire compassionate curiosity in your own self-discovery, to help you better understand yourself, and how best to navigate the group experience and dynamics.

Let the questions delight you. Journal, dance, sing or draw your responses. Let your responses float up effortlessly in their own time.

Relax. Ask. Listen. Reflect. Be curious. Go deeper. **Keep the question alive. EnJOY!**

Reflect and journal about your 'Group' self:

- When I think of 'a group,' what comes to mind?

- What group situations make me shine, and why? (An intimate dinner with friends, a large family reunion, work party, nightclub, church event, etc.)

- What group situations make me close down, and why?

- What would help me feel safe or safer in a group?

- How do I move in a group situation when I feel safe? (Demeanor, style, expressions.)

- Where do I like to place myself in a group, and why? How does it make me feel? (As the center of attention? In the furthest fringes and corners?)

- In a group, do I give and receive in equal measure, in balance? (Love, acceptance, kindness, courage, support, joy, etc.)

- Do I allow myself to be vulnerable in a group?

- Do I allow and trust others to hold me just as I am? Why or why not? (Do I speak up, emote and express my truth?)

- Do I hold and reflect unconditional space for others? How do I do this? Why or why not?

- Do I hold my center, my power, my joy, in a group situation? How do I do this? Why or why not?

- How can I be the most loving, shiniest, juiciest, smartest, boldest, best me in any given situation, regardless?

- What do I LOVE to do... what makes me SHINE?

- Who are my people? (What do they love, how do they act, where do they live, what makes them tick?)

- How can I find my people? (In person, online, networking events.)

Collective Joy Playlist

Get your groove on. EnJOY. Invite your friends to join you.
*Dedicated to David Mancuso and The Loft.

1. **Behind the Groove**, Lady T (Expanded Edition), by Teena Marie
2. **Funkin' for Jamaica**, Funkin' for Jamaica, by Tom Browne
3. **We Got the Funk** (12" US Re-Edit Version), Journey Into Paradise: The Larry Levan Story, by Positive Force
4. **The Joy** (Fundamentalist Mix), The Joy / This Too Shall Pass, by Joy Jones
5. **Ain't No Stoppin' Us Now**, McFadden & Whitehead, by McFadden & Whitehead
6. **Ring My Bell**, Ring My Bell, by Anita Ward
7. **Now That We Found Love** (Single), Journey to Addis, by Third World
8. **It's More Fun to Compute**, Produced With Love, by Joey Negro
9. **Roots** (feat. Jazzie B), Roots (feat. Jazzie B), by Copyright
10. **Afolabi**, It Began in Africa, Vol. 2, by Rauschhaus
11. **Move Your Body**, Move Your Body, by Marshall Jefferson
12. **Madan** (Exotic Disco Mix) (feat. Salif Keita), Suite, by Martin Solveig
13. **Move Like This**, David Ospina Classics, Vol. 1, by NYC Live & Direct
14. **Rose Rouge**, Tourist (Remastered), by St. Germain
15. **Paradise**, The Best of Change, by Change
16. **Let the Music Use You**, Frankie Knuckles Presents: His Greatest Hits, by The Nightwriters
17. **Right In the Socket**, Big Fun, by Shalamar
18. **The Groove Line**, Club Epic - A Collection of Classic Dance Mixes, by Heat Wave
19. **Happy** (from "Despicable Me 2"), G I R L, by Pharrell Williams
20. **We Are Family** (Single Version), We Are Family, by Sister Sledge
21. **Good Times**, Risqué, by Chic
22. **Going Back to My Roots** (12" Version), Greatest Hits, by Odyssey

Go to: www.EricaRoss.com/playlists

Fifth Turn

The Magic of Letting Go

*"Knowledge is learning something every day.
Wisdom is letting go of something every day."* Zen Proverb

Mama Ocean

There are three things I want you to know:

One, I was terrified of the ocean.
Two, there are strong undertows around the island of Bali: In the three years I lived there, a number of people were, terrifyingly and tragically pulled out to sea.
And three, I was feeling really, really, did I mention REALLY, good in my life.

So let's begin.

Life was pretty fantastic.

It was the late 80s and I was living an inspired island life. I was living on two islands, worlds apart. I lived in Bali, "Island of a Thousand Temples" and in one of the most exciting cities in the world, Manhattan.

In Manhattan, I co-owned a clothing boutique in the East Village. My business partner at the time and I were designing and producing our own clothing line in Bali. When she was taking care of the business in Bali, I'd be in Manhattan running the boutique and soaking up the juiciness of life in the East Village - going to clubs and great restaurants and late night parties, you know, all things NYC. Then we'd switch: She'd come back to Manhattan and I'd go to Bali.

(Occasionally we'd both be needed in Bali together, so we hired one of my dear friends to be our boutique manager. But for the most part, we swapped locations.)

My stays in Bali became longer and longer with each visit as my desire to be in the slower pace and natural beauty of Bali grew. My partner had kids in New York, so she was fine to be in Manhattan more and Bali less.

In Bali, we rented a sweet two-story, one-bedroom house with a porch and balcony. The house was in a beautiful compound (a Balinese term for a walled enclave where families, often up to three generations, live together, with buildings, open space and a family shrine). In our case, the compound was built in a very large garden owned by and situated behind the home of a Balinese family. It was lush with palm trees and tropical flowers. Houses for tourists and business people were scattered around the garden, separated by vegetation and grassy pathways.

It was a secluded paradise right off the main strip north of Kuta, the biggest tourist area, in Legian. Clubs, shops and restaurants were at our doorstep, and yet, the beach was a mere five-minute bicycle ride away. Perfection!

And a 15-minute scooter ride from our house, through small villages, bamboo-lined paths and rice fields, there was another compound. It was the production compound for our clothing line, which we had built as soon as we arrived to house our new-found tailor and her community of seamstresses.

Fifth Turn: The Magic of Letting Go

Business in Bali meant working six days a week. But trust me, it was no hardship! I'd spend my days happily tripping around the island overseeing our production - banking and buying fabric in Denpasar, the capitol city, supervising the dying and printmaking with the batikers and screen printers in local villages, and managing quotas with the shippers. And of course, making sure everything was going well with the pattern-making and sewing at the production compound.

I had an assistant, a young Balinese man, and because I didn't feel comfortable driving a motorbike, he'd take me everywhere on the back of his bike. At the end of the day he'd drop me off at home and I'd change into my bathing suit and sarong and ride my bicycle down to the local beach for the sunset.

My nights were just as wonderful. After soaking in the meditative sunset vibes with friends, I'd cycle home to start my nightly ritual of languidly preparing myself to go out for dinner with friends. The options were vast - from small, local, family-run *warungs*, to big, trendy international restaurants where jet-setters and clothing designers came to eat, but mostly, to see and be seen. (It reminded me of NYC.)

After dinner, the night continued. If clubbing was on the agenda, which it was at least four nights a week, I'd go home to change into my short leather boots, black tights and top, and a leather belt-skirt I'd hand-stitched and painted. Then I'd bike down to the beach to my favourite dance club, Double Six, to dance into the wee hours with the ocean just steps away. More perfection.

When I wasn't at Double Six, I'd either be at the other local dance club Gado Gado or relaxing with friends at their home or mine. And occasionally I was asked to perform solo improvisational dances for special events like birthday or going away parties. I'd show up with a portable cassette player (yes, those were the days of cassette tapes!), and a make-shift costume with makeup, and do my thing. I even co-created a larger dance performance with three other dancers at Double Six (a highlight).

It was pretty idyllic. I had the best of both worlds. Beach life and city life, Bali and Manhattan. And I loved it. I was in such a good state of mind. It's against this backdrop of beauty and bliss that I learned one of the most enduring lessons of my life.

Bali, it turned out, was going to bring me to my knees.

+++

It was Sunday, another perfect day in paradise. I was enjoying a little beach time on my day off. As usual, the beach was hopping. It was filled with swimmers, sunbathers and surfers; Bali was, and still is, famous for its surfing. The crowd on the beach was made up mostly of foreigners and business people like myself, but not that many Balinese. For the most part, and as I understand it, the Balinese aren't that fond of the water due to their spiritual and mythological beliefs. (I'll explain that later.)

Me, I'm not that fond of the water either. Pretty much my entire life I've been scared of the ocean. I like being near the water, but not in it. Not so much. I mean, I can swim; I'm just not a 'swimmer.'

Beach time for me is about soaking up the sun and taking in the sounds and scents of the surf, usually relaxing on my sarong. Maybe, just maybe, I'll wade into the water, usually only up to my waist. That's my comfort zone. I'm definitely not someone you'll find out there swimming, and I'm certainly not surfing.

On this particular perfect day at the beach in Bali, I went to the edge of the water and decided to wade in. Just like every other time, the ocean gently slapped around my ankles and calves. The sun sparkled on the water and I was completely enjoying myself.

It was bliss.

Pure bliss!

Until all of a sudden, it wasn't.

Suddenly, and I mean suddenly, the gently lapping water around my shins was up to my thighs. And then, again suddenly, I couldn't feel the sandy bottom under my feet. And for the third time, suddenly, I realized I was being pulled out into deeper waters. The ocean I feared and loved was taking me on (and in).

I started to panic. All I could think about were those people who'd been pulled out to sea. I tried swimming back to shore, pushing against the current in a kind of front crawl. I just wanted to get to a spot where I could stand up. Instead, the water was pulling me away, further and further from shore. The harder I pushed against the current, the worse it seemed to get.

I cried for help. I could see people playing on the beach and sunning and doing their own thing. Surely someone would hear me. Someone would see me. But nothing. No one noticed me at all.

Pure panic set in.

I was swallowing water, mouthful after mouthful. I was being tossed and tumbled by the waves, turning somersaults under water. I couldn't tell which way was up. I was totally freaked out, gasping and screaming and thrashing around.

And then, all of a sudden, I got pissed off.

I mean, really pissed off.

I couldn't believe that Mama Ocean had picked me - that she was carrying ME away!

'No way. Fuck that! What? Not me! Are you kidding me? I am not going to die. NO!'

'NOT NOW!'

'NOT ME! NOT ME! NO, NOT ME!!!'

I adored my life. I adored my friends. I adored where I was living. Everything.

I kept fighting and raging, and fighting and raging, against Mama Ocean.

"Help!!!! Help me!!" I was yelling at Mama Ocean as much as to the beach bathers on shore.

More water was swallowed. More tossing and turning. I was upside down and inside out. It was chaos.

Chaos!

And I was terrified.

One of my greatest fears, a true nightmare for me, was to be pulled out to sea, and here it was coming true.

But after fighting and fighting and fighting for so long, I was exhausted. Absolutely and utterly exhausted. I was losing the fight, and I knew it.

In that moment I made a decision I'll never forget.

I threw back my arms, flopped backwards, and bellowed, "Okay, Mama. You want me? You got me. I can't fight you anymore. You are way too powerful. I don't want this - I don't want to die, but what the fuck else can I do? You've got me."

And there it was.

I let go.

There's a kind of peace that comes with letting go. A quiet. I stopped the flailing and screaming. The yelling stopped. The fighting against the waves stopped. I just gave in. There I was facing my worst fear of being pulled out to sea and I felt peace and quiet.

I'm not sure how much time had passed, but it seemed like only seconds later, I noticed a young Balinese boy paddling towards me on a surfboard. I couldn't believe my eyes. He looked about eight years old, maybe a little older, but he'd seen me and he was coming to get me.

He paddled up beside me, grabbed me and somehow pulled me onto the board. This eight-year-old got me up on the board.

"Oh my god, you've saved me," I cried in total disbelief. I was lying there belly down on the board completely exhausted, when all of a sudden a huge wave washed over us and knocked us both off the board.

Chaos, again. Panic, again.

I truly thought it was over for me. Over for both of us.

Yet somehow, and I don't know how, the young boy found me and managed to pull me and himself onto the surfboard. With my limp body slung crosswise over the board, we started - he started - to paddle us back to shore.

I have no idea how much time passed, I just know he paddled me right up to the beach. When I felt and heard the scraping of the board on the sand, I knew I was safe. I rolled my exhausted body off the surfboard, got to my knees and kissed the ground.

I had never been more grateful in my life.

'Thank you! Thank you! Thank you! I'm alive!'

I lifted my head up to see the Balinese boy; I was ready to hug him and kiss him and thank him. He'd saved my life! I couldn't believe how lucky I was. But when I looked up, he wasn't there. Nobody was there. No one. Nothing. Not the surfboard. Not the boy. Not a soul.

'What? Wait. What?' It was crazy. I didn't understand it! I got up and looked around. He wasn't on the beach. He wasn't in the water. He was nowhere to be found.

And then, suddenly, I had this overwhelming realization.

The young Balinese surfer boy was an angel, my angel, that day.

+++

In the days that followed, I often wondered about that Balinese boy. I remember thinking that it didn't even make sense that it was a Balinese boy who saved me. Not only was there the question of how someone so young could pull me up on to that surfboard; it's that the Balinese, the majority being Hindu - a unique mix of Hinduism, Animism and Buddhism - have a fear of the ocean.

From my understanding, their aversion to the sea comes from a distinct religious and mythological belief that the sea is a hazardous place where the demons live, and the mountains are revered as holy places where gods live. So generally speaking, the Balinese aren't big swimmers and rarely surfers (at least at that time).

Yet, it was a young Balinese boy on a surfboard who came to save me. Not that I ever doubted it - that he was an angel, I mean - it's just that it sank in even more deeply that I had been saved in a remarkable way.

But this story is not about being saved by an angel. I don't share it in order to speak of the existence of them. Not at all. The idea of angels didn't really come naturally to me. I grew up in a secular Jewish family where angels weren't part of our family's lexicon, not even a little bit.

Nor is it about the terror. I was more afraid in that moment in the sea than I'd ever been in my life. That terror could easily linger to this day. But, it doesn't. Quite the opposite.

Instead of shunning the sea after that day, I embraced it. When I visited Australia a couple of years later, I dared myself to learn how to scuba dive. And I did. I became an accredited diver at the Great Barrier Reef. Fear. Confronted.

No, that miraculous day is not about the existence of angels, nor about confronting fear.

For me, it's about something else entirely.

It's about letting go.

It's what saved me that day. I know it. Letting go saved me.

When I gave in, when I stopped fighting, when I said "Take me," that's when the way out appeared. That's when the answer became clear. That's when the magic happened.

I've often wondered what would have happened if I hadn't let go. What if I'd continued to fight and fight and fight? It's not hard to imagine that I would have fought to the end, to my end. If I hadn't let go I don't believe I would be here today. By surrendering and letting go I was saved.

The experience of that day has as much power now as it did then. Every time I find myself in a situation where I'm fighting and fighting and fighting, I remember the lessons of letting go. I learned there are times when the answer is not within my power and that sometimes the answer is beyond my understanding.

I know now that when I soften and let go the answer will appear - not necessarily as an angel, but as an answer of some sort: a new idea, a stranger with a word of advice, an unexpected opportunity. But before the answer can appear, I have to give up the 'fight' and let go.

It's why I share this story and why I LOVE this story. Not only is it a mystical, wild story that if it hadn't happened to me, I'd say, 'Oh, come on, are you serious?,' it's a story of the Magic of Letting Go.

Letting go can change everything! One of the definitions of magic is a shift in perception and that, to me, is exactly what happens when we let go.

Many, many times since Bali, my experience at sea that day has inspired me to let go. When I do, something miraculous always happens. Boom. Doors open. Boom. Magic happens. And sometimes, even angels appear. It's truth for me.

That day in Bali, I received three gifts:

The gift of life - Mama Ocean didn't take me that day.
The gift of my daughter who was born three years later. She wouldn't exist if I had died that day.
And the third gift is the lesson of the magic of letting go.

Yes. Bali brought me to my knees, but it was in gratitude for this amazing life.

Reflections

"To live in this world you must be able to do three things: to love what is mortal; to hold it against your bones knowing your own life depends on it; and, when the time comes to let it go, to let it go." Mary Oliver

Welcome!

A soft and magical doorway awaits you here in the Fifth Turn of our spiral journey: the portal of letting go.

'Letting,' as in allowing. 'Go,' as in movement.
'Letting go,' as in allowing change, choosing receptivity and honouring release.

Now is that time. A potent time of renewal and magic.

Because your 'letting go' is a sacred act, an offering, a giving of yourself to the divine, to the universe, to the wisdom of your intuition and higher/deeper knowing, and un-knowing.

Letting go is both an outward act - saying when 'enough is enough' and walking away, burning the photos, or cutting things loose - and a spiritual practice, of softening and releasing so we can be stronger, more flexible, more receptive, curious and creative as we navigate through life.

Regardless of who or where we are, whether we're fighting 'the good fight' to make a more just and beautiful world, studying in university, working the land, or caring for aging parents, letting go is unavoidable and essential. It allows flow to move us forward.

Letting go is an everyday, life-long practice - there's *always* something to shed and clear. There's always room for more lightness and clarity. Always.

*If the whole idea of 'letting go' feels too much, too big, or too hard for you to take in or do, I invite you to reframe it, to find your own words for it. How about 'receiving' or 'granting permission to'? Maybe it can be about being held and supported - by a loved one, by your own heart, or by spirit. Find what works for you, so you can access the magic it holds.

In the 'letting go spectrum,' there are countless ways it arrives and is experienced. And it can come in gentle layers, warm, spacious and expansive, like a spiral going deeper and deeper into the healing. It can come as a complete abandon, a collapsing, an undoing and a relief, like when I was at war with the ocean. From the subtlest, almost undetectable, to the earth-shattering storminess, and everything in between. A full whoosh or like a leaf falling from a tree.

And if it comes intensely in the form of a meltdown, it can feel disturbingly unsettling and scary, but that's okay. You will survive! It's like the snake shedding its skin. She's vulnerable through the process, losing her ability to see. But once she's shed everything, every last inch of her skin, she's shiny, new and ravenous. You, too, once through the letting go and releasing, will become shiny, new and ravenous for life. I promise you.

What does letting go look and feel like for you? Does this feel possible for you right now?

The first kind of letting go that comes to mind is the surrender of my ego wanting to control everything. Not just because it happens to be my 'area of expertise.' (Just kidding!) Actually, it's my greatest teacher. It seems to be in my personality type... stubborn by nature. Some might say it's because of my five planets in the fixed sign of Scorpio.

All I know is, and it's clearly and especially in this story, LETTING GO is my lesson, the key, the magic... and continues to be an essential 'personal practice.'

For all of us, I'd add, letting go is fundamental to our human experience: The letting go of perfectionism, the letting go of thinking we know, the letting go of harsh self-criticism, bad habits and playing it small, just to name a few.

We all carry the weight of these concepts, expectations and beliefs. We constrict and constrain. And sometimes, we suffer with profound pain, angst and immobility. We're never good enough. Never where we think we 'ought' to be. Never right. Never, ever.

Where's the room for compassion, curiosity or courage? Where's the space for getting wild, creative and feeling free? What becomes of our true self, our messy ideas and juicy desires? Who are we doing this for, anyway?

That, my friend, is Amaterasu's boulder - the big rock in front of her cave (the once sanctuary turned jail). It's what holds us back from experiencing any semblance of self-love, joy and light.

We must let go. Something. Anything. It could even be a surrendering to the possibility of letting go.

What is the ocean in your life at this time? What are you fighting against? What's your fear? What's the situation you are struggling with the most? What needs to be let go?

After all, as far as I can tell, ALL healing requires some amount of letting go. Just like every breath needs its exhale. Two parts to this natural life process, in and OUT. That's what it takes. And you know what happens when you don't breathe? Yup. It's over. Life is done.

And when you don't consciously choose to turn your holding into softening, fullness into emptying out - turning the boat downstream - guess what happens? You'll get paid a visit by the magnificent deity Oya, the Yoruban Goddess of storms and tornados. She's been watching.

And without warning, for the higher good, she'll sweep into your life laughing, scoop you up in her wild embrace, and lovingly fling you to the side and force you to let go, to change. Oh yes, she will!

It's best to go with it. To soften and open your body and throw your arms up into the air and say, "I let go to spirit, to grace, to flow." It's best to accept. And don't forget to give thanks to Oya with a bow of deep gratitude because you'll find liberation and freedom after the storm.

Regardless of how letting go happens - intentionally or involuntarily, happily or hesitantly - life will respond to it. Life will call in your squad of benevolent helpers, surprising answers and magical solutions.

Who could be the Balinese boy in your life at this time? I don't mean who is the angel, although that could be true for you. Rather, I mean who or what in your life could be the unexpected answer to your situation, your ocean? It's worth letting go of to find out. And again, give thanks.

And for those of us (me included) who find it hard to let go, I'm here to tell you that you CAN do this. You can let go. Practice. And practice again. It does get easier once you see the results.

Now... repeat after me:

I am trusting.
I am softening.
I am releasing.
I am surrendering.

I am letting go.

Fifth Turn: The Magic of Letting Go   183

Practices for the Fifth Turn

- Be with Your Exhale
- Shake it Loose
- Release Your Voice
- Transform Your 'NEVER!'
- Become an Open Vessel
- Tell Your Future Self

Playlist: Shake it Loose

"We must be willing to get rid of the life we've planned, so as to have the life that is awaiting us ... The old skin has to be shed before the new one is to come." Joseph Campbell

Be with Your Exhale

Buddha said, in a nutshell, that our suffering is caused by our attachments. (In my words ... all the ways we hold and hold back, harden and tighten, restrict and bind, control and possess.)

I agree with Buddha.

And that's why it can be excruciatingly difficult to let go. Because we do get attached; to our ego's point of view (about everything), our need to control outcomes or people, our desire for things, our need for approval, to pretty much any and everything.

You know what I mean, right? Or maybe you're so 'enlightened' this doesn't apply to you. In that case, why are you even reading this book? (Just kidding!)

But seriously, here's an interesting nugget of truth...

We've been brilliantly designed. Yes. One of our many automatic reflexes is to BREATHE. In two parts, two ways. We breathe IN. We breathe OUT. Each with its own unique gifts.

In order to receive, we need to make space. We need to exhale. We need to let go. That's the beautiful dance of existence. It's like the Vedic dance of Lila - the divine play of the feminine and masculine, of receiving and giving.

Breathing in... we take in the world and are inspired, endlessly.
Breathing out... we let go and make space for the new, effortlessly.

So when you really think about it, aren't we all naturally built not just for being inspired, but for releasing? Aren't we all experts in the field of letting go?

Yes! You've been letting go all your life. Every few seconds. And you can draw on that wisdom anytime, anywhere. It's free and always available. In fact, your exhale is one of the most powerful tools and exquisite resources and allies in your possession. All yours. How blessed are you?!!!

To remind yourself of this exquisite resource and super power, and to demonstrate how easily you can let go, to effortlessly release, this short practice is to focus on your exhale.

Be with your exhale: Approx. 3 minutes

1. **Find a space** where you won't be distracted or disturbed.

2. **Get into a comfortable posture** and relax your face and body. You can keep your mouth closed or slightly open, breathing out from your nose or mouth, as you wish.

3. **Notice your first exhale.** Give the fullness of your attention to it. Follow it from beginning to end, letting your inhale happen naturally afterwards.

4. **Keep your focus on the next few exhales**, noticing the sounds and sensations of air releasing from your mouth or nose.

5. Now **lengthen your breath out**. Just a little. Slow it down.

6. **Invite a softening** to your body, mind, heart and soul. Let it feel delicious. Embody peace, healing, and nourishment. Feel the surrender.

7. Explore the possibilities of letting go in your mind as you continue to follow your exhale. Ask yourself: '**What am I releasing?** What is being let go? What am I sending away with each exhale?'

8. **Let each exhale be a gift, a giveaway.** Name what you are releasing and send it off with love. Send it out to the universe. Send it down into the Earth, to our magnificent Mother Gaia, to use as compost.

9. And if you feel inspired, **invite soft movement** to follow along with the rhythm of your exhale. Let your exhale carry with it any stress, worry, doubt, fear or pain. Let it cleanse you in any way that feels good and right and perfect for you.

10. At the completion of this practice, feel free to complete this sentence, silently or out loud, "**I just let go of ...**" And affirm, "I let go." Or "I let go effortlessly."

11. **Give thanks.**

How do you feel now? Let this practice take you into your day/night. Remember, your exhale is there to support you.

Keep breathing. Keep letting go.

I bow to your breath.
I bow to your wisdom.
I bow to your life.

I bow to you!

Shake it Loose

*"Dance with all the might of your body, and all the fire of your soul,
in order that you may shake all melancholy out of your liver;
and you need not restrain yourself with the apprehension that
any lady will have the least fear that the violence of your movements
will ever shake anything out of your brains."* Lola Montez

In Peter A. Levine's *Waking the Tiger*, a book about the somatic healing of trauma, animals are our teachers. Their ability to rebound after a threat, for example, teaches us an instinctual, biological and somatic process for healing and rebalancing - they shake!

What amazing innate wisdom they have. They seem to do a better job at getting on with life without carrying years of emotional scarring, traumas, and other forms of pain and duress like we do.

We have much to learn from them, and cultures and communities that already understand this wisdom. And maybe it's also about remembering or accessing what our animal-body already knows but has forgotten along our evolutionary path.

In any event, we, us brilliant humans, have a tendency to not let go, and no, we don't tend to shake it off, shake it loose. Instead, we carry the wounds of abandonment, of loss, of hurt, deeply lodged in our bodies. We wall up our hearts. We clamp down. We tighten up. We freeze. Who's the clever one now?

If we look to the intelligence of our animal relatives, and our own animal instincts and lineage, we see a better way, a cure, a respite. With shaking we can give quick relief and life back to our entire system - body, mind, heart and soul. We can shimmy our way to renewal and refreshment, like a bottle scrubber gently cleaning and clearing us from the inside out.

Shaking may not be well known in our 'modern' culture, but it is a form of healing still practiced in some parts of the globe - in Indigenous communities and ancient lineages. Shamans know about it. Sometimes it's used as a way to enter a trance state, to access information from other realms for the wellbeing of their communities. It's cellular. It's visceral. It's spiritual. It's that powerful!

For me personally, I love to use the dance of shaking in my ecstatic dance practice as the climax of the spiral path, when the tempo of the music is peaking. (In fact, every ecstatic dance practice I know uses it. The invitation is to release and let go, inviting another layer or two or three to drop away. It's my version of the dance of the seven veils!

In this Shake it Loose practice, the invitation is to shake off a specific issue or *to* dive in with no intention or outcome, and allow it to be a powerful tool and container for burning off what no longer serves you, for surrendering the walls of your heart, the trauma from your stories, and the stresses in your body.

Within, and because of, the chaos of shaking, it quite deliciously and miraculously boggles the mind into complete presence. It's like the mind needs to find the here and now in order to stabilize and ground as it lets go. I love that about it!

Shaking can be done in a more gentle watery way too, but there's nothing quite like the release inspired by fast tribal drums that stokes your breath to hiss and gurgle, and your blood to bubble and boil.

Into the fire and cauldron it all goes. Everything...

Fears. Permission. Niceness. Silence. Scars. Tears. Indignity. Certainty. Desires. Dreams. Fierceness. Love. Laughter. Exhilaration. Curiosity. Celebration. Presence.

Through this shaking practice your body becomes a moving prayer. You become Shaking Woman. Oya. Kali. Shapeshifter. Liberator. Destroyer.

And when you're done you'll feel spent, shiny and free. Ready to fly. Or sleep.

Want to give it a spin? Let's do this...

(And not just for YOUR liberation, but for the liberation of all people who aren't free to dance for themselves! Because your liberation is their liberation. Yes?)

Shake it Loose: Approx. 15-20 minutes.

1. **Get your music ready.** Use the **Shake it Loose Playlist**, or add some of those tunes to your own playlist.

2. **Find a safe and clear space** where you won't be disturbed or interrupted.

3. **Start your music.**

4. **Stand and plant your feet**, imagining the earth is below you, to ground and stabilize you before you begin.

5. **Choose an issue or situation you wish to let go of** or set a general intention to let go. Your choice.

6. **Soften your knees** so your entire body can shake freely.

7. **Relax your neck, face and head** so they're free to shake too.

8. **Begin to shake your head** in ways that feel good.

9. **Slowly move down your body** gently shaking and vibrating different body parts,

from head to toe - your heads, shoulders, arms, hands, back, chest, belly, hips, legs and feet.

10 With your whole body now, **quicken the pace** of your shaking.

11 **Find your exhale and let it be audible** - sighs, hums, oh's and ah's. Hear your exhale.

12 **Stay with your exhale and let go further.** Keep shaking. Set yourself free. *Personally, I love to go down to the floor and shake on my back. That way my back is supported and I can lift my arms and legs up towards the ceiling and really let my hands and feet shake out.

13 **Honour your body's wisdom,** bearing witness to any emotions, sensations or memories that come. Let them go with love.

14 **Keep going until you feel you've had enough.**

15 **Slowly bring your body into a quiet stillness.**

16 **Close your eyes.** Give yourself the wonderful gift of awareness. Feel what you feel. **Notice what you notice.** (Qualities of thought, feeling, sensation, knowing.)

17 **Give thanks** and open your eyes. Be extra kind and gentle with yourself if you're feeling tender or shaky.

Kudos to you. You've done good work!

And when it feels right...

Record your experience: What was released? How do you feel?

Free Your Voice

"And the day came when the risk to remain tight in a bud was more painful than the risk it took to blossom." Anaïs Nin

Self-expression is a birthright. And that birthright includes how we express our feelings, experiences and ideas in all aspects of our life - our art, our dance, our writing, our music, and... our VOICE!

Sadly, though, it seems the world rarely appreciates and respects the fullness of a woman's vocal expressions. We've been called bitches and witches (which actually isn't an insult in my book, but that's another story) for being bold, daring and independent. We can go back as far as the dark times when women healers, midwives and teachers were burned and hanged for speaking up and wielding their power.

I strongly suspect that we still carry that trauma deep in our cellular memory, as a part of our collective consciousness of the female experience. (Some say that the word 'history' comes from his-story. As in, not her-story. As in, our stories didn't matter. Our voices didn't count.)

And we don't even have to look back in history to see how women have been silenced. The raw truth is that we have sisters around the world today facing real and dire consequences for using their female voices. Justifiably, their voices must stay quiet in order to feel safe. (I pray for their/your liberation.)

For those of us whose lives allow for more freedoms, we are amongst the lucky ones. And yet, we still struggle with finding and freeing our voices. Perhaps it's that collective trauma. Perhaps we're still entering new territory, safer territory.

For whatever the reason, we tend to dial it down. We temper ourselves. We make our voices smaller and often higher than they naturally are. We're less threatening, and more likable and acceptable. We decide to not speak out or speak up. We choose to not raise a point or raise our voice. We constrict our mind, heart and throat, and suppress our truth, dignity and courage.

How dare we be so confident and powerful? How dare we be so bold as to own our sovereignty, and tell our stories and truth? But then again... who are we not to be? And who's going to speak up for those who can't?

I confess, I've been challenged to speak up and tell my truth most of my life. I've never wanted to make waves, hurt others, or be rejected. Even after years of spiritual and emotional work on myself, and living with all the privileges bestowed upon me as a 'liberated' woman, I'm still working on this. Argh. I'm in my 60s, for goddess' sake. And yet, those old damn fears have a way of temporarily dismantling my confidence.

As a result, I remain tight in my bubble of silence. It's safer and less painful there, but only for a hot minute (the benefit of all the good work I *have* done on myself is I rebound fast). Ultimately, I know closing down doesn't serve, doesn't liberate, and is the antithesis of how I wish to live in the world - with courage, love, joy, truth and freedom.

And so, yes, I understand the wounds we carry in our silence, my dear friend. I get it. But, trust me, I also know what it feels like to speak up. Life gets exponentially sweeter, increasingly richer and more authentic. The gifts are as radiant as the summer solstice sun.

I have witnessed firsthand what happens when we're given or give ourselves permission to let our voices go. At first it might be challenging, I'm not going to lie. But that's okay. It's part of the process of liberation and power.

In my ecstatic dance practice, when I lead women in the release dance of shaking, which includes the release of our voices, it can be overwhelming for some, especially for first-timers. The cacophony of a room full of women fearlessly releasing their voices like screaming banshees, or the unfamiliar territory of releasing our own voice in front of others, or both, can surely evoke deep feelings of embarrassment, vulnerability and shame. It can take many sessions to get there.

For others, it's as if they've been waiting their entire life for someone to say 'go for it.' They explode unabashedly. They roar like lionesses. Their souls sing. Their hearts open. Their entire being says YES! Full power. Full bodied. Emptied out.

This is what happens when we free our voice. It's ecstatic and joy-inducing, and it's powerful beyond measure because our voice carries great power and creative fire. Just as it can shatter glass, so too can it shatter and reawaken stagnant energy. It can set us free.

We must free our voice to free ourselves fully, without apology or exception. It's essential to having a clear and authentic voice. Without it, how can we create boundaries, ask for what we need, or allow others to know the real us? So…

Your task now, and yours alone, is to befriend your unique and precious voice to come out of hiding, and set it free to be heard in the fullness of its truth and expression; to nurture it, and fall in love with its beauty and resonance as an exquisite resource of empowerment, wholeness and love.

Because **YOUR VOICE is a sacred messenger, a peace-maker, a conduit of love.** It's vibrational healing that's needed in the world. Use it wisely. And continue to practice loving kindness. There's no need to be incessantly vocal, or overly loud and intrusive (although sometimes, that's what's required). Give space for listening so you'll know when to speak, when to be quiet, and when to be silent. And when you DO speak, you will be heard!

(One of my favourite quotes goes something like this… *"The difference between knowledge and wisdom is: Knowledge is knowing what to say, and wisdom is knowing whether to say it or not."* Good advice.)

To help you free your voice, here's an exercise from my 21-day virtual ecstatic dance program, **DAILY DANCE**. Feel free to incorporate this with the **shaking practice**, or get creative and playful with it. Get wild. Go deep, go slow, or whatever you need.

Free your voice: Approx. 20 minutes

1   **Find a safe and private space** where you can make sounds without feeling inhibited. (Turn off all phones and devices.)

2   **Stand, sit or lie down.** Close your eyes.

3   **Get grounded.** (Feel your feet if standing, and imagine the earth below you, if you're not actually on the earth.)

4   **Gently move your head** from side to side or in soft circles.

5   **Bring attention to your mouth**, jaw and tongue. Notice any tension or pain there.

6   **Soften and relax your throat and voice** as you begin to **sigh, hum, yawn**, whimper or groan - any sounds that arise naturally and effortlessly.

7   **Delight in letting sounds come** up and out. Move your body with the sounds if it feels good to do so.

8   **Open your heart, and let the sounds grow.** Let them get wilder. Let them go.

9   **Sing. Chant. Dance.** Move around the room.

10   **Let your voice travel.** Be loud. Be soft. Be heard.

11   **Keep going until you feel you're complete.**

12   **Come into stillness**, close your eyes and take a moment to notice how you feel.

13   **Give thanks.**

Keep Going:

- Keep releasing and freeing your voice by singing and sounding throughout your day/s: Take a voice class. Serenade a lover. Sing a lullaby to a baby. Go to a kirtan. Chant mantras. Join a choir. Join friends at a Karaoke bar.

- And most of all, **speak UP!** Speak your truth. Speak your truth with love. Always with love. (*Do it for those who can't!*)

Transform Your 'NEVER!'

Where in your life have you said 'NEVER'?

I will never marry. I will never be alone. I will never feel safe. I will never let my heart be broken again. I will never be able to dance. I will never... (fill in the rest).

Holding those vows of 'never' will most surely keep us locked and frozen in time. No movement. No breath. No life.

Is it possible you have one, two, some, or many vows of *never* that are holding you hostage? Promises that are freezing you in time and strangling your growth, your desired outcomes, your joy and your bliss?

In our Amaterasu myth, dear Amaterasu, feeling injured and betrayed, locked herself away in her cave vowing NEVER to come out again. EVER! And for very good reason. And in time, surely, her hurt had hardened into defiance, a stuck place - fixed and righteous.

I can see her now, sitting with arms crossed over her chest, lips sucked in, grimacing, saying to herself, 'You're never going to see my light. No way. You don't deserve it. I don't trust you. You're on your own.' (Even getting stuck in a place of injury is life-shrinking.)

Luckily, something new swept in and stirred things up. It was the contagious force of laughter. It was collective joy that ultimately broke the spell, the hold. Amaterasu *had* to surrender in order to come out and join the rest of the world, and realize the brilliance of her own nature. Thank goodness she did!

In our human experience we've all been Amaterasu. We are Amaterasu. We create caves. We create walls based on our wounds and beliefs, which are counterproductive to feeling love, peace, connection and joy. We tell ourselves that it's safer to *never* allow another to really see us, to really know us, to really feel us, like Amaterasu did when she vowed to never come out.

And what about Amaterasu's brother, Susanoo? Can you see an aspect of yourself in him too - trapped by or over-identified with anger, a sense of victimhood or powerlessness - where you've (unconsciously) vowed to *never* lay down your rage, or show your vulnerability or the truth of your sense of unworthiness?

Can you see how these 'nevers' hold us back from living in alignment with our dreams, from healing and reclaiming our power, our wholeness and radiance? We must be willing to examine our shadow or unconscious core blocking beliefs and vows. We need to soften, relax open, and let go, to come home to our true, shining self.

So, my friend, what age-old never/s could you soften and let go of?

Fifth Turn: The Magic of Letting Go   193

Where have you told yourself you could never have it, never do it, or never allow it? At the time you probably felt you had good reason to, like Amaterasu, but think about how her story would have ended had she not let go. The dark would have prevailed.

Below is a healing and transformational process designed to help you release those outworn, life-blocking 'nevers.' <u>Document your answers in your journal.</u> Let this be a sacred experiment.

Imagine what could happen. What if you let go? Let's melt away our nevers, and cast a new spell of expansion, release, adventure and openness to new possibilities.

Let the magic begin: Approx. 30 minutes

1. **Think about a broad or specific DESIRE** - i.e., a desire for more joy, a new love, or a creative partner to collaborate with. Meditate on it. Take your time.

2. **Relax** and feel into the desire. Use all of your senses to embody it. From this deeper space of reflection, **listen for any vows of 'NEVER'** that come up for you around that desire. Notice how your body responds as well.

3. **Write them down.** Let it flow spontaneously and uncensored. Your soul is speaking. Take, for example, your desire is to find a new love, and your vow is, "I will <u>never</u> be loved."

   Use these prompts to get you going: **I will never …   I never …   I can never …**

4. **Look at your statements** and let your intuition guide you. What pops out for you? What 'nevers' might be influencing the outcome of your chosen desire? Be your own sacred sleuth. What beliefs, past behaviours, wounds and feelings do you have around that? Any golden nugget/s of wisdom arising?

5. **Acknowledge the beautiful insights** and deeper knowing.

6. Thank yourself for creating these vows of protection and for being open to the process. **Be compassionate with yourself.** You did the best you knew how.

7. Use your intuition again, and **choose ONE of your vows of 'never' to release and transform.**

8. **Write** and say aloud, **"I let go of my belief that I never……"** or "I let go of my belief that I will never……"

9. **Send this affirmation out with love,** for the highest good. Imagine these words floating out into the ethers, into the sky, or down into the Earth to be used as compost. Feel into the release.

10. Now, **transform that old vow into a NEW affirmation** related to your desire. Keep it present tense, simple and positive. So in the example, your vow of 'never' was, "I will never be loved." Your vow of letting go, "I let go of my belief that I will never

be loved", becomes the affirmation "I am loved", "I am lovable", or "I am love."

11 Write this new affirmation down on a piece of paper and keep it somewhere nearby so you can read and say it again and again. Repetition is the key. Rewire your brain. Rewire your life.

12 Take action. Show up for yourself and the world in ways that assert your affirmation, moving you towards your desire. Invite a friend to support you on it. Be courageous, curious, compassionate and creative. Keep rewiring.

13 Give thanks.

To recap:

1 Write your vows of 'never':

I will never …
I never …
I can never …

2 Choose one vow of 'never' to let go:

I let go of my belief that I (will/can) never …

3 Transform it into an affirmation:

I am …

*If you catch yourself reverting back to old vows of 'never,' see if you can transform them on the spot. Rewrite the script. Act on your behalf - for your beautiful life!

Become an Open Vessel

The more open and empty we become, the fuller we can be filled.

This is an old Zen Buddhist story illustrating the importance of continually emptying out...

"There was a man who travelled many miles to be at the foot of a great Master. He tells the Master that he has travelled far, with the wish to be his student. The Master asks him to sit before him and have some tea. He begins to pour tea from the teapot, and keeps pouring until the tea overflows onto the floor.

The student sits with amazement, holding his tongue, until he can't take it anymore and says, "Dear Master. Why are you still pouring the tea when the cup is full? You are spilling it all over the floor." The Master stops pouring and sets the teapot down.

He says, "You are that tea cup. You are already full. I cannot teach you anything until you empty out. Until then, all that is given to you will just be wasted, spilling onto the floor. Go away, and when you have emptied your cup, then I will teach you what I know."

Isn't that a great teaching? See yourself and your life as that tea cup. Where are you too full?

What do you need to empty out to become an open vessel?

As you witnessed in my story, I gave up my battle with the ocean. I couldn't carry the fear and fight any more. It was too much to bear. I tried everything I could think of to survive but nothing worked. It was pointless. I had to give up.

I was surprised to find an unexpected sense of peace, stillness, and utter presence in the midst of my greatest fear and struggle to live. Everything went soft. Everything opened. Open arms, and floating on my back. No thoughts of past or future. I was completely present. "Here I am Mama Ocean. If you want me, I'm yours."

In my struggle I emptied out. I found spaciousness. I was free. It was a spiritual high. In other words... I became the open vessel. And that's when the magic happened.

You don't have to empty out in a grand way. You don't have to sell everything and become a nomad with a satchel, unless that's what your soul is prompting you to do. But you do need to continually check in to see how full you are, and adjust along the way.

If you're anything like me, I have this wonderful ability to take in a lot! That's a beautiful thing because it means I feel, and I empathize, and I respond to life, but... I don't necessarily let those pieces, energies and feelings go. I often don't even notice I'm carrying them until I'm overwhelmed or in pain.

So, you see, it's essential to be curious about the weight of your soul, of the fullness of your heart, of the denseness of your mind. It's essential to be aware and clear out the unnecessary burden of over-filling and over-holding.

How?

- **Draw on the power of your exhale.**

- **Shake yourself loose.**

- **Free your voice.**

- **Release emotions.** As the expression goes, "Better out than in!" So go ahead and let it out in any safe way you can. Cry. Laugh. Rant. Sigh. Howl. Allow your emotions to move, and flow out. Make space within.

- **Say, "I don't know" often.** Because, when you assume you know, you've filled the cup. There's no room for new growth, new possibilities. Letting go of your knowing opens you up, making way for the magic.

- **Ask Byron Katie's question, "Is that true?"** Similar to saying, "I don't know", there's magic in this. It prompts a curiosity and emptying out of old stories, often untrue. It's powerful to release the weight of that untruth, that old and stale story you've been carrying, sometimes for decades or a lifetime.

- **Empty out your shoulds, coulds, nevers and nos** by reframing and rewording the way in which you see yourself and life. Invite yesses and maybes, and all that feels like love, peace, expansion and joy.

- **Create more space** in your day. Pause. Take breaks. Slow down. Gaze at the sky. Stare into space. Meditate, rest, sleep. Drop the to-do list.

- **Get creative.** Find different ways and doorways to empty out, such as art, music, journaling, sports, affirmations, or laughter. Do it alone. Do it with friends. Do it in community. Just do it!!!

Tell Your Future Self

"Right now, there is a stronger, more vibrant, more inspired version of "you" that is wanting and waiting to emerge." Debbie Ford

Your FUTURE SELF, waiting with deep love, compassion and curiosity, wants to know what you're willing to let go TODAY, in order to create a brighter and lighter world for her (your future).

As an act of self-love and devotion to her (you, use these questions below to get clear on, and committed to, what you're ready to let go of (emotionally, mentally, physically and spiritually. What potent answers do you have for her? Lay it down. Do it for love.

- Where am I too full, too tight or too constricted?
- What am I carrying? What's weighing me down?
- What grudges and resentments am I holding on to?
- What judgments, biases and prejudices am I perpetuating?
- What stories about myself am I willing to surrender and change?
- What do I need to empty out?
- What am I ready to let go of? How can I let it go?
- What am I willing to let go of with my breath, to the wind, to spirit?
- What am I willing and ready to make space for?
- What am I ready to give up to experience the magic of letting go?
- What prevents me from truly being me? What's holding me back?
- What would love do?

"You wanna fly, you got to give up the shit that weighs you down." Toni Morrison

I **let go**.
I release.
I trust.
I **let go** with ease.
I **let go** with joy.
I **let go** with love.
I **let go** with power.
I **let go** for us all.
I release what no longer serves me.
I am an open vessel.
I am open to receive.
I am spacious.
I am free.

Fifth Turn: The Magic of Letting Go

Shake it Loose Playlist

Release. Set yourself free. What are you ready to let go of with love?

1. **Release**, Release, by Random Rab
2. **Sufi Groove**, Lost At Last, by Lost At Last
3. **Song of the Stars**, Spirit Chaser (Remastered), by Dead Can Dance
4. **I Exist Because of You**, (Henrik Schwarz Live Version), Coming Home (Mixed by Boozoo Bajou), by Henrik Schwarz & Amampondo
5. **Get It**, Futurizms, by Matt James
6. **Shake It** (Shaikh It), Fusion, by Adham Shaikh
7. **Josimar** (feat. Fila Brazillia), Brazilian Explosion, by Arakatuba
8. **Nerve** (feat. Claude Chalhoub), Electrojerk, by Beirut Biloma
9. **Another Station** (Todd Terje Remix), Another Station - Single, by Hans-Peter Lindstrøm
10. **Re-awakening the Spirits**, Without Within, by Bob Holroyd
11. **Breath Connect Us All**, Shaman's Breath, by Professor Trance & The Energisers
12. **Didgedelik**, Trancelucid HLT005, by Hilight Tribe & Whicked Hayo
13. **Dorset Perception**, Tales of the Inexpressible, by Shpongle
14. **Riding The Waves**, Volume 2: Release, by Afro Celt Sound System
15. **Sweet Surrender** (DJ Tiësto Remix), Remixed, by Sarah McLachlan
16. **Two Hoboes** (Detroit Grand Pubah's Remix), The Remix Album, by Champion
17. **Soy Como Soy** (feat. Cleydys Villalon), Soy Como Soy, by Makossa & Megablast
18. **Furka**, Urban Angel, by Sonicjoy
19. **Restless**, Head Cheka - Single, by Nok, DJ Fabio & Moon
20. **Shiva Moon I** (The Crescent Moon Mudra), Mudra, by Prem Joshua
21. **Air**, MIDIval PunditZ, by Midival Punditz
22. **Beyond the Senses**, Artcore, by Astrix

Go to: www.EricaRoss.com/playlists

Sixth Turn

Touch the Wild

*"Promise to stay wild with me. We'll seek and return and stay to find beauty and the extraordinary in all the spaces we can claim.
We'll know how to live. How to breathe magic into the mundane."*
Victoria Erickson, Edge of Wonder

Spreading My Wings

I'd never seen Christian hippies before. The couple who drove us from Istanbul to India, they were big Bible readers. The driver's girlfriend read the Bible out loud to her boyfriend in German all day long as he drove the mini-bus. I'd never seen anything like it.

'Oh,' I thought to myself, 'they must be really good people if they're reading the Bible. They must be religious. They must be kind.' Nope. None of the above. They were not the least bit nice. Nor friendly. As we got to the end of our trip from Istanbul to India along the 'Hippie Trail,' they revealed their true colours.

We were just days away from our destination. After four long weeks of travelling together, we were actually almost there. Our final destination was one of the central beaches in Goa, and we were so ready for it. So, so ready.

As it turned out, there was one more hurdle to overcome before finding freedom. And the hurdle was mine, all mine.

I didn't know what it was. Well, I did know it happened in Bombay - it was called Bombay in those days. I'd slept at a hostel and woke up the next day with a few itchy bumps on me. They looked like mosquito bites. No big deal. The next day, more bites and more itch. But I hadn't noticed any mosquitos. The third day, worse again. Bites all over me including my face, and because I was scratching in my sleep, I was bleeding. It was grim!

We were driving through Panjim, the capital city of Goa, just a couple hours from the beach - so close to our destination - when our driver pulled up to a sidewalk in the middle of nowhere – well, certainly nowhere that any of us knew. He got out of the bus and started doing something on the roof, creating quite the racket. Then, I saw a knapsack drop to the sidewalk. Mine.

"There's something wrong with you. You need to go to the hospital," the driver said to me. "I know there's one somewhere here in Panjim."

That was it? I mean, that was it. That was all he said.

I was kicked off the bus. Just like that.

I'd become an 'untouchable.' Me, and my knapsack, dumped on a sidewalk, in some unknown-to-me part of Panjim.

It was by far the worst part of the journey for me. We'd been together a whole month. You'd think people would care about each other at that stage; we'd been through a lot. But, no. They didn't even have the kindness to drive me to a hospital. Those Christian Bible readers ditched me.

They reminded me of the couple who drove me to Istanbul instead of Athens. "Don't worry," they said. "You're with us. You'll be fine." And then, they abandoned me. It was the same with this couple (and the rest of the passengers who stayed silent through my

Sixth Turn: Touch the Wild

exile). "Something's wrong with you. Get to a hospital." And off they all went - without me!

Of course I was stunned. And of course I was scared. I didn't know where I was. I didn't know what was wrong with me. I had to wander through streets completely unfamiliar to me. It was hot - around 32 degrees Celsius. I had a huge knapsack on my back. And I had to look for a hospital. I felt completely alone, miserable and afraid.

I asked anyone I could find, "Hospital? Hospital?"

People kindly kept pointing me forward. I walked for over an hour, dazed and fearful, but I eventually arrived at a hospital. It was an outpatient hospital and it was bursting at the seams.

Imagine a walk-in clinic, only it's a large hospital and every room's packed with multiple patients and their families. Every hallway, every nook, and every cranny, packed.

I asked the person at reception, "Where do I go?"

They took one look at me and sent me to the Clinic for Skin and Venereal Diseases.

Seriously? Skin and venereal diseases? The name alone horrified me. I had no idea what to expect. When I walked into the crowded room, I found people with skin falling off their ears. 'Oh, my god,' I said to myself, 'please, don't let anyone touch me.' I was afraid I'd leave the hospital with more diseases than when I'd arrived. (They were probably just as afraid of me.)

I was just a kid, 19 years old. In a country I'd never been to before. With bumps, or bites - something mysterious - covering my body. Just two hours from my long-awaited destination. And I was all by myself. I felt dejected and utterly alone.

Hours went by. I watched people come and go. At first, they were the people who'd come before me, but then it became clear that I was being ignored, passed over.

For the first time in my life I spoke up for my rights, demanding to be seen. Hesitantly, the staff responded to my loud and furious plea and shuffled me into the examination room just in the nick of time. The hospital was closing at 6:00 p.m. and it was 5:30! (I'd been there over eight hours!)

And then, it got worse.

After the doctor gave me a good once over, looking at every inch of my body, taking my blood pressure, weight, and all that good stuff, he said, "It's either syphilis or scabies." I knew what syphilis was, and that was not good. "What (the hell) are scabies?" I asked. "Microscopic bugs that crawl under your skin, biting." 'Lovely!' I thought. 'Microscopic bugs or syphilis. Perfect.'

He then gave me a slip of paper, a requisition, to take down the hall to the lab to have blood work done before the lab closed, and handed me a cream for the scabies. He said, "Come back in a week. If it's scabies, it'll clear up. If it doesn't, it's probably syphilis." I'd had sex one time in Delhi. One time! (And with someone named Mirage. Mirage! Nothing imaginary about him or the situation I was in.) I realized this could go either way for me.

I left the hospital feeling like I'd hit rock bottom. It was an awful moment. I had no idea what might happen. I had no idea where to go - or what to do. Do I just sit in some hotel for a week and wait it out? Oh, and I looked a mess. I had bumps everywhere. I felt ugly. Alone. Scared... again.

And then, I met a guy.

He was beautiful. He was a South American man a little older than me, and by that I mean mid-20s. He found me walking along the street. He must have thought I looked miserable - believe me, I felt miserable! He asked me with a kind voice, "Why are you so sad? Where are you going?"

I said, "I'm thinking of going to a hotel. I don't know what's wrong with me," and continued to explain the whole sad situation.

After hearing my story he said, "Nope. You're going to the beach with me. I'm going to take you on the public bus and we're going to go to Calangute Beach. It's just a couple hours away and you're going to stay at my friend's house." He scooped me up, and did just as he promised.

It was a huge turning point. After the isolation of my long journey from Amsterdam to Istanbul to India, I was finally beginning to feel a connection with someone. Someone who cared. Bit by bit, every day things got better, including, yes, the scabies. Thankfully, it did, in fact, turn out to be scabies and the cream worked like a charm. (I never looked back, nor did I return to the hospital.)

+++

Goa became my home for the next three months. It was one of the most incredible times of my life - a personal awakening. It changed me.

After a week sleeping on a porch in Calangute Beach, I decided to move two beaches up (north). I'd heard it was the central hub of Goa's hippies. I took a big hike over a hill and arrived at what was to be my home for the next three months.

When I moved to Anjuna Beach, the first place I stayed was in the ruins of an abandoned house. All that was left of it was the cement floor and four-foot-high walls. It was the domain of Eight Finger Eddie, the first hippie to call Goa home. He was a legend.

I, along with a few other young hippies, joined him in his ruins. I have sweet memories of drawing a headboard in chalk on the wall where I made my bed - marking my little spot in heaven! It was complete trust that nothing got stolen, since we were completely exposed without doors or roof or even full walls.

I then wanted a room of my own, so I bought my own woven palm-leaf hut on the beach for $50 US. That 50 bucks bought me four walls, a roof and a floor, situated on the beach not far from the ocean's edge and a few other huts. There were no toilets. No showers. No electricity. (There was no electricity anywhere in Anjuna.) It couldn't have been more basic, but I couldn't have loved it more. We were wild hippies living on the beach and we were free.

Anjuna was filled with travellers from all over the world, hippies like me who were searching for freedom. There were no rules. No restrictions. We'd eat, sleep and play whenever and however we wanted, thanks to the warm and friendly Goans (Portuguese Christians, Hindus and Muslims) who allowed us to be there, to be 'freaks' - to do and act however we wanted.

As I look back at it now, I wonder what they truly thought about us. I'm sure it was strange at first, maybe even intriguing, and possibly disturbing. They somehow found a way to tolerate our wild and carefree behaviour. Perhaps it was the revenue - we rented their homes, rooms and huts, and they provided shops and restaurants for us - or perhaps they were particularly open and tolerant people.

My days were fluid and peaceful. I'd start my morning off with a sand bath and a rinse in the ocean. Then I'd wrap a sarong around me and saunter inland through the palm trees to Mrs. Rodriguez's home for her delicious fruit salad filled with papaya and mango - two fruits I'd never tasted before.

After that I'd wander over to Joe Banana's, our local restaurant, shop, post office, you name it, to smoke a *chilm* (an Indian pipe for smoking hash) and drink a chai (Indian tea). And then, it was back to the beach to relax and play the day away.

And happily, for the first time on this solo journey, I felt part of a community of FREE spirits! Finally, I found a place where I could belong. I enjoyed nightly communal meals and bonfires on the beach where we'd sit in a circle enchanted by the sweet beats of drummers playing *djembes* (African drums), while others played guitars, sang songs, told stories or danced.

Life on the beach felt like a full-time festival. Full moon parties. Acid parties. Smoking hash every day. A parent's worst nightmare. My first taste of real freedom.

I had many firsts in Goa (almost everything was a first).

It was my first exposure to divination - the tarot and I Ching - and it was my first encounter with ecstatic dance, djembe drums, and showering with a bucket around a well. I had my first taste of banana pancakes and prawns, and the infestation of fleas and lice.

It also was my first and only experience of living in a community where being naked was the norm - at least while the sun was out. I mean, I learnt to let it all hang out like all the other hippies. It felt amazingly liberating, and to be honest, it was sexier when we wore our clothes at night. What a revelation!

And without electricity, I had my first taste of the moon's capacity - her brightness and her darkness. For most of each month I'd navigate the nights with a small candle cradled in a coconut shell, being super careful not to fall off of the ragged rocks on my way home to my hut. But when the moon was full... Wow! The entire landscape would be lit up with the most beautiful light and shadows, exposing every tree branch, rock and shell.

It was there in the Goan paradise where I fell in love with nature, with the wild, with life, and with India.

Anjuna was renowned, even back then, for its epic parties, and every month we'd hold the biggest party of them all - a celebration to mark the full moon. Hippies would come from all the other neighbouring beaches. We'd prepare all day for them, making buckets of fruit salad for everyone. Using a giant generator, rock and roll would boom from speakers all night long as we danced under the full moon. (I was told that The Who had been in Goa and they'd left those speakers, but there are numerous myths about it.)

To juice up the party, a few hippies would dance around the beach handing out acid to anyone who wanted it. We tripped, danced, played and swam all night long. The next morning, a group of us would hand out little hand-woven palm-leaf plates filled with the fruit salad we'd made the day before.

It was quite a scene; it was a beautiful scene. It was freedom in the extreme, and it was exactly what I was looking for. Sex, drugs and rock and roll. It's what I'd set out to find when I left the suburbs of Toronto. I had no idea I'd find it in India. A place I barely knew anything about when I started out on this journey, had become the place that felt most like home to me.

It was the place where I first spread my wings, and let myself feel wild and free.

+++

After three unforgettable months in Goa, the 1973-74 season was ending. By April, pretty much every traveller was leaving Goa with the plan to return the following October. It was getting too hot to stay and the monsoon would be arriving. Most of the people I knew were going to Bali, Kathmandu or Ibiza. I had no idea where was next for me, but I left also, and headed back, by boat, to Bombay to decide.

I'd heard about islands off the coast of Kenya, the Seychelles, and there was a boat from Bombay direct to Mombasa, Kenya. I was gravitating toward Africa, to take that route for my next journey. However, I bumped into a friend from Goa, Mick, who was heading through central India by car, up to Kathmandu and the Himalayas. He asked me to join him. I preferred the idea of travelling with someone so I said yes! Yes to the mountains. Yes to not being alone. Yes to staying in the East!

I left Bombay for Nepal to go trekking. But, I trekked right into a hospital instead.

The doctor said, "Look up."

I looked up.

"You're not going anywhere," he said. "You're jaundiced. You have hepatitis."

And that was that. For two weeks I was laid up in hospital. It was a Christian mission hospital run by very kind nuns. And if it wasn't for being sick, I'd say I was staying in the best resort ever! You see, the hospital was full. They had one room on the roof which they only used if they had to. Well, they had to, because they weren't going to let me leave.

So there I was in the best room with a view in Kathmandu. The walls were all windows, and being in a valley I had a 360 degree view of the mountains. Insanely beautiful.

I thought I was getting better, and then they gave me the bad news. They said, "We're not going to let you leave. You have to go home. You need to call your parents and get them to buy you a ticket to fly home."

It felt like I was given the 'Go directly to Jail' card in Monopoly, a huge blow to my psyche. I didn't want to go home. I'd fallen in love with India and Asia. I was a different person than the one who left Toronto nine months earlier. I didn't want to be part of the Western, commercial world any more. My life was going to be in India. I had a plan. I had dreams. Oh, but I was so sick.

They said, "You will die if we let you go. You are too weak. There is no one to take care of you. (Mick was gone.) We will not let you go without a ticket from your parents."

(In fact, the hospital had already contacted my parents, through broken telephone, literally, which sent my mom and dad into a 24-hour nightmare - not knowing if it was actually me who needed the ticket, or where exactly I was, or why I was in the hospital.)

And so it was.

The ticket arrived, and I was returning home to my parents, to their horror and my own, in a terribly sick state. The long journey back to the suburbs began.

I flew from Kathmandu to Delhi, staying overnight in Delhi. Delhi to Rome. Rome to Frankfurt. I was so sick they took me off the plane in Frankfurt on a stretcher, put me in the hospital zone at the airport and hooked me up to intravenous for an hour or so. Then, they put me back on the plane and we flew from Frankfurt to Montreal and from Montreal to Toronto.

After nine months of freedom, and discovery, and being in charge of my life, I was back in my old bedroom in my parents' home in the suburbs. But, I was a completely different person.

The charge of the hippie - peace, love and freedom - was now etched in the marrow of my bones and emblazoned in my soul forever more.

Reflections

"We are volcanoes. When we women offer our experience as our truth, as human truth, all the maps change. There are new mountains." Ursula K. Le Guin

Dearest...

I'm honoured to meet you here in the clearing. Into this next turning. Into the wild. From letting go to freedom. You've earned this place. It's a glorious reward for doing the great work of emptying out, and all you need is to be in this present moment.

You've cycled yourself back to a place of innocence and curiosity, like the beginning turns of the spiral. We find spaciousness again, or perhaps, for the first time. A veil has been dropped. You're in the sweet spot after the storm, after the orgasm, after the release. What a beautiful place to be.

In this clearing, I hear deliciously evocative words. I love them, utterly: **Freedom. Liberation. Untamed. Unfettered. Wild. Wilderness. Wild Heart. Wild Woman.**

Ever since my adventures in India those many years ago, I've been attracted to juicy experiences of freedom, creativity and the wild. It's been a thread, a life-line, a sacred calling. To be free. To be wild. To be free again.

I followed this calling to NYC, to Philly, back to NYC, to Indonesia, to Toronto, to Wales, and back to Toronto. I followed freedom. Freedom of expression, creation and movement. Freedom to be me. I followed it with my body, mind and soul. With my wild heart.

Along the way, in the early '90s, I discovered what would soon become my 'bible': Clarissa Pinkola Estes's book *Women Who Run With the Wolves*. Clarissa named for me the one who has been my life-long companion, the one who has been there all along:

"Within every woman there is a wild and natural creature, a powerful force, filled with good instincts, passionate creativity, and ageless wisdom. Her name is Wild Woman."

I had no idea until that book that the calling I felt to roam, to love fast and hard, and to create always was the call of the 'Wild Woman.'

And in order to reclaim her (from the old French word 'reclaimer' which means 'to call back the hawk which has been let fly'*), we need to call back our intuition, our instincts and our voices, our passions and our imagination... to call back the wild within us.

Thanks to Clarissa's book, I understood Wild Woman in a deeper more potent way. I was over the moon excited and grateful to find someone who could put a voice to her, to my experience as a woman living outside the box, often on the fringe, carving my own path. Bohemian. Wanderer. Artist and dancer.

To my delight, over the years I noticed *Women Who Run With the Wolves* becoming a quintessential go-to resource and source of inspiration not just for me, but for thousands longing to come home to their innate, instinctual, wild and intuitive self.

* If you've never read *Women Who Run With the Wolves* and long to connect to your 'Wild,' I highly recommend getting yourself a copy. (You'll come back to it again and again, so don't just borrow it from a friend.)

Do YOU know Wild Woman too?

Have you met the one who shapeshifts, animates, creates and roams as she pleases? Who sees into dreams, into the mythic, and the unseen?

The one who is mutable. Sacred. Resilient. Rooted. Timeless. Awake. Elemental. Natural. Feral. Keen. Resourceful. Innovative. Radical. Dangerous. Daring. Vibrant. Liberating.

She who creates original works of art, and expresses a full range of emotions. She who fuses fierceness with heart, instinct with acumen, and belly with imagination. She's a protectress, alchemist, change agent, messenger, liberator and goddess. She's a spell-breaker and rabble-rouser. She lives in us all, and has done since the beginning.

Have you heard her howling from the fringes of your mind and depths of your womb, calling you home?

If so, how have you responded? Do you dance and chant with your sisters under the full moon? Do you create talismans, prayers and sacred altars in the sanctity of your own solitude? What is your way?

And if you've not yet heard the call of Wild Woman, or you've heard the call but didn't respond, no worries. You're not late. It's all divine timing. All perfect. My hope is that you'll be open and curious enough to lean in and make a resounding 'HELL YA.'

Even if you're thinking, 'I don't know if I can do that. It feels too far from my experience, too many miles for me to travel from where and who I am, to the wild.' That's okay. You're exactly where you're meant to be.

Or you're terrified, asking yourself, 'But what if I go too far out in the wilds? What then? What if I get lost and never return?' Have no fear, my love. As real as those fears are for you, please trust you are safe, you will be safe. Your wilder self loves you. She knows the way through.

Scared or not, she's available to us all, regardless. I truly believe it's our birthright to embody her, like the right to self-expression and the right to love ourselves. Her awakening is YOUR right!

The secret lies in the subtle and even seemingly ordinary moments of tuning in to hear your own thoughts, or softening your gaze to watch clouds float by, or going dancing every Friday night.

Wild can be as simple and as powerful as connecting to your own presence and being in your own skin, your own sensuality. Wild can be the animal at rest in the jungle. It's an act of self-care. It's a state of mind. A state of minding, mending, and re-membering.

Finding the wild comes when you lay down the strategizing and analyzing of your brilliant mind, and instead, pause, relax and open to the present moment, and follow your body's cues. That's enough of a kick starter in finding YOUR Wild Woman.

Because the truth is, she's been with you since the start, back when you were born - curious, whole and intuitive. As you grew up, you became a foreigner to your own inner landscapes. It happens to us all.

Even if you've lived for decades acting mostly out of your head - being reasonable, careful and discerning - you can find and embody the wild. You can learn to live in both worlds. Wild AND discerning. Spontaneous AND safe. One does not negate the other.

Because... the wild in you doesn't want you to jump off bridges (unless there's a bungee cord.) It doesn't want you to get hurt. It also doesn't worry about playing safe. It just plays. It just does. It trusts.

And let me be clear: There are potential risks associated with the wild, it's true. Risks affecting all your relationships - to yourself, to others, and to the larger world. The wilder you get, the more chance you have of being rejected, ostracized or shamed.

Society won't like it, unless you're a famous rock star or artist, someone known for your eccentricities. Especially if you're a woman. As you and I know, the world functions with agreed upon structures and behaviours. As long as we act within those parameters, we're usually accepted. For the 'greater good,' we're encouraged to stay clear of the wilds.

Your loved ones probably won't approve of it either. Becoming Wild Woman may alienate your family and friends, co-workers and community members. That can be a hard pill to swallow, to feel misunderstood or rejected because of who you're becoming, who you've become, or who you are.

In my story in Goa, in the wake of being free and living wildly, I got sick. Very sick. I was willing to take that risk, even though I had no idea what the repercussions and dangers were of living so free and wild. I was naïve. Mind you, I was only a teenager. The teen years are often precarious and precocious times of pushing limits, exploring boundaries and living without a sense of balance.

One more risk in acting on Wild Woman's behalf is the possibility of turning your whole world upside down. Because it will connect you to your wildest dreams and soul's longings, you might find unmet desires and a calling towards a completely different life than the one you've been living. You may need to either relinquish the truth you just found or change your life. And that can be incredibly painful. A big letting go that can break your heart open wide.

So... if you don't want change, be gentle with your calling in of the wild at first. Take small steps. Don't look too closely at Wild Woman quite yet. Don't sing loudly to her bones, or ask her to dance too close with you. It's safer that way.

But when you're ready and willing to offer yourself to her magic, go ahead and invite Wild Woman home for tea. And wait as long as it takes.

Believe me... she will in her own time slip in through any door or window you leave open just a crack, slide down the chimney, or rise up from under the floorboards.

And when that happens, turn off your phone, stoke the hearth fire, fluff the couch cushions, and put on the kettle! Because, the risk of NOT making her feel at home, of not listening with both ears and an open heart, is truly unfortunate.

For to live without her is to live on the surface, never really diving deep enough to truly know who you are, what you're capable of, and what brilliant gifts you have to share. Our souls, communities and nations are impoverished, starved of soul, art, freedom and bliss. We need your wild.

Without her... without the wild... There'll be far less birthing, singing, loving, roaming, dreaming, laughing, crying, touching, moving, awakening, flying, sensing, emoting, remembering and releasing.

Far less fire, spirit, kindness, joy and courage. Far less making love, following heart, shedding of skin, weaving of stories, breaking of taboos, and living in the depths.

So let her in. Sit for a while, and you'll be touched. You'll notice something different about yourself... a certain sparkle in your eyes you've never seen before. You'll feel freer, less inhibited, less ashamed or apologetic.

You'll know how Amaterasu, Goddess of the Sun, felt as she danced herself out of her cave.

You'll enliven the world with your bedazzling rays of light and life-giving gifts as...

Wild Woman supreme!

Practices for the Sixth Turn

- ◎ Live Life Unscripted
- ◎ Touch the Wild
- ◎ Encounter the Wild Goddess
- ◎ Connect with the Gifts of Animal Wisdom
- ◎ Create Beauty
- ◎ Dance Your Wild / Dance Yourself Free

Playlist: Touch the Wild

"And forget not that the earth delights to feel your bare feet and the winds long to play with your hair." Kahlil Gibran

Live Life Unscripted

*"This is also the story of how my soul found me, and it was a wild soul.
I wasn't prepared for how wild it was."* Anne Hillman

I had a stressful dream last night, most likely created by my psyche's reflections on this very subject.

I was acting in a play. It was night time, so quite dark. I had my personal <u>script</u> in hand, and I was prepared for the performance. I knew it was my script because it had the collage I'd lovingly made for the cover.

While I was hiding behind the audience under some kind of structure, the play began. I was nervously scanning the pages looking for my lines, trying to figure out when I came in, and what I was to say. I was in deep confusion because for the life of me I couldn't find my place. It also was so dark that I found it hard to see what was happening on the stage.

The entire play came and went, somehow still intact, in spite of my absence. I was gutted. I felt ashamed to have missed it. After it was all over I realized that the script that I had, even though it had my personal cover, was in fact the wrong script! Someone had switched them up. I was so relieved to know that it wasn't my fault. And then I woke up.

As I interpret this dream, I'd say that it has some important teachings and warnings for me about how to 'act' in the world, on the world stage.

- **Don't put all your trust in the script** you've been given. It might hold you back from being in, and sharing yourself with, the world.

- **Question and pay attention to the script** you're holding. It might not be yours, even if it looks like it is! You'll be less anxious.

- **Give yourself permission to throw away the script** sometimes. Get familiar with your own impulses. Liberate yourself.

- **Trust in yourself to act on your own behalf**, perfectly. Your words. Your expressions. Your way of participating in the world stage.

On a more collective note...

Since day one, we've all been fed lines from scripts to follow - with instructions on how to act, how to dress, how to talk, how to be. We grow up learning not to listen or trust ourselves, and dismiss our own inner prompts and desires.

Our scripts can be useful and keep us safe, it's true. But their structures and stories eventually become outworn - no longer applicable or helpful to our soul's path. The older the script, the less likely it was written by us in the first place. It's more likely to have been filled with other people's agendas, beliefs, expectations, fears and desires for us.

Old scripts also can tie us down to a history which becomes challenging to live beyond. When I lived in Goa, and later in NYC, one of the many blessings was having no history there, no threads to the past. (It was easier then, before the days of the internet.)

Having no one know me gave me freedom from expectations. No story to live up to. I was free to invent myself, unscripted and untied.

Having said that, I'm not suggesting that you need to run off to India or move to NYC to live your life unscripted. There's a spectrum of possibilities in authoring your own life.

Below are some small and big prompts to inspire you to toss out the script and live life unscripted.

Begin exactly where you are. After each one, don't forget to give thanks to the experience and to your magnificent courage, curiosity and willingness to live on behalf of your wilder and juicier self. I bow to your commitment to being free. Brava!

Take Small Steps:

If you're unfamiliar or uncomfortable with leaving the script behind, or your life is particularly restrictive (time-wise, economically, culturally or politically), start small. Start by crossing out one or a few lines at a time, rather than tearing out whole pages or chapters or burning the whole damn thing. Be gentle on yourself, always.

- **Follow your own pace and rhythms**. Sleep without an alarm clock. Eat when you're hungry. Slow down when you feel rushed. Be alone when you need solitude.

- **Clear an hour, a morning or a whole day** in your calendar and do something that's not on your to-do list.

- **Travel without a map.** Travel off the grid - your grid. Point your bike, your feet or your car in a new direction and go.

- **Surprise yourself.** Do the opposite of what you habitually do. Speak up when you usually stay quiet. Let go when you normally hold on. Make a decision when you usually don't.

- **If you feel a *no* coming on**, but obligation tells you yes, **go with the *no***. Try it on for size.

- Whatever you're doing, **do it your way.**

Take Bigger Steps:

If you're well practiced at living life unscripted, the invitation is to keep going. Give yourself permission to take a big marker and scribble all over the pages or burn a few books. Be your own author. Create more sacred, wild freedom. Be kind to yourself along the way. And give thanks for the privilege of living so freely.

- **Give yourself a long extended holiday,** travel around the world, or live in a new country for at least six months.

- Spiral back to the practices in '**Dare to be Impulsive.**' Yes. Be daring.

- **Look at the top of your bucket list** (things to do before you die) and do that.

- **Go to Burning Man,** or any festival that calls you to throw away the script and live on the fringe!

- **Do what feels radical for you.** Shave your head. Go skydiving. Change professions.

Record the experience of living your life unscripted. How does it feel when you throw away the script? When you just think about it? As you do it? When you return from the adventure?

And continue to stay open to NEW opportunities for living your life unscripted.

Touch the Wild

The world NEEDS your wildness. It contains your power, your truth, your vitality and your passions.

Not all of us have had the kind of intensely liberating experience like the one I had, all those years ago in Goa. But... I'm quite certain that you, yes YOU, have experienced the embodiment of Wild Woman in your own way.

In the ebb and flow of life, you've experienced moments of freedom where you've felt untethered and uncontained. Where you've tapped into the natural you. Where you've touched a sense of home within your own skin. You've felt her alive, unpredictable, electrical and present.

Even for a few inescapable and palpable seconds - in the soft delicious purr as you relaxed from a soothing touch, in the aliveness of being caught in a windstorm, or in the loud belly bellow as you said 'not now.'

Or perhaps it was in that quick reflection of yourself as you breezed past a mirror. It might be a rare sighting but you know you've seen her. And even when you're not aware of her presence, she IS there. She's patiently waiting for you to name and claim her. And she wants more than anything for you to come home, to return to your soul-home, to return to your wild nature.

In *Women Who Run With the Wolves*, Clarissa illustrates the importance of that home-coming in her version of the story of 'Sealskin, Soulskin.'

In this story, a seal comes onto land, strips herself of her pelt and transforms into a woman. While in her womanly form her beautiful pelt is stolen and hidden away by a lonely man. He coaxes her to stay with him, and she agrees. They marry and have a child.

Slowly over time, her skin begins to dry up and crack, and she becomes increasingly tired and worn out. By the seventh year of womanhood, she realizes she can no longer remain on land and must return to her original home, her original form. Her son helps her find her pelt. She slips it on, transforms into the beautiful seal she once was, and returns to the water.

Have you ever lost yourself like that? Have you lost that sense of home, of soul?

Clarissa says, *"Home is a sustained mood or sense that allows us to experience feelings not necessarily sustained in the mundane world, freedom from demands, freedom from constant clacking. All these treasures from home are meant to be cached in the psyche for later use in the topside world."*

She goes on to say, *"Whatever revivifies balance is what is essential. That is home."* And when we come home, it takes us *"to a nutritive inner world that has ideas, order and sustenance all of its own."*

As for knowing when to return home? Clarissa says, *"Each woman knows in her heart how often and how long is needed. It is a matter of assessing the condition of the shine in one's eyes, the vibrancy of one's mood, the vitality of one's senses."*

This is a powerful reminder to us all to pay attention, to listen softly, to notice the quality of our 'shine,' our vitality. And to reclaim and call back the wild. We must!

How can we do that? **How can we touch the wild in a contained world?** How can we stay in touch with its beauty, power and truth while still thriving in the mundane life? There are countless doorways, big and small, to move us in and out of the wild, to remind us of home, of soul, of heart.

Take this short list below and run with it:

Use your natural instincts. Sniff around. Sense into them. Listen to your inner prompts and curiosities. And if none of these tugs at your wild heart, never mind. Do it your way. Trust. Explore. Touch the Wild. (For at least a moment.)

- **Get drunk on life. Every day!** Let the world take your breath away and render you speechless. Let the wind and stars intoxicate you. Dance wildly in the rain. Fall madly in love with everything and everyone. Whatever causes you to be dizzy with delight and awe, to be high on life, do that! Today, and for the rest of your life.

- **Unleash your creative juices.** Activate your soul's wild and radical expressions, languages and creations. Get playful, emotive and innovative. Immerse yourself in a creative community or project. Call in your Muse. Rent a studio. Say YES to not holding back. Whatever it takes to ignite and unleash your passionate creative fire, do that!

- **Free your mind and imagination.** You were born a visionary, so activate and liberate your wild and fertile mind and imagination to carry you deeper into your wild self, into worlds seen and unseen. Be curious. Inventive. Read mythic fairy tales and children's books. Watch sci-fi movies and find visionary art. Day-dream. Fantasize. Whatever it takes to free your mind and imagination, do that!

- **Get turned on.** Your sexuality is wild, electric… and sacred. It's primal, natural and powerful. Let the wild animal of your body love what it loves. Set it free to feel and express its aliveness, with or without a partner. Experiment. Let pleasure heal you. Have orgasms. Be more responsive. Move. Dance. Play. Become the embodiment of love, of pleasure, of connection, of bliss. Whatever makes you hum, purr or moan, do that!

- **Go au naturel!** Your wild self is natural. She loves to be naked. Sky-clad (a Pagan term for being naked during spiritual rituals). For her sake, feel the wildness of your body in motion, unhampered and unrestricted. Get naked and dance under the moon. Get naked, body paint, drum or swim. Get naked and awaken your wild nature, au naturel. (Like Uzume and her wild dance!)

- **Get close to your shadow.** The wild comes in ALL forms - through the full spectrum, from shadow to light. In order to heal, awaken and ready ourselves to co-create with the wild universe, we must make peace with and take responsibility for our shadow - the unknown, undeveloped, unrealized and unconscious. Do dream work. Find a great therapist. Be curious. Whatever supports your courageous dive to meet the shadows of your wild soul/psyche, do that!

- **Return HOME.** Do What You LOVE. If you've been lost, or away for a long time, come home, my love. Come home to your soul's wild heart and the rooted yet mutable truth of your soul. The place where you can lick your wounds and find your vitality and shine again. Put your seal skin back on and dive into the waters of home. Whatever you did, perhaps as a child, that made you feel whole, beautiful and home, but you no longer do now, do that!!! Again and again.

- **Create your own *Book of the Wild*.** Record your journey into the wild. Capture feelings, memories, stories, sensations and experiences in a special book or journal - through writings, drawings, photographs, and/or mementos. Keep this book near and dear to you.

How do YOU 'Touch the Wild'?

Encounter the Wild Goddess

*"She changes everything she touches
and everything she touches, changes."* Starhawk

Woman! You are a force. Contagious and wild. Magical and kind, touching everything and everyone.

The world may have seen you, and named you, differently - as terrifying, intimidating, too much, too wild, and too strong. The actual truth is that you're none of those things. In fact, you are beyond measure. You are divine.

This world has also tried and still tries to control the uncontrollable nature of the WILD - the wildness and wilderness within and without. You and I know that that's just plain fear talking, right?

It's fear created by the old collective paradigms of patriarchy, colonialism and sexism that have misaligned our hearts and minds (brothers and sisters alike), our relationship to the wild, to the wild feminine, and to our beautiful home - our Mother Gaia - for millennia.

The good news is... We're waking up. Individually and collectively. We're starving the dragon by turning our gaze away from its 'nonsense' (I'm being polite here!) and saying 'No more fear. Only love.'

Yes!!! We are rising up and remembering our intrinsic worth. We're remembering who we are. And we're honouring our Mama Earth the same - As sacred. As wild. As feminine.

We're remembering that the wild, the feminine and the sacred are beautiful allies intricately woven and alive in each other. Whole. Divine. Magnificent. Powerful and radiant.

They belong together. They belong to us all. And they are needed in the world. Her/your wild truth, her/your divine body, her/your sacred voice and her/your stories connect us to the soul of the world. To the invisible. To the mythic. And magic.

And so blessed we are to live at a time when her mythology, her presence - like the way in which the moon cycles into fullness - is returning to us to remember our sacred and precious existence and place in the world. Full expressions. Fullness of being.

Meanwhile, The Wild Goddess is there smiling, cackling and dancing. She sees you. She loves you. She is in you. You are in her. Be not afraid of her. Be not afraid of yourself.

As I'm writing about the feminine and the wild, my mind circles back to Amaterasu's story, specifically the part where she's in her cave. I see two different scenarios playing out for her:

One... the longer she stayed inside the less powerful she became. Her light slowly dwindling, her soul and life slowly shrinking and dying. The only way she could survive was by being rescued by Uzume and her community. And thank goddess for that!

But... What if there was something else happening? Something quite different. What if, in fact, it was Amaterasu's initiation? Like the descent of Inanna.

Maybe, just maybe, after the initial painful withdrawal from the world, she began to connect to her Wild Woman essence - her true nature, power, creative fire, and soul's light, in the darkness of the cave, a metaphor for her soul/psyche. All the while, finding wholeness and balance of both light and dark, preparing herself to re-emerge even brighter.

She arrived lost and wounded, and within her cave she found herself, healed into wholeness from her womb, from her depths; a reclamation of her true, sacred and powerful essence. What a powerful reminder of our innate abilities!

Goddess myths do that. They are, after all, wisdom teachings. They are gifts from our ancient ancestors - each goddess holding their own unique flavour, appearance, symbols, perspective and magic. Their stories help us better understand and experience ourselves. With limitless possibilities!

Take the Wild Goddess. Being the shapeshifter that she is, she comes in many and magical forms - animal, elemental, mutable, dark, light and feral - even with three heads to better see the past, present and future! There's no telling how she might show up, or what she might teach us, or what mischief she might get us up to.

From the far reaches of our planet, here are a few beloved Wild Goddesses. May they whet your appetite and inspire you to learn more about their powerful and healing stories and teachings.

I am honoured to introduce to you...

Muso Koroni. She's an Earth Goddess from Mali. Her name means "pure woman with ancient soul." She's an ancestral mother who gave birth to all life. She's a Night Goddess sometimes seen as a black panther or leopard. She's both tame and wild. (I love that!) She rules wild places, even the wilderness within the human soul, which in Mali is called *wanzo*.

Vila, an Eastern European Shapeshifter Goddess, is another wild one who lives deep in the woods. She speaks the many tongues of, and is fiercely protective of, her wild animals. She has animal instincts and acute perception, changing in and out from snake, to swan, falcon, horse or whirlwind as she pleases. She's fully present, fluid, aware, discerning and resilient.

You may already know **Artemis**, the Greek Moon Goddess. She loves the wilds of the woods where she roams with her band of nymphs. She comes in many forms, assuming different roles at different times. She's virginal (a woman unto herself), instinctual and promiscuous, and a protectress of women. She's sometimes seen as Lady of the Beasts or a many-breasted Bee Goddess, or she's found in the form of a tree, bear or the moon.

The wild ones can also be found in the mountains of Tibet in the form of the **Dakinis**, the sky-dancing ancestral pre-Buddhist Goddess spirits. They hold skullcaps full of blood as they dance wildly, cutting through illusions and all that is not real - creating and destroying as needed. They have their own secret language and wield great, wild, divine feminine power.

And then there's **Baba Yaga**, the Slavic Goddess of the wild, of magic, of intuition and the dark. She lives deep in the forest in a wobbly house surrounded by a picket fence made of bones and skulls. She's the older aspect in the trinity of the Triple Goddess. She is the crone, the great grandmother, the wise elder, the witch.

To round off the list of Wild Goddesses, there's **Kali** from India, **Anat** from Syria, the **Erinyes** from Greece, and **Xochiquetzal** from Mexico. And many more worth knowing about.

Now that you've had a taste of HER as she has been seen and loved by many for millennia, it's fitting for me to now ask you three juicy questions. I'm hoping you're up for the challenge. And if now isn't a good time, no worries. I'll be right here when you're ready!

How can YOU connect to the Wild Goddess?
How can you embody and BE her?
How can you more easily and consistently be led by your Wild Sacred Feminine essence?

Feel into these questions. Sit with them. Dance with them. Be with them.

To help you answer, consider these prompts:

They will help you remember… you are her.

- **Create an altar to her.** Just as you did for Aphrodite in the Third Turn, create or re-create an altar as a sacred container for the Wild Goddess to be welcomed home. Use it as a focal point of her remembrance. Include whatever feels wild, juicy and holy.

- **Invite her to join you.** Give yourself ample time (**20 min?**) to get up close and personal with her, with no expectation of how, when or if she'll come. Here's an abridged version of what I do…

    1. **Sit or stand, allowing you to move** in a soft and receptive way. (By your altar would be delicious.)

    2. **Close your eyes, ground, and relax your breath.**

    3. **Invite the Wild Goddess to join you** when you're ready. Say, "I am ready to receive you now. I welcome you with open arms and heart."

4   **Notice any sense of her presence** - a shift in energy, a feeling, an image. Take your time. If and when you do, acknowledge her: "Thank you for your presence. I feel you. I see you. I love you."

5   **Ask her to sit and be with you.** Ask her: "How can I embody and be led by my/your wild, sacred feminine essence? What do I need to do?"

6   **Listen for her wise and potent answers.**

7   **Give thanks** to her and let her go back from where she came.

8   **Take 3 full breaths** and **open your eyes.** Slowly come back. Notice how you feel.

9   **Document** the experience. Turn it into art. Write. Draw. Dance. Sing.

*If you felt she never arrived, or you received no answers, take heart. It doesn't mean she wasn't there! She may show up later in a dream or the answer will come another way. See this as a sacred experiment. Keep your heart open, regardless!

◎ **Create a ceremony in honour of her.** In your own way, design a personal love offering to your Wild Goddess within.

1   **Reflect on the Wild Goddess** and what she means to you. Get clear on the attributes you desire to embody or know. (Instinctual, timeless, feral, rooted?)

2   **Narrow it down to three key attributes to guide you** in the creation of your ritual - your intentions, location, sacred objects, writings, etc. Choose to be indoors or outdoors, alone or with others. Keep it simple and short, or wildly elaborate and long.

3   **Decide if you will script it out, go with the flow, or both.** My suggestion... have a basic structure - a beginning and end, and a few ideas you wish to include - and then go with the flow. Trust your intuition. Let the Wild Goddess guide you. She might want incense, candles, or rose petals all around. She might want to hear Goddess chants, read Rumi poetry, or play with oracle cards. The sky's the limit.

4   **Prepare the space.** Prepare yourself.

5   During the ritual, let the outer expressions be a mirror to your heart's longing to BE the Wild Goddess. **Make it as juicy as possible.** This ritual is for your Wild One, after all!!!!

6   **Stay in the ceremony until you feel it's complete.**

7   **Give thanks.**

8   **Take some time to process and reflect on it** afterwards. Journal or be in si-

lence. Have a bath. Whatever you do, take good sweet care of yourself. Loving kindness is in order here.

- **Dress her up.** How does your Wild Goddess want to feel? What style, clothing, accessories, makeup and hair suits her fancy? Does she want to feel sexy, soft or edgy? Does she love clothing that's loose, tight or stretchy, ancient, classic or hippie? Does she like flannel, silk or denim? Does she want ruby red lips and coal black eyeliner, or does she want to be natural and untouched?

    What's your Wild Goddess's desire? This might mean investing in a few new things… a new dress, a new hairdo, or new shoes. Who knows? It's a sacred playful experiment, after all.

- **Read up on her.** We're so blessed to live in a time where books about the Divine Feminine are flourishing and easily accessible. (My library alone contains about five thousand goddesses… Seriously!) Deepen your relationship with her through her stories. She's waiting to be found, seen and known.

- **Create a Goddess feast** - a feast for you alone (or invite a loved one, or a few friends). Go wild with the possibilities. What foods would **excite your senses** and make your inner Wild Goddess go 'mmmmm'? How would she like to eat, and in what setting? Prepare the space and food as a love offering for wild pleasure, delight and joy. Oh, and **dress up** as your Wild Goddess self!

- **Join up with others** in a collective remembrance. Coming together to remember, honour and love the Sacred Feminine, and Wild Woman, is powerful, healing and juicy! You can find groups, courses, trainings and retreats all over the world now. (What exciting times!)

It's amazing what you'll find when your heart and soul align with something, so I suggest, if this is what you're looking for, and hope it is, that you ASK around (or to the universe in prayer), search the web with key words like goddess, wild woman, wild sisterhood, red tent, goddess circles, and see what unfolds.

And don't necessarily jump on the first thing you see. Listen to your inner compass that says YES! Look for inclusivity and diversity of cultures, backgrounds and experiences. And if nothing feels right… **create your OWN Goddess gathering.** Get some books, or find ideas on the net, and go for it!!

Connect with the Gifts of Animal Wisdom

"Birds have ceaselessly inspired us with their mellifluent voices and polyphonic exchanges, undoubtedly instilling some of our earliest impulses toward song and spoken language." David Abram

All animals - feral, domestic, real or mythic - have great wisdom for us, if we're open to receiving it. I'd even go as far as saying that it's vital and essential to the well-being of our modern existence to do so. **We need our more-than-human relatives.** Wild Woman needs them. You need them.

Without the intelligence of our brothers and sisters of fur, feather and scale, we lose connection to our ancient heritage, our roots and lineage, and forget how fertile we really are. We forget the power of our cyclical and instinctual nature.

We need their presence. We need their resonance in our own electric body, and in our heart. We need the whale's siren song and the hiss of the snake to activate our imagination, inspire our art, and remind us of our place. To feel home.

With them, we remember all life is sentient, responsive, sacred and interwoven. With them, we find healing and love. With them, we find reflections of our own true self - our own wildness, untamed, inquisitive and pure.

If you've ever had a pet, you know what I mean. Our pets offer us companionship through unconditional love, and comfort and loyalty, joy and connection. I learned that from growing up with a dog Ginger, a cat Smokey, a budgie (parakeet) Boodgie, and a number of gerbils and hamsters. Since then, I've had some beautiful cats, most recently, Biba and Gem. I loved them all. They were family. All animals are.

When I lived in New York City I had the most unconventional of all my pets, a beautiful ball python named Secret. It was - she was - unexpected. One day, a friend came to the boutique I co-owned in NYC and asked if we'd take his male pet ball python, Monty. Unexpectedly, we both said yes. And unexpectedly, he turned out to be a she and we renamed her Secret.

Secret was an incredible companion and shy teacher for me. I loved to dance with her, and wore her like a necklace most days. I loved Secret dearly. It was through her that I learned patience and the sensual wisdom of slowing down.

As with shaking, the somatic release inspired by animals, Secret taught me her way of letting go, in the shedding of her skin. In the process, she secretes a milky substance that coats her entire body including her eyes. She becomes blinded, vulnerable, and needs to hide. She then rubs and rubs against rocks until all of her old skin is sloughed off. It doesn't look easy, but when she's complete, she's magnificent. Spectacularly shiny and beautiful. And ravenous.

I give thanks to Secret for teaching me to have compassion for myself when I need to hide in the cave, like Amaterasu, to retreat and protect myself when I feel acutely vulnerable and blinded by pain, confusion or fear. It gives me hope and trust that it's part of a natural process, and I'll not only survive it, but I'll come out of the cave dancing, shinier, and hungry for life again. Thank you, snake healing wisdom!

Animal encounters have been a huge blessing in my life. Like Secret, each one has gifted me with their own sweet elixir, evoking in me a direct connection to my own humanity in the wild web of life.

Some of my most memorable encounters are...

Falling in love with a horse in Canada; seeing wild ponies roaming freely in Wales; feeding and bathing rescued elephants in Thailand; watching orcas breach in Alaska; living with a gecko in Bali; scuba diving with parrot fish and grey sharks in the Great Barrier Reef and seeing dancing peacocks in full plumage in Australia.

I would be remiss to not point out the role animals play in the sacred, spiritual, mythical and ancestral realms. They, too, hold great wisdom.

In my treasured book *The Language of the Goddess*, by the late archeologist Marija Gimbutas, Marija deciphers the earliest signs, symbols, and images of the Old European, Neolithic, Great Goddess civilizations.

It was, and still is in Indigenous communities around the world, a time when **animals, plants, the cosmos, and the sacred feminine were inseparable and integrated**. A time when women were seen as mother bears, she-bison, mares, crows, butterflies, Mistress of Animals, and Frog, Fish, Bee, Snake, Bear, Deer, Octopus and Bird Goddesses (Crow, Owl, Vulture, Bird of Prey). They were symbolic of the natural seasons and cycles of life - of birthing, becoming, emerging, nourishing, transforming, dying, and regenerating. A reminder of our powerful life-giving heritage as women.

Mythology from around the world is full of animals. In Hindu mythology, birds, bulls, goats, peacocks, swans, tigers, elephants, snakes, shrews and lots more are often helpers, carriers or companions of the gods and goddesses. Animals are also deities in their own right - Hanuman, the Monkey God who helped rescue Sita, is symbolic of loyalty and courage. Lord Ganesha is the elephant-headed God of Wisdom and Protection. Lord Hayagriva, an aspect of Vishnu, is the horse God of Knowledge and Wisdom.

You don't have to look far to find our animal cousins sitting center stage in some of our favourite legends, fables and epic tales. Who doesn't love the White Rabbit of *Alice in Wonderland*, Baloo from *Jungle Book*, or the Bengal tiger from *Life of Pi*?

As you see... animals, whether as deities or companions, mythic or real, virtual or live, feral or tame, carry archetypal energies, powerful teachings and boundless love. So let's pay homage to them, and connect in to their many and diverse gifts and blessings.

Here are some ways to connect to the gifts of animal wisdom:

(Zoos and aquariums didn't make this list. I'm no longer enchanted with them, and haven't been to one in years.)

- ◎ **Get up close with animals nearby.** Go into nature. Enjoy your own or others' pets. Cat or dog sit. Go to a cat café. Take up dog walking. Visit a local farm or animal sanctuary.

- ◎ **Seek out wild animals in their natural habitats,** such as in nature reserves, parks and sanctuaries. Here are just a few: Volcanoes National Park, Rwanda (mountain gorillas), Churchill, Canada (polar bears, beluga whales), Monteverde Cloud Forest Reserve, Costa Rica (400 different bird species).

- ◎ **Explore animal mythology.**

- ◎ **Invite animals to enter your dreams.**

- ◎ **Do the Animal Wisdom Visualization** on the next page.

- ◎ **Divine with animal wisdom cards.** I love the Medicine Cards by Jamie Sams & David Carson, or Animal Messages by Susie Green.

- ◎ **Watch nature and wildlife documentaries and films.** Follow SafariLIVE on YouTube.

- ◎ **Whenever and however animals cross your path, give them your respect, gratitude and love.** It's a beautiful practice.

Animal Wisdom Visualization:

Find a private and quiet place to settle into. Ground to the earth. Follow your breath for a few minutes, to invite a soft and relaxed space to tap into the power of your imagination. When you're ready...

"Imagine you're entering a magical realm where animals live. *Feel the earth under your feet. Look around and find a spot where you can sit and relax. Take your time. While you relax, you sense there's a special animal waiting just for you. You feel safe to imagine this animal, any animal at all, feral or tame. Four-legged, feathered, scaled - flyer, swimmer, creeper, rover or hopper. Who will it be?*

Take a moment to visualize it arriving. ***Welcome it in your own way.*** *Notice the way it moves. See its shape, colours and texture. Notice any smells or sounds.*

How do you feel in its presence? *Do you feel a sense of heightened awareness, relaxation or excitement? Are your senses more alive? Do you feel inspired to engage with them - to fly or play with them, or curl up beside them? Imagine you're doing just that. Follow their lead, or invite them to follow you. Your intuition and instincts know exactly what to do.*

After a while, you settle down together. Look deeply into their eyes. You know they've come to share their unique genius with you - their essence, wisdom, instincts and power. You know they are a wise and loving friend, guide and healer with much to teach you. You are ready to receive whatever they have to offer.

Ask them what wisdom they have for you. *And listen. Listen to their messages with an open heart and mind. They may come through their own animal language, sounds or song, or through symbols, words or colours, or as a deep-felt sense. Trust that it's all perfect, just right. Feel free to respond and ask other questions you need.*

When your conversation is complete, ***they hand you a gift.*** *They say, 'This gift is for you to keep. Whenever you need support, just remember it, remember me. I'm always with you. I love you.' Receive it with deep gratitude. Take your time with it. And then with a smile they disappear. As you look around this magical place one last time, take three breaths, breathing in gratitude and emptying out remembrance. At the end of your third exhale open your eyes. Welcome back!"*

++

Take your time to come back and to ground in the here and now. Reflect on your experience of connecting to the wild through Animal Wisdom. Record what you found, your gift and teachings, in your journal.

Create Beauty

Great goddesses from around the globe have been known in their mythology to create and destroy universes just by opening and closing their eyes.

You too wield the potential to change life around you because whether you like it or not, you ARE a Creatrix (feminine form of creator). You are, in your own distinct way, powerful beyond measure.

Right here, right now...

Creatrix you, you are a breathing, pulsing, creative embodiment of life, love and the wild. It's in your DNA. And as a divine Creatrix, your body, mind, heart and soul, hand in hand with spirit, are temples made to express love, truth and beauty.

The divine instructions are clear and bright: CREATE! But not just anything or for any reason. The instructions go deeper - Create BEAUTY! Because...

Beauty is love made manifest.

I say...

Create whatever would make the Wild Goddess howl and bellow with excitement.

And that's anything that makes YOUR eyes sparkle and water with joy. Anything that makes you moan with pleasure and delight, or puts a sway in your hips.

Anything, and I mean anything, that makes YOU feel beautiful, powerful, whole, shiny, resilient, present, alive, purposeful, wild, intuitive, and shamelessly you.

Because beauty is deeply personal. Your sense of beauty is completely subjective. It's yours, and it's part of what makes you unique. Your attractions, desires and loves are what sets your unique soul ablaze, so follow them.

Follow what catches your eye. Follow your senses. Follow your inner spark, inner vision, inner knowing. **Follow the trail of Beauty. Soul. Truth. Art. Love. Power. Radiance. Life. Yes!**

Don't let anyone or anything sway you from that. Your sense of beauty is yours, just like the way you move or speak. It's your body, your voice, your taste.

You may love the sight of a crumbling wall over a fresh new one, or the sound of a saxophone over the piano, or the taste of cinnamon over ginger, the feel of denim over silk, or the smell of sandalwood over lavender.

Whenever you see, create, wear or feel what you love, you're creating beauty. You're activating your heart and wild soul to shine, to dance and sing. You're igniting your senses and sense of your true self to flourish and come alive. To be seen, heard and felt.

Give yourself permission to notice what you love, to notice what makes you zing.

What's your pleasure? Draping yourself in jewels? Wearing only black? Dying your hair purple or shaving it off?

Maybe it's making shawls out of home-spun wool. Moving your bed to the middle of the room to watch the stars at night. Getting a snake tattoo down your spine. Creating malas out of pearls and garnets. Writing a love poem (maybe to yourself!) in coloured ink.

In the name of beauty. In the name of love. In the name of what's holy...

Create beauty out of nothing.
Create beauty out of the wild.
Create beauty out of pain.
Create beauty out of mystery.
Create beauty out of prayers.

Go ahead...

Adorn
Brew
Build
Craft
Disassemble
Embellish
Experiment
Invent
Move
Play
Refine
Shape
Simplify
Tear
Upcycle
WEAVE

Whatever it is, do it! Do it with love and passion. Do it for you!

And then bless it. Thank it. Be with it. Let it inform, uplift, heal and inspire you with its beautiful magic.

Right now, as I am writing these words, I'm marvelling at the exquisiteness of the silver rings on my hands - a beautiful cut-out of a lotus, a tiny Wheat Goddess with spiralling arms, and a labradorite stone wrapped in twisted wires. They feel delicate and striking against my well-worn, aging hands.

And my wrists give off a jangling metallic sound as my Indian bangles clang together. I love the sound and feel. It makes my heart and soul sing. I'm creating beauty for me, which in turn vibrates out into the world. It's my own personal blessing.

I love many symbols, styles and expressions. I love what I love. I'm sure you do too.

I love Zen gardens, and Moorish and Balinese architecture.
I love pearls, wild headdresses, and all goddess imagery.
I love sacred and flaming hearts, mermaids, and mirrors.
I love sacred geometry, ancient symbols and carvings.
I love silver, hand-woven tapestries, and soft scarves.
I love Indian kitsch, praying figures, and visionary art.
I love mosaics, labradorite, and cobalt blue glass.
I love snakes, birds, and anything with wings.
I love tattoos, lotuses, and spirals.
I love the odd and unusual.

And that's just the top tier of what makes me shimmer and shine.

What about you? What do you LOVE? What brings you incredible pleasure and delight, and makes you come alive? What sets your Wild Goddess soul on fire?

Your task for this practice is this:

Love what you love, and...

Beautify your life with creations only you can make.

Go ahead, Wild Goddess.

Bring it on.

It's why you're here.

Dance Your Wild / Dance Yourself Free

"You were once wild here. Don't let them tame you." Isadora Duncan

I honour and respect the wisdom-teachings of all spiritual and yogic traditions. I truly do. Their messages of love, compassion and forgiveness, along with their practices of mindfulness and living in harmony and balance, are exquisitely nourishing, inspiring, healing and life-supporting. I celebrate and bow to that!

I also sense sometimes, and maybe you do too, that there's a missing piece, something *not* being taught, not being attended to that stems from a deep fear of the wild, our wild. As if our roots connecting us to Earth have been cut off. This fear feels pervasive to me.

In the beautiful pursuit of the transcendent, the devotional, the bhakti heart, the focus tends to rest in the upper chakras, from the heart up. The loins, the deep, the dark, in other words, the wild, remain unexplored and unexpressed. (Does this feel balanced and whole to you?)

Please don't get me wrong… as I said before, I honour all wisdom-teachings, and have practiced different forms of yoga on and off since the 90s, although it's not been my main squeeze.

In the last retreat I attended at a well-known and beloved yoga center in Canada, I enjoyed it immensely. I loved the early morning readings of holy texts, the ecstatic chanting accompanied by tambourines and shakers, and the mindful breathing, meditations, and asanas. It was all very beautiful and healing.

However, I couldn't help but notice there was the absence of dance. In fact, it turned out to be forbidden. Even in the state of ecstasy through the chanting, it was not condoned. Being the inquisitive dancer that I am, I asked one of the main teachers why dancing was not allowed.

His answer? It was too provocative. Too primal. Too sexy. It's not the collective energy they want to raise. (I also sensed that it was a territory too uncomfortable and unfamiliar to the teachers there that they wouldn't know how to hold safe space for it, so best to not engage.)

I bless them for what they know and how they wish to explore the divine, the union of oneness, but, my friend, I have a different truth that resonates in my bones…

Dance ALSO is treasure for the soul, for the wild heart. I believe it is a sacred feminine practice. Dance carries us home. It's a prayer. It's healing. It's an expression of love. It's pure Shakti embodiment.

So the invitation to you, right now, is to **dance with your wild one.**

Dance until you've set yourself free. Free from fear. Fear from doubt. Fear from pain. Fear from fear. Uncaged, untamed, unspoiled. Breath and heartbeat connecting you to all of life, to the Earth, to the stars, to the wild.

Grow wings.
Take flight.
Set your spirit bird freeeeeeee!

Get WILD and DANCE yourself Free:

Version 1: Approx. 20 minutes

1. **Find a place to dance** with lots of room, inside or out. In the kitchen or studio, or in the rain, under the sun, or moon. Alone or in public.

2. **Put on some upbeat music** you love; use the **Touch the Wild Playlist** or dance without music.

3. **Take a moment to ground** yourself in whatever position you like. Grow roots.

4. **Begin to move.** Relax your breath and invite your body to soften and relax.

5. **Invite your Wild Woman to dance.** Coax her. Tell her it's safe to express herself.

6. **Feel your wild nature** moving, and moving through you. Feel your Wild Woman BEING MOVED all the way down to your feet.

7. **Allow any natural sounds to come,** especially the ones from your belly. Howl. Hiss. Moan. Growl. Hum. Yawn.

8. **Feel the beat.** Feel your hips. Feel everything. Be real. Be raw. Be here. Be now.

9. **Let go.** Go dancing into the wilderness of your own SOUL.

10. **Dance until you feel done.** Satiated. Free.

11. **Come into stillness** and give yourself the gift of awareness.

12. **Notice what you notice.** Qualities of thoughts, feelings, sensations.

13. **Give thanks** to yourself and your wild dance. Give thanks to the Wild One Within.

Sixth Turn: Touch the Wild   233

Version 2: Approx. 30 minutes

1   Start with <u>Shake it Loose Playlist</u> from the Fifth Turn. Keep it on or start the **Touch the Wild Playlist**.

2   Instead of dropping into stillness at the end, **keep going.**

3   **Allow your dance to transform** by following any impulses that feel natural and easy.

4   Imagine, sense and **feel your wild nature, your Wild Woman,** moving you, moving through you.

5   **Allow sounds to come.** Howl. Hiss. Moan. Growl. Hum.

6   **Feel everything.** Be real. Be raw. Be here. Be now.

7   **Let go.** Go dancing into the wilderness of your own SOUL.

8   **Dance until you feel done.** Satiated. Free.

9   **Come into stillness** and give yourself the gift of awareness. **Notice what you notice** - qualities of thoughts, feelings and sensations.

10 **Give thanks** as always.

May you know your WILD.

May the ancient Wild Ones support your passage into
the realms of nature and spirit, heart and soul.

May you feel held by their deepest embrace
and highest vibrations of love, joy, flow and freedom.

May you feel celebrated, loved and adored in
all your natural expressions, creativity, and instincts.

May you know your wild is a great blessing.

May you wield and share your wild power wisely and generously.

May you value, treasure and support the wild in others.

May you be wild for those who cannot!

May you be wild, as wild is for you.

Here's to your divinity, dear Wild Woman!

Blessed be!

Touch the Wild Playlist

Dance your Wild Woman. Be wild & free.

1. **Wild Woman** (feat. Jens Gad), The Goddess (feat. Jens Gad), by Amiya Inspiration
2. **There's Nothing Wrong**, Galactica Rush, by Jhelisa
3. **Return To Paradise** (Mark De Clive-Lowe Remix), Verve Remixed, by Shirley Horn
4. **Take Me Up**, Chill House, by Ralphi Rosario
5. **Dibiza** (Island Groove Remix), Elegant & Fabulous, by Danny Tenaglia
6. **One Brief Moment** (Klute Remix), One Brief Moment - Single, by David Arnold & Natacha Atlas
7. **Rakandao** (Remix), Buddha Bar X, by Shaman's Dream
8. **Black Betty**, Disco Super Hits, by Ram Jam
9. **Adouma**, Aye, by Angélique Kidjo
10. **Indusufi**, Buddha Bar IX, by Bahramji
11. **Cores** (Bomb da Bass Club), Cores (feat. B-Fonic), by Ana Flora
12. **Wildcats Gotta Move**, Night Over Rio - Latin Flavoured Lounge & Club Tunes, by Brenda Boykin
13. **Shut Up and Dance** (Tavo Remix), Electro Swing VI by Bart & Baker, by Kitten & The Hip
14. **Bad Girls**, Bad Girls (Deluxe Edition), by Donna Summer
15. **Magalenha**, Magalenha, by Sergio Mandes
16. **Lost In Music**, Journey Into Paradise: The Larry Levan Story, by Sister Sledge
17. **Heaven**, Ambient, by Moby
18. **Munsen's Main Mix**, The Thing About Deep (Can Drum), by Agev Munsen & Roland Clark
19. **Oshun**, Gathering One, by Hamsa Lila
20. **Naked**, Raise a Holy Fire, by Lakshmi Devi
21. **Womyn**, Rise of the Phoenix Mermaid, by The Floacist
22. **Freedom**, Stars, by Simply Red

Go to: www.EricaRoss.com/playlists

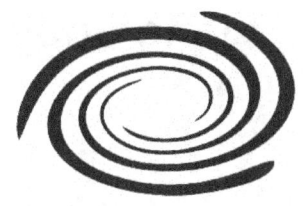

Seventh Turn

Return to Self

"If you feel lost, disappointed, hesitant, or weak, return to yourself, to who you are, here and now and when you get there, you will discover yourself, like a lotus flower in full bloom, even in a muddy pond, beautiful and strong." Masaru Emoto

Into the Soup

What is the point of pain?

It's a question I've been asking myself for over eight years.

Pain - chronic and immobilizing, began for me in my 50s, in my back, and my right hip, leg, knee and foot. I couldn't work. I couldn't dance. And for a dancer not to dance, it made my spirit ache. Dance is my life. It's who I am. It's how I see myself, and how others see me.

Not since the break-up of my first marriage 30 years earlier had I felt so much pain. Not that my break-up caused physical pain; it didn't. But, it broke my heart. And the chronic pain in my body was slowly breaking not only my heart, but my spirit.

A form of depression set in. Dance is joy to me. It's one of the most powerful ways I experience joy and express it. You could call it my superpower. Even during the most difficult times in my life, I have felt an innate sense of joy available to me and dance is how I lived it. Pain not only dulled my joy, worse, it sometimes obliterated it. Instead, in its place I felt exhaustion and sorrow. I was in mourning, grieving the loss of everything dance meant to me, which is everything that has been central to my life.

Since I can remember, dance is where I found my friends, my community, my lovers, my bliss. It's how I found the divine, god/goddess. It's how I prayed. It's how I found freedom. Having pain wrapped up in what is supposed to be my bliss - in the freedom, the love, the wholeness and healing I felt when I danced - was crushing. I had no idea where else to look for bliss. If it wasn't dance, what was it?

I sought help for the pain, relentlessly. I worked with physiotherapists and chiropractors, acupuncturists and bodyworkers, medical doctors and surgeons. I met with channellers and shamanic healers, energy workers and diviners. I searched science and the cosmos looking for treatments and cures, advice and care.

"Please, somebody. Somebody! Help me!"

+++

Pain doesn't happen in an orderly way. It's been much more of a roller coaster ride. There were times when the pain receded into the background - when, if I adjusted things just enough, I could forget about it, or find a way to manage it. Sometimes, for hours, or even days at a time, I would be pain-free. Sometimes, the treatments would work. Often, they didn't, or at least, not for long.

But, pain or not, life carries on, and I had to as well. I didn't retreat completely from life. I worked when I could, modifying every step along the way. I lived and loved as best I could. But the dancing, it seemed to be coming to a close. (Exit, stage left.)

Pain came to a head in the autumn of 2015. I'd just arrived in Bangkok with my beloved partner, Rob, to begin a six-month sabbatical in S. E. Asia. I was so excited to be back in a part of the world I truly love. I envisioned us on new adventures together, creating sweet memories of play and delight. Six months of bliss.

On our very first day, Rob and I were strolling down a narrow lane filled with travellers, street vendors, massage salons and restaurants, exploring what was to be our new 'hood for the next week or so.

It was mid-morning, hot and sunny. Our senses were alive and taking it all in: the bustling sounds of the city were mixed with the pungent smells of coconut curry, and the birds were dancing all around us. We were chatting about the smells and sounds, and what and where we wanted to explore first, when, without warning, pain shot through the lower part of my body, from my back to my hip, down my leg and into my foot. I froze. I literally couldn't move. One single step was agony.

With the support of my beloved, I limped my way back to our hotel room to rest and figure out how we would navigate and carry on our plans. For the next few days my pain ebbed and flowed in intensity, and I somehow managed to take in some very slow sight-seeing - mainly by boat so I wouldn't have to do much walking.

We even connected up with friends, Marla Slavner and her daughter Kasha, who were on their own six-month journey to film "The Sunrise Storyteller", a documentary on the resiliency of communities overcoming adversity. However, the pain I was experiencing, plus the bustle of the city, was too much for my nervous system.

We decided to fly north to Chiang Mai - a place we'd heard was beautiful, and imagined to be less noisy and fast-paced - hoping to stay until our two-month Thai visa ran out. We settled into the perfect hotel for us - a smallish, modern and clean oasis in a local Thai neighbourhood just outside the tourist area. I began a series of treatments at the Physiotherapy Department at a hospital, which really only helped me by prescribing pain meds and anti-inflammatories. To help manage the pain, I found a new rhythm - one day of activity, one or two days of rest.

The big blessing came when an ex-pat living in our hotel introduced me to her son, Andrew Innes, a master acupuncturist from England practicing just 15 minutes from our place. I jammed in as many sessions as I could - 13 to be exact. He also mixed in other techniques beyond acupuncture - trigger-point therapy, fire cupping and ear bleeding (don't ask). It was often extremely painful but it enabled me to walk more easily and continue the journey when our two months were up.

Our beautiful sabbatical, initiated by pain and struggle, continued that way for the entire six months. I was in so much pain, physically and emotionally, that it got to the point where, for the first time in my life, I went into the metaphorical 'soup' - I had a complete melt-down of my identity. An identity crisis at 60. I had never experienced one before.

Somehow, I always knew what I was doing and how to be in the world. It's not that I knew from one month to the next what I was doing - I was always very spontaneous. But for years and years I've always had movement in my life - forward momentum. Whether it was to become a jeweller, or a boutique owner, a dance teacher, or a dancer, a mother and a partner, there was always an opportunity in front of me and I just kept moving forward. There was momentum and flow. But not so much anymore. Pain took over everything and it forced me to confront my life and my future.

No matter what I had done in my life, whatever businesses I had, whenever anyone asked me what I did, I always answered, I'm a dancer. My spirit is a dancer.

And in the last 20 years, my life fully reflected my spirit. I had an ecstatic dance practice teaching and leading ecstatic dance workshops and retreats, helping women heal their spirits and their bodies through dance. I'd co-created and DJ-ed for a large ecstatic dance community in Toronto - the largest one in Canada (I believe) - that met every week. And I'd trained women to become facilitators of my practice. Even my past website was named 'Dance Our Way Home.' Everything - everything - was dance.

Sometimes, I'd get stopped in the street, "Aren't you the dancer? The one who works with women and the goddesses?" I knew myself as a dancer. I was known as a dancer. Yet, I could no longer dance. And as dance disintegrated from my life, I felt like I, too, was disintegrating.

I had three questions...

*If I can't dance, how do I make a living? Dance has been my livelihood.

*If I can't dance, what becomes of my community? Dancers are my community.

*If I can't dance, where do I find my bliss? Dance is my bliss.

We were getting close to the end of our sabbatical. We'd travelled through Thailand, Laos and Cambodia, and then settled in central Vietnam for the last three months. We found a perfect space in Hoi An - a small UNESCO town close to the beach and not far from Danang. It was utterly enchanting and beguiling with its riverside, colourful silk lanterns, pedestrian-only streets, delicious food, a gazillion tailor shops, lively markets and ancient tea shops and Chinese temples. It was idyllic.

Our home was a brand new, New York-style loft with a huge and expansive covered balcony, above a furniture store. As soon as we moved in, there was a ripple effect: the store owners' family moved in to their own rooms, all of us living above the shop. There were cousins and children and a grandfather who loved to write poetry. We were quickly adopted into the family. We were so happy there, and it felt like home.

But still, there was pain, and just like the snake when its shedding of its skin, I felt blinded. (Refer back to '**Connect with the Gifts of Animal Wisdom**.') Like the snake, I was shedding my skin. And, like the snake, I couldn't see. I couldn't see what the future held for me. I knew what I was losing, but I couldn't envision my future.

I'll never forget it. One afternoon, when Rob had gone out for a while, I was out on our beautiful balcony. Around me the air was humid and fragrant. I could smell the incense and flowers wafting up from the avenue below. Lush climbing vines draped over the balustrade. I was surrounded by beauty, and burgeoning life. But, on the inside, I was coming completely undone.

The frustration and the grief I'd been feeling for so long, and the wear and tear of the pain in my body, all finally caught up with me. I literally crumbled to the floor. I wept and wept, giving my tears over to Kuan Yin, and all the goddesses I knew so well. I was crying for answers. I was on my knees, begging the universe to tell me, "If I'm not a dancer, what am I?"

And then, I got an answer. Seriously.

You know, like in *Eat Pray Love*, when Elizabeth Gilbert is curled up on the floor of her bathroom, and she heard a voice? Yeah. Like that. That's what happened to me, too. I spoke (make that sobbed) and someone... something... spoke back. I know. It may sound strange. But it's true.

It felt like a beam of light shining down on me. Like the heaven's parted, just like in the biblical stories. God-dess was pointing at me and she had a message. I know it might sound unbelievable. This stuff is hard to explain, but that's exactly how it felt.

"If I'm not a dancer, who am I?" I cried.

And in response, I heard these words...

"You are love."

I mean, it felt bigger. More like, *"You are **LOVE!**"*

It's not like I had to wait for it. Well, it took months for me to get to the point where I was on my knees. Months. But, when I got there and asked the question, the answer was prompt. You are **LOVE**!

And, the moment I heard it - right in that very moment - I knew. I knew everything would be okay.

Not that I knew what it meant in terms of the practicalities. I mean, okay, if I am love, how the heck do I make a living? Do I just say, "Hi, I am love, here's my card." I don't think so. But, you know what I mean. Everything would be okay.

I remember thinking years ago that I have this practice that's dance-based. But really, what I'm doing is just loving up every single person who comes into the space. 'Bwahaha. You think you're coming to dance, but really you're coming to be loved. You don't know that's what I'm going to do, but that's what's happening. You're gonna be loved.'

I know it's how the healing happens. The healing comes because they're being held in a space of love. Dance is the vehicle, but love is the thing. And now, unequivocally, I understood that I *was* the thing. I was love.

Still, there was a huge letting go required - the letting go of everything dance meant to me, including the 'bliss factor.' That was a big loss. The loss of my mobility meant the loss of my bliss, the bliss I experienced when my body was fully capable - capable of twirling, and spinning and flowing and flying, moving from down on the floor, to up on my toes, to leaping, to lift off and to flight.

Through pain I'd come to a place of recognition that I am more than my body - that this big, bright, spirit of mine was/is love, but it needed a new form of expression. I needed to find my way back to bliss. I mean, there's no way in hell I was giving up my bliss. Who wants to give up bliss!!!!!???

And so, just like in my Bali story, I let go. I let go of my wings in order to make peace with myself and to become earthbound for as long as needed. I decided it was best for my wellbeing to stop fighting my new self, and allow a new teacher to guide me - TURTLE. Like me, she's slow and steady, and close to the ground. Low became my new high. A shell became my new home.

It's been four years since that pivotal moment on my balcony in Hoi An, and I'm still on my healing journey. My pain is much better thanks to a culmination of therapies - most recently, with Alvaro Esteban, a student of Osteopathy (who I call 'my angel') - but I still have a way to go, not just physically, but emotionally and mentally. My return back to myself, back to love, hasn't been an easy ride.

You see, I miss flying and leaping. I miss looking and feeling light, agile and sensual, and more than anything, being flexible and graceful. Instead I often feel stiff, heavy and tired. It's taken pain, and the hormones of menopause which came at the same time (and changed the shape of my body), to really understand what it feels like to see my body through a harsh lens, and to be estranged from it. I sometimes wonder, 'Whose body is this?'

Because of this journey I have a deeper compassion for every woman I've held safe and sacred space for, and all beings who suffer with the same issue. Perhaps you can relate. I think most women, if not all, have issues with our bodies. For me it was pain and menopause (Barbara Marx Hubbard calls it 'regeneropause' for its regenerative nature) that opened that gateway for me in a big way, and I still struggle with fully accepting, appreciating and loving my body as it is - pain and all.

And so… I practice returning to self-compassion, and count my blessings at every turn. I return to find comfort in the mystery and in the chaos. I return to find juiciness in small things, and treasure the shape of my own (slow) wildness, magic and wisdom.

And ultimately, I know that I AM love, regardless. It's an extraordinary thing, and I don't take it for granted. I am filled with wonder, curiosity and fascination, and have no idea where it all will lead. ("I allow. I trust.")

Pain has taught me much, but most importantly - I am love. It's my discovery. It's the expansion of, and the return to, myself at the same time. It's the end of the journey, and the new beginning.

Reflections

"You may return here once you have fully come to understand that you are always here." Elizabeth Gilbert

Well my love, you have arrived!

You've arrived at the Seventh Turn, the potent point on the spiral where, if you were to see the spiral in three dimensions, it has spiralled back on to itself - either ascended over or descended under the First Turn. Either way, it's the return to the beginning but on a different plane and time, to a new threshold.

You can look at it this way...

Imagine the spiral was your day. You wake up in your own home. It's deeply personal, and it's just for you. Then, as you continue your day you venture round the next turns, going out into the world, connecting with others and encountering life. And then when the day is done, you go back home, back to yourself, carrying with you all that you've experienced.

In other words, you meet yourself, you meet others, you meet life, and then... You return back from where you came.

So here we are. Here you are... in the return.

And oh how I love the return. There's something special about it. Regardless if it's a hotel room for the night, a weekly room rental or your own dream house, there's still some kind of comfort in it. It's our domain, our bed, our sanctuary. It's ours for as long as we're there.

(I have to pause here and do a quick shout out to divine timing, for as I sit here musing about the magic and potency of the return home, I realize two things: 1. I've newly returned home from a two-week journey. 2. It's almost Spring Equinox here in Toronto, which marks the return of Persephone from the Underworld! How perfect is that? Thank you, oh great universe! I trust in your perfection.)

As I was saying...

The return, the blessed re-turn, is potent with possibilities. It's powerful, sacred and miraculous. It's spiritual and mysterious.

You see, our return holds deep insights and teachings for us. With every new experience, every person, every encounter, every breath and every thought, we're touched and changed, consciously and unconsciously. And not just for that moment. No. In fact, we carry what and who's touched us back home with us. Their presence is now a part of us. Every experience is a part of us. A part of you. We truly are connected.

(Even if you lived in a cave in the remotest place on Earth you'd still be connected to the great pulse of life!)

And so... Your task at this sacred stage is to pause and let things land, and then find the new shape of yourself by weaving together the new shiny threads with the old frayed ones into a brand new, richly soul-infused fabric of you - an expression of who you are, where you've been and where you are going.

Yes, your task is to become a sacred weaver, and to wear your magical tapestry as a personal healing blanket, a prayer shawl, a love wrap, a blessing way as you dance down your exquisite path of self-love, inner strength and divine wisdom. Radiant. Soft. Yours.

Take full advantage of this powerful juncture, this Seventh Turn. And as you did in the First Turn, relax into a softening and listen well. Get curious. Get creative. Get courageous and compassionate.

And most of all... because this is a time of reintegration, please be gentle and easy on yourself. This restructuring (and re-membering) can be challenging to your system. You might be more sensitive, more open, more emotional, or more confused. Anything is possible in the realms of the spiral - in the realms of healing, integrating, owning, deepening and growing.

Notice what you notice with ease and love. Notice the obvious and subtle changes, the whisperings and inner stirrings. Find and ask new juicy questions. Invent new languages of light and love. Make prayers and songs. Create art and altars to your inner worlds and visions. Shower yourself with all that is juicy, alive, nourishing and healing for you. Give thanks.

Whatever you do, bless it with the depth and fullness of your heart and soul, for your return home is vital and essential to your wholeness. Let me say it again...

Your return home is vital and essential to your wholeness.

It's essential to your holiness, and to healing for all of us. This return is a return to love, after all.

And while you're at it, bless and drop into your gorgeous, boundless heart. Remember you are loved. Breathe into the truth that YOU ARE LOVE. I feel this deep in my bones. Yes, you are love. We are love.

Your life is sacred. Your life is a divine mirror for all that moves with and through you, with nothing left out. Your life is a grand and sacred experiment.

Can you see life as a sacred experiment? (This is one of my favourite practices. It changes everything. You'll see further on.)

Which brings us to the all-mighty and expansive word, 'acceptance'; a key to opening to more love, more peace, more understanding, and more joy.

Can we/you accept all that is - all the connections and experiences in your life as you spiral in and out, home and afar, returning home again and again, new and transformed?

Even in my story, at 60 when it was pain that returned me home, back to self. When the pain melted me open, forcing me to drop down to my knees, let go of my ego and question my self-identity, it was perfect!

Because, one of my greatest life-changing questions, "Who am I?" and the immediate answer "You are love" came through me that day, and my life was changed forever. I knew then that I'd be fine. Love was my super power. I am grateful beyond words.

And it was pain that gave me another great gift - the gift of living in the moment. Living in the present without needing to know, which brings it all back to letting things land and accepting where I am. Trusting and celebrating in the mystery.

Still to this day, I don't have clarity about my future. I only know what's happening right now. And I'm okay with that. And when I drop deeper into gratitude and self-compassion, I feel more than okay with that.

May you...

Return...
to begin again.

Return...
to ask new questions.

Return...
to behold the mystery of yourself.

Return...
to see life as a sacred experiment.

Return...
to remember you are love.

Return...

Practices for the Seventh Turn

- Create a Gratitude (List &) Collage
- Accept What Is / See Life as a Sacred Experiment
- Keep Your Heart Open, Regardless
- Support Your Expanding Heart
- Trance Dance with Love
- Appreciate Your Unique Light

Playlist: Return to Love

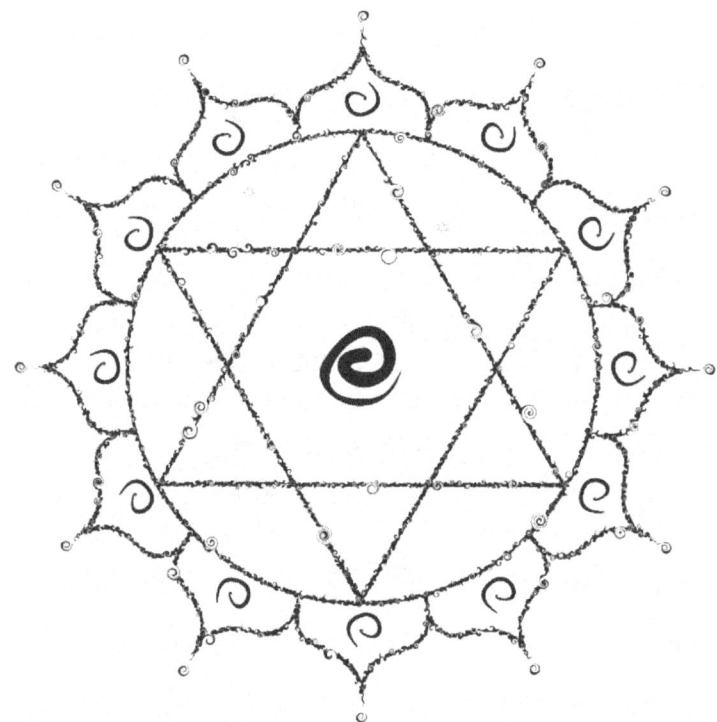

"And the more you become aware of the unknown self - if you become aware of it - the more you realize that it is inseparably connected with everything else that is." Alan Watts

Create a Gratitude (List &) Collage

"Gratitude is not a passive response to something we have been given, gratitude arises from paying attention, from being awake in the presence of everything that lives within and without us." David Whyte

Let's start with gratitude, because... well... it just feels so damn good.

It's a heart cleanser, lens changer, light inducer. It gives us good reason to pay attention, and fall madly in love with ourselves and everything around us! Gratitude changes EVERYTHING.

And yet... we seem to have a 'gratitude' deficit, *even*, and maybe especially, in places of great privilege, prosperity and abundance. Regardless of how much we might have and what our circumstances are, we are vulnerable to falling into the trappings of all the 'wantings' and the 'not enoughs.' (The path of consumerism hasn't helped.)

It's easy to forget how deeply blessed we really are. We don't notice all the ways the universe is showering each one of us with blessings. Every moment of every day.

And yes, there are times - maybe more often than not - when it just doesn't feel like that. At all! Your life may be very hard, right now or in general. I honour that. I'm not in any way wishing to dismiss that truth for you, and still... I believe there's always something to be grateful for. Always!

Finding reasons to be grateful and acknowledging and counting our blessings is a wonderful gift because it shifts our perception (a form of magic). It moves us from lack to fullness, worry to optimism, and discontent to appreciation. It opens our hearts and reminds us of what is good and working in our world, counteracting our longings and feelings of need and inadequacies.

Yes, there'll always be reason to complain about something not feeling right in our life, but... there's also always a reason to celebrate. Being alive is good enough reason to shout 'Hallelujah!' It's a miracle and privilege to have breath and a beating heart.

Even our challenges, pains and losses can be counted as blessings when we align with gratitude (don't I know it!). And that causes great ripples of healing, connection, compassion and loving kindness. The gift of your presence is an offering of gratitude.

So, this practice is an invitation to count your blessings in a Gratitude List, and then use it to inspire the creation of one of my favourite art forms - a collage, as a remembrance so you'll not forget!

The word "collage" comes from the French "coller" meaning "glue." Collage techniques go back to around 200 BC in China during the time of the invention of paper. How cool is that?

If you've never done a collage, you're in for a treat. It's both simple and powerful, and you don't need any experience at all. None! Your soul will love it too - it loves, communicates and responds to imagery, words, colour and light, so while you collage you're inviting your soul to speak and guide you.

You'll discover what your soul needs through the images chosen by it. It may only want a few images. It may want many. It may want only words. Every collage is an embodiment of a particular sacred soul expression. You can't get this wrong.

Supplies you'll need:

- Paper (or journal) and pen for your list
- Scissors and glue (white or clear)
- Magazines (photocopies are great too)
- Construction paper or poster board (whatever size you prefer)
- Drop cloth or extra paper to do your gluing

And here we go...

- **Set up your space.** Where would be a delicious place to create your list and collage? Trust your intuition. This is a loving creation, a holy ritual, a sacred act. You may wish to create an altar specifically for this gratitude practice, and create your list and collage by it.

    Wherever you choose - a table, a floor - let it be clean and uncluttered. Eventu-ally, it will become a lovely creative mess. That's part of the process.

    I recommend having some beautiful heart-centered music playing. Check out the **Return to Love Playlist** for this Turn. Infuse a sense of love and gratitude into this process, from set up to clean up.

- **Gather your supplies.** You're going to start with your Gratitude List, so have your paper (or journal) and pen front and center. Your drop cloth and poster board can be sitting under it, with your magazines in a few piles around or in front of you, and your scissors and glue nearby.

Create your Gratitude List: Approx. 15-20 minutes

1. **Relax.** Give yourself permission to trust in your own process and creative instincts. Breathe. Let go of any shoulds and doubts, or any attachment to outcome. Keep your body and mind soft and receptive. Drop into your body and feel into your beautiful heart.

2. **Ask yourself**, 'What and who brings me joy, pleasure and delight? What and who do I love? Where do I feel most alive? What and who am I grateful for?'

Seventh Turn: Return to Self   249

3   **Look at all parts of your life** - your inner and outer world, your passions, your talents, your beliefs, your home, your relationships, your business, your spirituality, your experiences, your choices.

4   **Let the words flow.** Begin to write without censoring yourself. Let the words flow from your heart, to your hand, to the page.

5   **Go beyond the shiny and beautiful.** Invite gratitude for your pain, your losses, your misunderstandings, and challenges. All teachings and lessons. They all count. They are all blessings. Bless them all. And don't forget all your relations – our beautiful Gaia, the stars, the waters, the animals, plants, etc.

Create Your Gratitude Collage: Approx. 2 hours

With your **Gratitude List** in front of you, meditate on your words for a bit. Let them sink into your body, mind and heart.

1   **Find images from your magazines.** When you feel ready, let your hands be guided towards a magazine, like you would choose an oracle card. Trust. Open to the flow of your heart, soul and hands to guide you. This is a creative act, and you are a visual poet.

With magazine in hand, effortlessly wander through it, flipping pages looking for any colours, shapes, words or images that resonate with your list. Stay fluid - don't get distracted by articles or bogged down in the details. Don't overthink this. Allow your collage to be a mystery to you. See what catches your eye. **Look for the feeling of YES.**

2   **Cut or tear those pieces out and set them aside.** Don't assign meaning - simply acknowledge your attraction to them. Trust your soul on this one. You're beginning to create a library of images for yourself. You may or may not use each one in this collage. It may be for future use!

Keep flowing from magazine to magazine until you feel you have enough pieces to create with. You might find that one magazine has all the pieces you need, or there may be none.

3   **Glue down your images.** There are different ways to do this. Again, as always, trust in your own creative instincts. Your soul knows!

One way is to find a central large image (could represent *you* for example) that becomes the base or background for your collage. All other images get glued on top of that. (This method is handy when there are words or objects on the larger image you don't want. You can cover them up with other images!)

Or, you can create your collage without a background image. Take whatever images you want to use and play with them, moving them around on your paper until they feel right, like pieces of a puzzle, overlapping or apart.

As for the gluing... You can wait until they are all in place and glue them all at the same time, or glue each piece one at a time, cutting and gluing as you go.

Très Important! From time to time, step away, take a break, do a dance. Why? So you can come back in your body, heart and soul. Because what often happens is, along the way your beautiful and smart mind/head will take over (it loves to be in control). You'll become less fluid and intuitive, and perhaps you'll even forget your original intention for your collage - to be an expression of GRATITUDE.

Here's a secret tip: Once you know which pieces you're using, explore both cutting AND tearing them for their final look. Using scissors gives a cleaner, smoother feel, while tearing gives a more organic natural shape. Tearing is also unpredictable, which I love because you never know exactly how it will tear. I love the balance and juxtaposition of both. The wild and the controlled. The feminine and the masculine!

4 **Bring closure.** This process is an embodiment of gratitude - to remember, acknowledge and celebrate all that you are grateful for. Complete your experience with a final bow of gratitude. Find a way to complete this in a sacred way, a sacred closing. Maybe it's with a gesture, a poem, a dance, an affirmation, or a song.

I'm especially fond of titling my collages. There's something powerful and magical about the act of naming. Oh... and date both your list and your collage (at the back) so when you look at it five years from now, you'll know when it was made.

5 **Keep it alive.** Place your Gratitude List somewhere special. Place your collage somewhere special also, either privately, or on an altar, or near your bed. Where does it feel right?

See how your world is touched by them. Allow new visions, ideas, writings or art to unfold from them. Journal. Invite your Muse to come forth. Keep her flow alive. See what else wants to be birthed through you. Art-making leads to more art, more possibilities, and definitely more magic.

"If the only prayer you said in your whole life was, 'thank you,' that would suffice." Meister Eckhart

Accept What Is / See Life as a Sacred Experiment

"I dance to the tune that is played." Spanish Proverb

Gratitude and acceptance go hand in hand. They both are heart expanders. They both evoke love. They both carry us more lightly on our path. If we can truly be grateful for every experience, we can find acceptance, and vice versa.

Acceptance, by definition, is the act of accepting, agreeing to, consenting, accommodating, or reconciling oneself to what is offered, such as an invitation or situation, and regarding it to be true.

Accepting all that is, therefore, means agreeing to, consenting, accommodating, or reconciling oneself to ALL that is offered to us in our life, in every moment. That's everything that shows up within us - emotions, sensations, thoughts, and feelings - and everything around us - people, relationships, circumstances, etc. That's no small task!

(Acceptance of outer circumstances, similarly to the practice of *letting go*, doesn't imply that you should give up on a just cause, become complacent or inactive. No! It's the quality and suppleness in which to engage with the bigger picture.)

Like a large polished mirror, we have the potential to accept and reflect the fullness of life, not just a small portion of it. Acceptance invites us to see, observe, notice, listen, feel, sense and reflect that wholeness and perfection - embracing beauty and pain, shadow and light.

Without distortion, want, or fracture from our smaller consciousness, narrow perceptions and understandings, we can practice walking a noble path of love, gratitude and acceptance.

<u>Seeing Life as a Sacred Experiment</u> is part of my secret sauce; my way of seeing and understanding the comings and goings on this path. It's the revelation that all is a) sacred, and b) an experiment.

In other words, it's a lens through which to see how life flows - the divinity, beauty and creativity in all that moves. When we approach life like an experiment, a sacred experiment, it evokes an expanded sense of curiosity, acceptance, delight and wonder. We ask ourselves, 'I wonder what will happen when...? What if....?'

And whatever happens, the sacred scientist, adventurer, artist and divine woman in you understands there's a bigger picture at play, and a broader, more relaxed and trusting perspective is needed. She trusts in the unfolding without needing to know the reason, outcome or even purpose.

The sacred explorer sees life as oh so mysterious, potent and deliciously interesting. And accepts life, and living, in a state of not-knowing and becoming.

But wait...

I know... it's easy enough to be in a state of acceptance, curiosity and creativity when things are landing right side up; when you're feeling loved, healthy and strong; having blissful adventures, living in comfort, and so on... no problem. Acceptance. Seeing the sacred. Easy. Check!

Unfortunately, it's not so easy to do when you're not able to sleep, are in pain, feeling lonely, hurt, depressed, scared, and so on. Acceptance? Seeing the sacred? Not so much. It's harder to justify challenges and accommodate pain or unwelcomed circumstances.

So how can we get to that expansive space of acceptance of ALL, and seeing life as a sacred experiment when clearly there are tripwires all around us, or in our mind? Even when the odds seem stacked against us. Can you still keep going in trust? Or when life feels dull, pointless and uninteresting. Can you invite a sense of wonder?

That's the practice right there: Seeing into the shadows and finding the light. Feeling into the pain and finding the gift. Moving with inertia and finding levity. It's possible. It's the practice.

Can you have faith when you're in the soup of 'I don't know'? Can you be okay with that? Practice. Acceptance.

Can you hold space for yourself, continue to find a way to be with it, to accept it, to accept yourself as you are right now? And love yourself, regardless? Practice. Acceptance. (As I ask myself. Right. Breathing love.)

Truth is... some days you'll feel whole and beautiful and shiny. Other days you won't. Some days you'll accept it all. And other days you won't. But all and all, if you can keep practicing showing up with whatever is alive in and around you, and shine some joy and curiosity onto it, you'll be fine. Believe me.

And when you have days that feel really blue and super challenging, see if you can turn it into art. Try it as a sacred experiment. You've got nothing to lose. Go ahead. Make art with it, create with it, heal with it, share it, dance it, write it, sing it. Use those stories for personal and collective healing, empowerment and liberation.

*Remember... Acceptance doesn't breed complacency. Acceptance of it all is a path of wholeness and healing within, AND it offers us a healthy grounding to make change, to act on loves behalf, to be an activist, a sacred activist and artist creating wellness within and around her.

Here are more practices for Accepting What Is:

- **Get familiar with what you don't accept.** Through awareness you can transform the unaccepted to the accepted, denial and rejection to acceptance and gratitude, and move your shadows into the light.

    Ask yourself: *Do I accept all that is a part of me? Do I accept all my emotions? Am I able to celebrate and move with anger, sorrow, fear, shame? Or do I fight or deny it? Do I accept change? Do I accept who I am? Do I celebrate who I am in my fullness? How does NOT accepting all of me impact my life? What do I not accept about my life and the world around me?*

- **Invite feelings of positivity.** Invite an optimistic attitude. Summon a sense of hope and resiliency into your being. Surround yourself with positive people and engage in uplifting conversations. Look for the blessings in everything. Find ways to bring a smile to your face, a lift to your step, a lilt in your voice.

- **See life as a sacred experiment.** Be endlessly curious and in awe of what unfolds within and around you. Be fascinated, appreciative, engaged and present. See how miraculously messy and divinely creative it all is.

- **Feel it all.** Don't judge it. Let emotions flow. Allow your heart to break. Welcome the tears and the laughter. Wonder at the fullness and breadth of your deep, living sensing body. Marvel at its wisdom and knowing. Let life in. Be touched.

- **Laugh and play a lot!** In other words, lighten up! Connect with your innocence, joy, laughter, pleasure, freedom, self-expression and wonder. Connect with your inner child - the playful one within - who loves to be silly, laugh and play.

- **Offer random acts of kindness.** Whatever will keep your own JOY alive, transfer it to another. Be a force for good. Spread it! Far and wide.

- **Relax and soften your inner judge or critic.** Give yourself a breather from judging so harshly, both to yourself and others. Invite a softening. Find and use kind, thoughtful and positive words. Forgive. Be gentle, loving and generous. Sigh!

Keep Your Heart Open, Regardless (For 28 Days)

"When you begin to touch your heart or let your heart be touched, you begin to discover that it's bottomless, that it doesn't have any resolution, that this heart is huge, vast and limitless. You begin to discover how much warmth and gentleness is there, as well as how much space." Pema Chodron

I'm so excited you've landed on this page. I get to tell you about my absolutely favourite, best and most powerful practice EVAH!

And honestly… if you were to do only one thing from my entire book of over a hundred different practices, THIS is the ONE! Do yourself a huge favour: Do this.

I've been doing it for over two decades. I can say, unequivocally, it's a life-changer. It will change every relationship you have, with yourself, your loved ones, strangers, and the world. Guaranteed.

And, actually… this practice is magic-making. When you do this practice it shifts your perceptions, and THAT is magic.

It's a kind of heart interruption, or better still… intervention. It's the practice of <u>keeping your heart open, regardless</u>.

And don't just try it once! **Commit to this practice for a good month, 28 days.**

In yogic tradition your heart is depicted as a twelve-petal lotus. I love that. It's an energy wheel, or chakra, where you receive, assimilate and give love. Its name, Anahata, which means unhurt, unstruck, and unbeaten, expresses its divinity and purity, and underneath it all, regardless of circumstances, it remains unhurt and unstruck.

I'm no expert or scientist but I have been paying attention to my heart for six decades. But, before I go any further, I want to share with you my view on the notion of OPEN and CLOSED hearts.

I see our hearts as mutable and fluid in expression, shape and movement. I believe no heart is completely closed nor all the way open; I see it as a spectrum of possibilities. As long as we are alive, our heart is open, even if it's to the smallest degree. It will close completely only when we shed our mortal coil.

As for being fully open… I see our hearts as boundless and bottomless, with no end to their capacity to be filled ceaselessly with love light, endlessly receiving and giving love. In other words, a heart can't be completely open because it has no termination to its filling.

I say this because I feel there's a lot of shaming in spiritual circles around how our heart performs, or how it 'ought' to be. Saying a heart is either open or closed feels judgmental, simplistic, and not useful to our growth.

Another good way of describing this is to see our hearts in movement, not static, always in a state of opening and/or closing. I truly believe we are fluid in nature, 'flickering flames,' all of us, and that includes our heart. It's beautiful to be in the dance, ebbing and flowing.

I also truly believe that YOU were born to LOVE! It's one of your birth rights.

Okay… 'nuf said. Back to the practice…

The best way I can think of to explain this is to take you through a couple of personal scenarios.

*Visualizing is my strong suit; my way. If 'seeing' is not yours, no worries… when it comes to your turn to practice, stay focussed on your feelings or sensations or energies, or whatever you need. Trust your intuition. Remember, this is a sacred experiment!

Two days ago I was waiting in a doctor's office. This was my first visit. I was told to be there at 10:10 a.m. sharp, and it would only be a 10-minute visit. Well there I was at 10:30 still waiting for the doctor to appear. I slowly became increasingly impatient. I grew more and more pissed off.

And then I remembered… 'Keep your heart open, Erica.'

So I closed my eyes and felt into my chest. I imagined the twelve petals of my beautiful heart lotus in my chest. I saw my heart lotus pink, and its petals open. And I felt it softening. I felt my heart softening. I felt my chest softening and expanding. And I felt warmth. I also felt like time was slowed down. I had all the time in the world; in fact, it felt like time didn't even exist in that moment.

I sat there feeling peaceful, calm and relaxed, no longer attached to any outcome. And I felt an outpouring of love for myself and the doctor I hadn't even met yet. And when she did arrive a few minutes later, I was able to receive her gently and kindly. Ahhhhhh…

Okay, let's take this up a notch in this next scenario, this time, a hypothetical one, but a real-life moment we've all been in.

I'm engaged in a deeply hurtful discussion with a loved one. I'm feeling misunderstood, betrayed and attacked. My mind is racing. My body is feeling overwhelmed with more and more fear and loss. I feel armour growing around me, protecting me like an armadillo's skin. My belly is in knots. Aching.

And my heart? Well, I can barely feel it other than a sickly squeezing kind of sensation. I feel weak, walled-in and ready to run. Freeze, fight and flight all at once.

(Everybody has their own responses. Yes, I mean every ... body. Yours might be different, but guaranteed you'll have them. Prickly. Mushy. Hot. Rigid. Flimsy. Whatever it is for you, those are the cues to pay attention to.)

I'm scanning my body. I'm listening both to the words being exchanged AND to my own body's wisdom. And I stop right in the middle of this painful discourse and say to myself, 'Erica. Keep your heart open, regardless!'

I breathe into my heart, and engage my visioning skills to see my heart expanding. My loved one may or may not even realize I'm consciously multi-tasking - listening, breathing and visioning! Doesn't matter.

That's what this practice helps you do: Notice. Respond. Continue.

By the way, that doesn't mean that I've stopped feeling hurt, or that I 'should' stop feeling hurt. I'm feeling what I feel. Usually, though, new sensations and feelings arise. Emotions change.

As my heart relaxes, a warmth begins to flow, melting my whole being. As I melt, the magic begins... I become connected back and available. I remember to give thanks to my heart and theirs. I return back to love, letting go of the outcome or resolution. I no longer feel pulled into power-struggles, rights or wrongs. Only love.

In my surrender, in my remembrance as an adept of the heart, the only thing that matters is to be love. To be love so big and bright that it heals a thousand hurts. That it eases the pain of separation to become whole and holy, again. To return to union.

And notice the word, 'regardless,' in keeping your heart open, REGARDLESS. There lies the golden key. It means... regardless of anything or anyone, any circumstance, situation, place or time, and regardless of any outcome, action or desire.

No matter what... keep my heart open. If I'm annoyed, keep my heart open. If I'm angry, keep my heart open. If I'm happy, keep my heart open.

I find it to be a really interesting practice to play with. It's asking our heart to respond in a counter-intuitive way. It wants to shrink up and protect itself in times of stress, anger, worry or fear. But... is that reflex truly natural, or something we've been taught and have practiced our whole life? I don't know.

So this is the tricky piece...

Can you practice keeping your heart open, more expanded and available, to allow more love to flow in and out and all around, regardless?

Can you do it in a situation where your heart normally would want to hide?

Remember when the beautiful Sun Goddess Amaterasu hid in her cave, feeling betrayed, upset and angry? Well that's kind of what your heart does. It feels safer to retreat, protect itself and hide.

But... remember also how glorious it was when the rock in front of the cave's mouth moved and out she came, shining her exquisite light, and saw her own beauty? THIS is what it feels like when you relax and let your heart-light shine!

And again, I'm not suggesting that you change your emotions. **Your focus is only on changing the quality or state of your heart.** That's what matters. Everything else will naturally follow.

That means being fully in your own heart and truth, powerfully feeling what you feel, AND being deeply connected to and in union with everyone and everything around you. It's an intoxicating feeling being drunk on love that way.

And seriously... do this not just when times are tough, but when everything is going RIGHT, when everything is flowing and there's synchronicity and everything feels perfect. It will open your heart up even more. It's life-changing stuff! It's the beauty and power of the practice!!!

Because, when you do this, you become a walking embodiment of light and love. You become a divine mirror that reflects the purity, divinity and wholeness of everyone and everything. It changes the lens through which you see the world. You can't help but see beauty and oneness everywhere, within and without.

When I got the answer to my question, "Who am I?" as "You are love", I knew I didn't need to know anything more. "You are love" was the re-affirmation I needed to hear. And that by continuing to do this practice, keeping my heart open, regardless, was essential to embodying fully who I am, a vehicle and divine mirror of LOVE!

Love is what I am. Love is what I do.

Will you join me in this love fest?

Come on... practice with me and let's meet in the radiant field of love, beauty, acceptance, kindness, peace, tolerance, gratitude and union.

My arms are open wide to receive you, my beloved.

I see us already, dancing, laughing, and drunk with love.

One heart.

One love.

Only love.

Support Your Expanding Heart

*"You've got to do your own growing,
no matter how tall your grandfather was." Irish Proverb*

Becoming and being love, loving, and loved, is a life-long practice. With awareness of this life-mission you'll find a bounty of tools and resources available to you along the way, many of which you already have in your magical tool box.

Believe me, if you've made it this far, in life or in this book, your tool box is already over-flowing. The key is to keep listening in so your heart, intuition and divine guidance can lead you to the practices and tools that are right for your present needs.

Be gentle with yourself always. Begin wherever you are. Soften any judgments about your own practice or others. There's no right or wrong path. Every heart has its own way of carrying and expressing love.

And because you are a shapeshifter, ever-changing, and so is life around you, your tool box will morph too. There will be times when you'll need to add to it, and other times you'll need to lighten it up by culling what no longer serves or resonates with your expanding heart. In that case, bless it, thank it and send it off with love.

In honour of your expanding heart, here are some sweet tools and practices:

Do one, or combine a few at a time. Tweak as you need - go deeper, lighter or slower. Your choice. Your pace. Your way. May they be of service to your beautiful courageous heart! May they inspire your inner Love Goddess to come out and play. May they invite love to permeate everything.

- **Practice Asanas (Yogic Poses):** I wouldn't call myself a Yogini by any means. I'm an Ecstatic Dancer! However, I do know a thing or two about yoga and have practiced it on and off for years - my first experience being initiated in Kriya Yoga, then studying some Kundalini, Shivananda and Hatha Yoga.

    When it comes to heart-expansion, practicing any asanas that open the area of the chest will benefit your heart. Cobra, Camel, Standing Bow and Cow Face are wonderful poses to do.

    *Always do them safely and read up on any restrictions if you're pregnant or have injuries, etc.

- **Sound AH:** AH is considered a sacred seed syllable. In many traditions it's considered the sound of the heart, and like the sound of a sigh, it's deeply soothing.

To do this, find a comfortable place to sit, close your eyes and relax into your body. You might wish to place your hands over your heart or in a prayer mudra. Breathe in, and on the exhale sound "AH" in whatever key or tone that feels comfortable for you. Keep breathing in and sounding on the exhale, going at your own pace. Allow peace to enter your heart. Let it soothe you. Sound for as long as you wish.

- **Chant sacred mantras:** With deep respect for the cultures they come from, chant the sacred Sanskrit sound for the heart, "Yum," the mantra, "I am Love," or the Tibetan mantra to help expand love and compassion, "Om Mani Padme Hum," commonly translated as, "The jewel is in the lotus."

  Begin as you did with the sound of AH... relax, close your eyes and feel into your heart. Whatever mantra or sound you use, repeat it 108 times, with a mala (a string of 108 prayer beads to keep count), if you have one.

- **Explore the colours of the Heart Chakra:** Infuse your being with the soothing, balancing and energizing colours of greens and soft pinks. Visualize with them. Wear, paint or create with them. Trust your intuition!

- **Use crystals:** Any gemstones that have the colours green or pink are for the heart. Each one has its own properties. You can wear them as jewelry - a gem pendant hanging by your heart or beads in a bracelet. Carry them in your pocket or purse. Place them on your body as you rest, hold them in your hand, or keep them by your bed or on an altar.

  Some of my favourite heart stones are:
  Emerald
  Green tourmaline
  Jade
  Peridot
  Rose quartz

- **Treat yourself to essential oils:** In the mid-1980s, for a hot-second, I dreamt of becoming a perfumer in Paris after reading Tom Robbin's bestseller, *Jitterbug Perfume*. And when I discovered essential oils soon after, I was hooked and excited to explore and craft my own intoxicating blends. (In fact, I have my own special perfume oil called 'Awakening Aphrodite' available at anarreshealth.ca. It's a blend of pink grapefruit, palmarosa, katrafay, vanilla and Peruvian balsam.)

  Ah... aroma AND healing, a perfect marriage. And magnificent for the heart. I especially love sandalwood and rose blended together (I have a bottle that was blessed by Amma, the hugging saint). It's sweet, earthy and heart-soothing.

  Some of my other favourite heart oils are:
  Angelica
  Jasmine
  Patchouli
  Ylang ylang

You may already have some or all of them, if not, you can find them in health food stores and online.

***Important! Dear Healer Woman...** Note this:

Most oils are <u>not</u> to be applied neat (without a carrier oil) directly on your skin. They're often too strong and can irritate you. Choose a carrier oil - almond, sunflower, grapeseed, jojoba, or anything else you have in your kitchen. A good ratio is roughly 4 drops of essential oil in 1.5 teaspoons of carrier oil. (My rule: never put anything on my skin that I can't eat!)

And speaking of eating... some oils are <u>not</u> to be ingested! PLEASE learn about each oil you use. Be safe!!!

Also... buy the <u>purest</u> oils you can find. You don't want synthetic. If cost is an issue, having ONE good oil is better than three oils of a lesser quality. Choose from a place of love, as an act of self-care.

Once you have your oil or oils, evoke your Inner Love Goddess, and anoint your heart and breasts (with or without the carrier oil, as required), or pour a few drops into the palm of your hands and breathe it into your heart and lungs.

Or... pour a few drops into your bath, rub it into your hair, or massage into your skin. Treat yourself to this sensual, heart-expanding act of self-love.

There you have it. Heart-expansion. Check!

Remember...

You are the beloved.

You are the one you've been waiting for.

YOU ARE LOVE!

Trance Dance with Love

"Love makes your soul crawl out from its hiding place." Zora Neale Hurston

Trance dance is a powerful, ancient healing practice used by Indigenous communities around the globe for thousands of years. Traditionally, like the practice of shaking, it's done by Shamans and healers as a way of altering their consciousness and awareness, to access new and vital information for the purpose of healing their communities.

With a blindfold wrapped around their eyes, to the fast and consistent beating of drums and/or rattles, while using special breath work, they dance their ego self into dissolution and drop the veils that separate them from the invisible realm, to see and know what's needed for their people.

In this case, this invitation and practice is a tool to turn inward - a slow dance back to yourself - to invite a deep, slow touch of love to dissolve within you, and to take you into the place of deeper intuition, soul-knowing, mystery and trust.

This is also an invitation to find stillness, your center, your grounding. It's a gentle, loving, deep experience for yourself. A moving prayer. A place of healing.

You are the beloved; beloved as in: adored, cherished, treasured, precious, valued and exquisite.

In this Trance Dance, be the lover offering herself to her beloved in the sweet temple of your being. Slow. Deep. Devotional.

Let's Trance Dance: Approx. 20 minutes

Tips:

- It's best for you to **stay in one spot** for the duration of your dance so you don't bump into things. Safety is important.

- If you at any time feel off balance or dizzy, drop down to the floor, or bring your awareness down to your feet, or stay down **on the floor** for the entire dance.

The Prep:

1. **Prepare a playlist** or use the **Return to Love Playlist**.

2. **Prepare your space.** Find a private space where you won't be interrupted. Clear enough room for yourself. Turn off your devices other than whatever you're going to use for your music.

3. **Find a bandana or scarf to cover your eyes with** (not too sheer, slippery or short).

The Dance:

This may seem obvious, but read through the instructions before you begin so you'll know what to do once you put the bandana on.

1. **Begin the music.**

2. **Place your bandana over your eyes,** knotting or tying it at the back of your head. Make sure it's tight enough that it won't fall off, and not too tight that you're uncomfortable.

3. **Choose to stand, sit or lie down.** *You can stay on the floor for the entire dance, or rise up or come down from your feet at any point. (You're in control!)

4. **Grow roots** down into the Earth to support your dance. (From the soles of your feet if standing, from your tail bone if sitting, or from your spine if lying down.)

5. Find your breath and **begin to move slowly.**

6. **Imagine, sense and feel LOVE flowing through you.** Let it fill you with warmth, light and grace. Dance with it. As the beloved.

7. **Bless yourself with this love,** touching and loving every part of you, especially your womb, yoni, belly, head and heart.

8. **Invite your love-light to expand, and send it out as kisses to everyone and everything.** Let your dance be an offering of love and devotion. <u>Don't keep it to yourself!</u>

9. When you feel close to completion, **bring your hands into a prayer or Namaste mudra** (hands pressed together in front of your heart).

10. Still dancing and moving, **ask your heart what it wishes.**

11. **Allow a prayer to come through you and dance with it,** as a moving prayer: 'May I be love.' 'May I love myself.' 'May I ...'

12. **When you feel done, come slowly into stillness.**

13. **Find and hold a shape, a shape of love.** Sink into it. Breathe with it.

14. **Notice what you notice.** Hold love there.

15. **Give thanks.**

The Closing:

1. **Slowly release the shape.**

2. **Take off the bandana and open your eyes.**

3. **Capture your prayer and experience** in your journal. And perhaps, pull out your divination deck and pick a card or two.

As always, be gentle and loving with yourself, especially if you feel fragile or vulnerable post-practice.

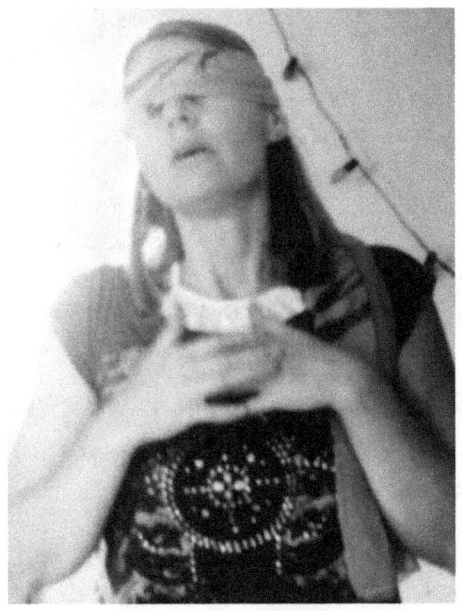

Appreciate Your Unique Light

"Even a small star shines in the darkness." Danish Proverb

Let me tell you a little story I love. It's the story of '**The Cracked Pot**,' author unknown.

*Heads up... I don't approve of the term or concept of 'master,' however, I chose to leave it as written and only hope you love the story, regardless - as in, keep your heart open, regardless!

Here it is...

"A water bearer in India had two large pots, one hung on each end of a pole which he carried across his neck. One of the pots had a crack in it, and while the other pot was perfect and always delivered a full portion of water at the end of the long walk from the stream to the master's house, the cracked pot arrived only half full.

For a full two years this went on daily, with the bearer delivering only one and a half pots full of water to his master's house. Of course, the perfect pot was proud of its accomplishments, perfect to the end for which it was made. But the poor cracked pot was ashamed of its own imperfection, and miserable that it was able to accomplish only half of what it had been made to do.

After two years of what it perceived to be a bitter failure, it spoke to the water bearer one day by the stream. "I am ashamed of myself, and I want to apologize to you." "Why?" asked the bearer. "What are you ashamed of?"

"I have been able, for these past two years, to deliver only half my load because this crack in my side causes water to leak out all the way back to your master's house. Because of my flaws, you have to do all of this work, and you don't get full value from your efforts," the pot said.

The water bearer felt sorry for the old cracked pot, and in his compassion he said, "As we return to the master's house, I want you to notice the beautiful flowers along the path." Indeed, as they went up the hill, the old cracked pot took notice of the sun warming the beautiful wild flowers on the side of the path, and this cheered it some. But at the end of the trail, it still felt bad because it had leaked out half its load, and so again it apologized to the bearer for its failure.

The bearer said to the pot, "Did you notice that there were flowers only on your side of your path, but not on the other pot's side? That's because I have always known about your flaw, and I planted flower seeds on your side of the path, and every day while we walk back from the stream, you've watered them. For two years I have been able to pick these beautiful flowers to decorate my master's table. Without you being just the way you are, he would not have this beauty to grace his house."

+++

Can you see now why I love this story?

Everyone is a unique being, a rare flower, a flawed gem, a cracked pot.

In our search for love, family, home and acceptance, it's easy to get pulled away from our center of knowing who we are, losing touch with that original spark we were born with by following gurus, teachers, shamans, yogis and yoginis.

Don't get me wrong; teachers are wonderful. However, I believe a great and true teacher, the kind of teacher you want to find and follow, has the heart-centered intention to guide you back to yourself, to support you in finding your own genius, your own uniqueness, and your own cracked but whole self.

When I was a new parent many years ago, I heard Deepak Chopra speak live in Toronto. My biggest take away from that talk was his comment about how he parented his son and daughter. I'll never forget it, and it inspired and informed how I raised my daughter. He said something like, "The best thing I can teach my children is for them to find out who they are, what they love and what their gifts are, and to keep supporting that search until they know."

I love that.

Do YOU know what your unique genius is?

It's up to you to find out, and make a life for yourself with what you find. The power is in your hands and in your heart. It's up to you to fall in love with your cracks, your peculiarities, your shadows, your gifts, your special beauty.

Your uniqueness IS your beauty, is your magic, is your power. It's the light of your existence made manifest in flesh and blood. Your special recipe can only be found inside you, from the tiniest of details of how you hold your pen to the wholeness of your entire life's journey. It's who, how and why you are so brilliant. So perfectly you. So sacredly you.

Your soul KNOWS it. Right now, she's holding your special shard of mirror. She's ready for you to gaze into it, to SEE your own Sun Goddess, and to dance yourself out of your cave. As love. As light. As joy.

It's up to you to allow yourself the right to recognize and celebrate your own unique light, your way. To ponder and delight at the miraculous beauty you are. To step into your goddess self and trust the myriad of expressions and experiences ready to bloom in, through, and around you.

As keeper of your mirror, and the mirror itself, it's your responsibility to keep practicing polishing it, and creating unobstructed space within yourself to be the clearest channel you can be - to reflect your beauty and holiness without distortion (not like the warped mirrors in the fun house at a circus).

It's time to polish yourself through praise and appreciation. To raise your spirits and see and step into your magnificence and radiance. Are you ready? Let's do this. May I call you Amaterasu? I bow!

The Self-Appreciation Practice: 5 minutes, many times a day

1. Find a time when you can be alone and uninterrupted.

2. **Go over to a mirror and set a timer for 2 minutes.** (Have a lovely timer sound set up!)

3. When you're ready, start the timer.

4. With love, softly gaze into your own eyes.

5. **Begin to shower yourself with loving words. Say them aloud.** You can say 'YOU,' or 'I.' For example:

    "**You are / I am ...** amazing, beautiful, a Goddess."
    "**I love how you / I ...** play, laugh, feel so deeply."
    "**I love your / my ...** body, creativity, sense of humour."

6. **Don't stop until you hear the timer.** Repeat the same words if you have to, but keep going.

7. When you hear the timer, **slowly end your words** and turn off the timer.

8. **Close your eyes, pause, and notice what you notice** with love.

9. Breathe into your heart. Honour your truth. **Be gentle with yourself.** (You may feel tender and emotional.)

10. **Bonus:** Write on a piece of paper this affirmation - **I am committed to my full shining** - and tape it to your bathroom mirror! Say it out loud whenever you see it.

Because...

You are a QUEEN. A Goddess.

A Rock Star. A Divine Light.

Return to Love Playlist

Return to self. Breathe and dance with your heart.
You are loved. You are loving. You are love.

1   **Breath of Love**, Enchanted Wind, by Suzanne Teng
2   **Prophecy Song**, Orenda, by Joanne Shenandoah
3   **Love Is All**, Pray Rain, by Pam Gerrand
4   **Moola Mantra** (Short Version), Moola Mantra, by DJ Taz Rashid & Ria Roth
5   **Love Belongs to Everyone/Gayatri**, Stars, by David Newman
6   **Higher Love**, We Don't Eat - EP, by James Vincent McMorrow
7   **Get Together**, Dreaming Wide Awake, by Lizz Wright
8   **Aap Sahaaee Hoaa**, I Am Thine, by Jai-Jagdeesh
9   **Mother of Mine**, Moon Shines At Night, by Djivan Gasparyan
10 **Heart Center Either**, Nyabinghi Anahata Yoga, by Sound Ambassador
11 **Alleluja**, Divine Rites, by Vox
12 **Gayatri**, Shiva Machine, by Girish
13 **Heart Sutra**, Opening to Bliss - The Meditation Music of Wah!, by Wah!
14 **Unbecome**, In the Garden Of Souls, by Vas
15 **Lokah Samastah Sukhino Bhavantu**, Compassion, by Jane Winther
16 **Divine**, Goddess Rising, by Jennifer Zulli
17 **Returning**, Yogawoman, by Jennifer Berezan
18 **Drawing Water**, The Zen Master's Diary (Remastered), by Darshan Ambient
19 **Compassion**, Signatures On Water, by Maneesh de Moor
20 **The End Of Suffering** (feat. Thich Nhat Hanh), Graceful Passages, by Gary Malkin & Michael Stillwater
21 **Om to the World**, Centering, by Deosil
22 **Long Time Sun**, Grace, by Snatam Kau

Go to: www.EricaRoss.com/playlists

Eighth Turn

Share Your Light

"The main thing is that you're showing up, that you're here and that you're finding ever more capacity to love this world because it will not be healed without that." Joanna Macy

She is My Prayer

I didn't grow up with prayer.

My family was, and still is, secular. Our home was filled with many gifts, of creativity, art, dance, and great love, but prayer wasn't among them. In the little understanding I had, I figured a prayer was like a wish - "May I pass my exam." "May I find true love." A formal ask, a hope.

But slowly through the years, from within my body and my dance, I began to touch and be touched by a sense of connection to myself and to everything. My heart melted open. I was moved and being moved.

I began to fall in love with love, and there it was... without looking for it... I found it.

I found my prayer. Not the asking, wishing, hoping kind, but the 'I AM LOVE' kind. I came to realize that I am a living, breathing, dancing prayer. Seeing my life AS a living prayer changed everything.

I became a devotee to love and life and all that is, in a fuller, more expanded, courageous and knowing way. I witnessed myself dancing with the universe, paradoxically, as completely and exquisitely me, AND dissolved into nothingness and everything. I was everything and nothing at the same time.

Sublime. Ecstatic. Mythical. Tantric. Whole. Divine. Timeless.

Through the years, as I stepped further along my path, I began to sense that my dance was no longer just for me, for my own pleasure, prayer or accomplishment. It was to be shared - as my gift, THE gift.

This revelation was new, yet came from what felt like ancient memories still alive in my blood and my bones, still burning in my belly and my heart, present in my every breath - in every cell of my being.

I knew I'd offered myself this way before. I knew I'd prayed like this before, for millennia. It was one of the surest feelings in my life. I knew I was BORN for this.

+++

In the late 80s, when I lived in Bali, around the time when I was swept out to sea, this 're-membrance' came shining through in my improvisational dance performances. I'd done improv dances for years, but they weren't consciously conceived and given as spiritual gifts. But there in the magic of Bali, that changed. My dance became a channel for spirit - an offering of love and light. I wished only to serve.

It was, undeniably, the deepest, holiest and shiniest love offering I could give.

And so it was… word began to spread about my dancing. I was invited to dance at discos, clubs, homes and farewell parties. I'd arrive with my boom box, in simple makeup and costume, ready to let go and be moved by spirit.

I trusted that whatever happened would be perfect because I had no attachment to the outcome. I'd say a quiet prayer before I began: "May I surrender and be a source of joy, light and love."

On one occasion, I received an invitation from my dear friend, Moon, to attend an evening in the home of his good friend. I was honoured to attend, as I'd heard his evening soirees were legendary.

Accepting the invitation, though, came at a price… the price of COURAGE and a willingness to be seen and heard. Authentically. You see, every person invited was obliged to participate with a capital P. That meant, we weren't there to just join in on lively conversations around the dinner table. Oh no. That wasn't the deal.

In order to be part of the evening, each one of us had to agree to take the spotlight - the floor - for at least ten minutes at some point in the evening. Each one of us would share a gift, something that felt alive in us. We could tell a story, do a dance, a mime, recite love poetry, sing or paint a picture. All offerings were welcomed, and there was no time frame. The night ended when it ended.

I loved the idea, and took the invitation seriously. I decided to do a dance (of course). When I found out that one of the guests was a tabla player, I jumped at the chance to invite him to accompany me. Lucky for me, he agreed.

Since the dance and his playing were to be improvised, the only parts that needed to be pre-arranged were the cues for the beginning and the end. So it was planned… I'd start down on my knees and he'd start to play, and when I came back down to my knees, it was his cue to stop playing. In between, I'd rise up and let spirit move me. Et voila. Done! Easy-peasy.

The evening arrived, and I was super excited and totally ready. Except for one thing… an uninvited guest came a knockin' - an old gatekeeper of mine, a mind-gremlin. He came to protect me and fill my head with fear: 'It's not safe. There'll be strangers. You'll be in an unfamiliar place. What if you don't fit in? What if you aren't the same caliber of the others?' Blah, blah, blah. You know what I'm talking about, right?

Even though my 'gremlin' made a strong case, I wasn't going to let him take me down. No way. Instead, I felt my nerves, gave thanks, and shook it/him off, literally, so I could return back to trust and light and love. (The power of shaking came to the rescue!) I chose courage over fear, and arrived at the soiree with bells on.

And that night couldn't have been more magical. The home was beautiful, the dinner was delicious, and the company (six others) was divine. I fit in just fine! And to add to the evening's splendor, some of us presented our offerings in a round, geodesic dome on the property, equipped with a stage and lighting, and incredible acoustics. The effect was womb-like.

Moon showed his powerful photographs, one woman sang songs from her birthplace of Madagascar (which literally brought us all to tears, it was so powerful and stunning). There were stories and mime performances.

And then it was my turn. The tabla player got up onto the stage and arranged himself and his drums on a carpet set back and off to the right. A small clock sat beside him. I placed myself in the center of the stage. The audience fell silent.

I got down on my knees and lowered my head. I could feel my heart beating as I said a silent prayer of protection and guidance, something like, "May I be a vessel of love. May my dance bring healing and blessings. May my invisible helpers and angels be with me. And so it is!"

And then, in the silence, BEFORE the tablas, BEFORE my dance...

I heard the sound of applause.

'Wait. What?' I didn't understand. I was completely confused. 'Why aren't they waiting for me to dance?'

I reluctantly raised my torso and head to see what was going on. The audience was on their feet, smiling and clapping. I tried to take it all in, to be gracious in front of everyone, so I just smiled back (in disbelief).

I slid over to the tabla player, who was also smiling and clapping, and asked why everyone was clapping when I'd not yet danced. He looked surprised and responded with a puzzled look, "What are you talking about?" pointing to the little clock beside him. "You've danced for 20 minutes!"

"What? No way! All I've done is kneel and pray. I was waiting for your tablas to begin. I have no memory of dancing at all."

But there it was. The proof - the clock, the clapping, the smiles. And the comments from my friend Moon, and the others, telling me how magical and beautiful my dance had been, especially the spinning. Apparently I had spun for a very long time. (Like the Sufi dancers?) Who knows who came through or where I'd gone for those 20 minutes that night? I may never know.

All I could say is, 'Thank you,' to whatever, whomever and wherever I was. 'I will continue to show up and be a vessel for love and a beacon of light.'

++

From the dance floors of Bali to the deserts of Nevada, my journey with dance-prayers continued...

It must have been a new moon. The desert night couldn't have been darker.

Eighth Turn: Share Your Light   273

It was 2002 and I had travelled to Black Rock City in the middle of Nevada's Black Rock Desert. It was "Burning Man", the famous week-long festival of self-expression and self-reliance. Close to 29,000 'burners' - artists, IT geeks, cultural creatives, healers and visionaries, children and adults - had come to play on the 'playa' (beloved term for the desert), and share something of themselves. It's a world of trading and gifting whatever you have to give: blueberry pancakes, fire-dances, pyro-sculptures, or body massages. All are welcome.

(By the way, Burning Man started in San Francisco with 20 people in 1986. What a testimony to the power of an idea!)

It was my first trip to Burning Man; after countless invitations from Raoul, one of my oldest and dearest friends - a long-time 'burner': "Erica, this place is made for you. You'd feel right at home. The art. The people. The scene. You've got to come."

Every year I'd decline due to the logistics: Burning Man happens around Labour Day and is located in the middle of nowhere, making it impossible to be back in Toronto for the first day of school. As a mother, my choice was simple - I'd always stayed home to be with my daughter, Caya, for her first day of school.

But that year was different. Caya was older, in high school, and much more independent. So, when the invitation came around again, I gave a resounding yes! A hell yes, in fact.

I joined Raoul and his friends - artists, actors, dancers, musicians, clowns and stilt walkers - who come to Burning Man every year to co-create together, in a camp located on the Esplanade - the inner ring of the C-shaped structure of Black Rock City. Our camp's offerings were performance and art installations based on the five elements (earth, air, water, fire and ether), with fire being represented by a large, metal pyro-sculpture - a fire tunnel to walk through.

Burning Man was alive day and night with art, music, lighting, and wild creativity at every turn. Kind of like Dr. Seuss meets Mad Max! Every year there's a theme and in 2002 it was 'Floating World' (in the desert, no less).

Imagine... Buses and cars transformed into pirate ships and breaching whales. Sea monsters poking out of the desert floor, and 'burners' on bicycles and on foot, dressed as mermaids, starfish and schools of dolphins. The nights were bedazzled with aquatic creatures big and small, lit up with moving LED lights. I'd never seen such imagination expressed in one place. Ever!

Raoul was right! I was totally at home at Burning Man. I was in my happy place.

Towards the end of the week, a blinding sandstorm swept through Black Rock City in the late afternoon. I quickly took shelter inside Raoul's big domed-tent with my mask and goggles. As a novice to whiteouts, it was intense and exciting, and it was only the beginning. What happened after the storm was even more extraordinary.

First came the cooling rains - making it possible for us to come out of hiding. And just as we were celebrating our return to the outdoors, Mother Nature gave us two exquisite gifts: a brilliant, full rainbow arched directly over us, AND, if that wasn't enough… one of the most beautiful sunsets I'd ever seen. The sky was ablaze in flaming oranges and pinks.

They both took my breath away. Mother Nature had outdone herself, and had outdone all of us as well. No human-made art could top that spectacular show of hers. 'Brava, Mama!'

After all that beauty, the temperature plummeted, as desert nights can do. I quickly changed into layers of warm clothing, and put on a scarf, gloves and boots, and my oh-so-cool vintage black-vinyl raincoat with matching black-vinyl head-scarf.

As I stepped out of the tent and into the dark windy night, I felt a wildness - an immense sense of aliveness and power, and reverence and gratitude all at once. I was ready for the magic to continue.

The winds began to sweep through me - hypnotize me - beckoning my soul to go wander into the wild darkness of the desert, beyond the shelter of our camp. I was being called to do my own elemental dance of earth, wind and ether (mystery).

Blindly, without opening my flashlight, I moved out and away from the safety of my camp. The surrounding mountains gave no protection from the forces, but I didn't need or want it. I wanted wind and wild freedom. I needed to trust and keep moving deeper into the dark mystery.

Soon enough, I became invisible. The night was pitch black. Other than the twinkling stars above, and an occasional flicker of flashlights or 'ship lights' crisscrossing in the distance, it was just me and the wind and the dark desert night. And there, in that deep, velvety darkness and blindness, I found my wild woman. I found my wild desert dancer.

My body was filled with a visceral, instinctive power - unpredictable and wild. I felt the flow of Shakti - the animating force of the universe - awakening and quickening my moves. My gloved hands drew spirals and sacred shapes, like sparklers, while my boots pounded out rhythms on the hardened and dusty desert floor. My body spoke directly to the stars and wind - a dialogue only I could have.

I danced and danced, and danced. I didn't want to stop, it felt so good. I felt utterly alive and powerful beyond measure. I felt whole and complete. I felt holy and merged with all that is. Eventually exhaustion set in. I'd exerted a lot of energy, and I knew it was time to return. I gave deep thanks to the dark beauty and wild embrace of the desert sky, and walked back to camp to continue the night.

Even though no one saw me or my wild and mysterious dance (except for a few passing strangers who almost bumped into me), it didn't matter. My dance was a prayer, for all of us, regardless if it had been seen or known. Regardless if it was just me, alone. The wind knew. The stars saw. The desert felt it.

++

I had a vision, call it a past life, or call it a dream. (Whatever it was, it was as real as real can be.)

I was a Temple Dancer.

I was in India just outside of Bombay (Mumbai). My home was a temple - a temple for Kali, the Dark Goddess, the Great Mother and Destroyer of Worlds, the Great Liberator. Kali, the Goddess of Endings and Beginnings. She Who is Beyond Time.

I was her Temple Dancer - a humble devotee and servant - for she was my Mother. My purpose and sadhana (spiritual discipline) was to stand on a stone at the corner of the temple just outside the main door, and silently offer prayers and divine truths through postures and mudras (hand positions) all day, every day. This was my life.

The stone I stood on was an altar, large and flat, just big enough to stand on, and unpolished and unadorned as I was. From morning to night, no matter the weather or season - scorching heat and humidity, torrential monsoon rains and winds - I was there. This was where I lived in complete surrender to my purpose, and complete devotion and service to Kali.

Every day, people came to gather by me. They came from near and far to witness my silent, holy sermons. They sat up close and quiet - to receive the soundless and healing mantras, messages and invocations emanating from every movement, shape and posture of my body. To be blessed by those transmissions - those ancient and embodied codes of the Divine Mother's love and sacred wisdom.

As they prayed and worshipped with me, I was present only to Kali Ma - my holiness, my queen. It was she who graced me with spiritual insight and knowledge. It was her rapturous Shakti energy that intoxicated and flowed through me. I was her beloved daughter, her initiate, her sacred messenger.

My congregation understood this. They understood how the mere touch of my lips, bend of my neck, or shift of my hips reassembled the intricacies of life, bringing heaven to earth through the magic of Kali's presence. They knew. And I knew. It was my great privilege and honour.

And as I disappeared into the great mysteries of her embrace, we all received her. We all felt her and were shaped by her. Nothing else mattered.

My Temple Dancer has lived through life-times, and lives in me today. Whether I am dancing or not, she is with me. She is my prayer.

Reflections

"When I dare to be powerful, to use my strength in the service of my vision, then it becomes less and less important whether I am afraid." Audre Lorde

I'm so delighted you're here.

The Eighth, and last, Turn of our sacred spiral journey is glowing with ecstatic possibilities for you. You've arrived at the precious place of giving, emanating and radiating the gifts of the return home. The treasures of your soul, of love, presence, and all that you are.

The internal, personal experience of the Seventh Turn now faces outwards, like in the Fourth Turn of Collective Joy, however, we've evolved/revolved since then. The gifts of what was received, gathered and celebrated through the entire journey so far now longs to touch and complete itself, like the inhale needs our exhale to be whole.

This longing is a gift. Your entire presence, and life, becomes an offering, conduit and conveyer, for something larger than yourself, given freely and boundlessly. This is where your personal soul journey merges with the world and cosmos. You, and the unique part you have to play in this luminous tapestry.

And so it is... As in the powerful and healing story of Amaterasu and Uzume, **we gather together with the promise of the light**... for everyone, and for all of life.

We've entered the realm of oneness and wholeness, in strength and devotion to our collective healing, for it is here where we become Amaterasu, Uzume, and every god and goddess holding their precious piece of mirror.

It's where we become reflections of the whole, of the light of the universe, of divine love, where giving and receiving are one.

It is here where whatever goodness you have found in your journey thus far, through the spiral path of these pages and practices, is offered up as your love offering to the world. Your unique shard of mirror. Your unique temple dance. (If you haven't read the practice in the Fourth Turn, '**Be the Mirror**,' check it out!)

Because, it's not enough to keep what you found to yourself. You must share it.

Let me be very clear:

Do not keep it to yourself... PLEASE!

If you found joy, share the joy. If you found love, share the love. If you found healing, share the healing. If you found liberation, share the liberation. Whatever has been of value to you, send it out.

Keep the ripples coming. Keep it alive. Let the essence and energy of your beingness flow and transmit: Wildly, tenderly, naturally, out and out and out, ever-expanding - like the nature of your big, magnificent heart.

This is a spiritual practice: Inclusive, boundless, free, available and shining. Oneness. Union. Within and without.

The world NEEDS you to keep returning back to yourself for what is true, again and again, and then, share the treasures you've found, always - beauty, belonging, kindness, gratitude, radiance, confidence, justice, softening, trust, wisdom, patience, power, generosity, forgiveness, acceptance, all of it - to be the divine mirror you were born to be!

Do it for the Earth. Do it for the sky. Do it for the animals. Do it for your brothers and sisters, blood or not, and all our relations.

You see… **your journey has never been in vain.** It's never been of little use or consequence, nor gone unnoticed. No, no, no!

You've been seen, heard, known and felt. The threads of your life have magically been interweaving with all of ours all along. Like the way the roots of a banyan tree entwine under the surface of the earth, we, too, are made stronger together. As above, so below!

It is up to you, along with all of us, to rewrite the old stories and tell your own. You have the light and the love and the power to create new paradigms and new realities. You can change the world, and ignore the great storytellers that tell you that you can't.

Remember, my beloved…

Your heart is as precious as star dust.
Your stories, truth and expressions are sacred and life-giving.
Your part of this enchanted life-weaving is essential.

I need you. We need you.

You who creates. For us.
You who glows in the dark. For us.
You who imagines the best. For us.
You who reflects generosity. For us.
You who leads passionately. For us.
You who holds the divine mirror. For us.

Thank you for not holding back.

278 She Reflects: A Spiral Journey for the Feminine Soul

Practices for the Eighth Turn

- What's Your Soul's Offering?
- Pass the Flame
- Heal Our Sisterhood
- Get Solar Powered, Sun Goddess
- Show & Tell
- Share Your Light in Amaterasu's Circle

Playlist: Share Your Light

"Shine so brightly that you illuminate a pathway for others to see their way out of the darkness." Dr. Stacey A. Maxwell-Krockenberger

What's Your Soul's Offering?

I've said this before, and I'll say it again: You are unique, precious and valuable, not only to yourself, but to the world. You are powerful beyond measure!

You are the only one who can offer what you have uniquely to give. They are yours, your own unique soul gifts - the kind that arise from the depths of your being, carried by your deep desire and longing to serve and to meet the world with something the world needs.

They are your gifts to give - offered freely, honestly and generously. Offered with breath, intention, purpose, presence and devotion. Their messages arrive ready to do their magic - to heal, to spark, to grace, to touch, to reveal, to release, to awaken, to celebrate and to unite.

And they come as they must - flying, slithering, shimmering, tiptoeing, laughing, howling and whispering. From the heart, in pieces, through lyrics, by hand, and by surprise:

Bright. Raw. *Crunchy*. TRANSLUCENT. Shadowy. Fierce. *Liminal*. Indescribable. Fragile.

Your offerings come through in the way you hold space for others, the way you serve tea, the way you love and the way you live. In fact, here's a bigger lens to see this:

YOUR ENTIRE LIFE is an offering!!!

From your first to last breath. One. Beautiful. Offering. Like the morning song of a bird, the light of the full moon, the scent of a lilac, each of us has our own humble and perfectly irreplaceable offerings - the ones we were born to share. And oh how the world rejoices in the presence of the magic and beauty we've made manifest.

As you can see, the possibilities of how, why and what we offer are limitless. In fact, the vehicle really doesn't matter, although of course we love to be awed and enticed through beauty and our senses. But the essence of the offering is what we long for, what we need.

One of the most powerful offerings I've come to know, comes in the form of prayer. As you've read, my form is through dance. What about you? How do you pray? Is it through song? Is it through touch? Or poetry, love-making, cooking, drumming, chanting? Do you pray on your knees? In a mosque? In a yoga class? Under the full moon? With sage? With a rosary?

However you pray, say a prayer for all of us!! For your loved ones. For your neighbours. For your sisters. For future generations. For our planet. Bless us with your words and heart-felt intentions so our prayers can unite with yours. Pray for peace, wellness, kindness, magic, liberation, strength, wisdom, joy, and love, and all that is good, healing and whole-ing for us all. (And of course... follow it up with action!)

And prayer may not be your way (or only way) - how you share your soul with others. Maybe your way is through creative impulses and endeavors. That would be wonderful because the world needs you to take the gorgeousness of YOU - your unique and exqui-site soul shine and expressions - and create for us! That's right! For US!!!

We need your STUFF. We need your services. We need your mind, body, heart and soul creations. Your soul offerings. We're going to buy stuff and services from someone, somewhere, so why not from you? It's a win-win situation: You flourish in your livelihood, and we are elevated and nourished in return!

We know you put your heart and soul into what you love, and if what you love is made manifest, we want some of that.

Your creations bless us. We want to see, touch, taste, smell and hear the beauty you make manifest. And if you're thinking you have nothing to create for us, you're dead wrong. You have PLENTY to create. It's not just about the tangible or seen.

Aren't you the Mother of Invention? Don't you have tricks up your sleeve, and magic in your visions? Sure you do. We want your innovative, provocative, beautiful, sustainable, equitable, playful, life-giving ideas, plans, services, objects and designs. Every. Last. One of them.

We want to...

- Savour your cherry pies.
- Be haunted by your music.
- Bathe with your handmade soaps.
- Be intoxicated by your love poetry.
- Cry from your courageous story-telling.
- Chart our cycles with your moon calendars.
- Do deep ceremony in your Goddess Temples.
- Melt our bodies on your massage tables.
- Make love on your batiked sheets.
- Join your social justice movement.
- Divine with your oracle decks.
- Adorn our walls with your art.
- Wear your organic makeup.
- Play with your toys.

Whether you're an architect, a tree planter, a trip-planner, a wedding photographer, a mid-wife, a comedian, a chef, dog-groomer, peace maker or film maker. Or maker of scientific breakthroughs, babies, festivals, rites of passage, revolutions, and sacred spaces. We want what you've got.

We want to be uplifted, soothed and astonished by your creations. And then, share them. We want all our relations to be touched by your creations too. And that's how we create a world we want to live in: We buy from each other. We love the experience. We share what we love. And so it goes.

And if you feel you don't have the means to create or buy, no worries. There's always a way. Get creative with how you can participate in this exchange. Stay positive and hold the idea as an option, and see how the universe provides. One way is to barter. It's a beautiful, mutually respectful and beneficial exchange of creations or services, without the ole' mighty dollar.

And what about collaborations? There are many ways of creating new paradigms of mutual exchange based on kindness, respect and inclusivity. (This is a way bigger topic to dive into. I'm just offering some alternative thinking.)

So there it is... Create, barter, swap, buy and collaborate. And keep on creating and sharing. We're waiting... for you to clear off your drafting table, sharpen your tools, fire up your kiln, lay out the drop cloths, and put on your apron. What's it going to be? When can we see it? Feel it? Taste it? Hear it? Smell it?

Which begs the question, my love…

What's YOUR soul's offering?

What soul offerings are bubbling up to be expressed, heard, seen and felt?

To inspire a deeper inquiry into your magnificence, here's a provocative bundle of questions I had pinned to the corkboard of my home office for a couple years. It was found in Bill Plotkin's fabulous book *Nature and the Human Soul*. (And if you don't know who he is, you've got to check him out!)

So, go ahead. Lean in. Ask yourself…

> ***"If my only criterion were to deliver my soul gift
> to my people as magnificently and fully as possible,
> how would I do it? Through what forms?
> With what voice? In which settings?"***

Sit with it. Meditate on it. Dance with it.

What do you find?

More Soul Inquiries

If you need some other prompts, complete the sentences below.
Without editing or judging. Write until you feel complete.

- ◎ I am most myself when ...

- ◎ My soul longs for ...

- ◎ One of my shiniest offerings to the world is ...

- ◎ I love sharing ...

- ◎ I am following my bliss when ...

- ◎ I experience the presence of the Divine when ...

- ◎ My soul's calling is ...

- ◎ I am ready for ...

- ◎ I am committed to ...

- ◎ I am guided by ...

- ◎ If I could do anything, I'd ...

Pass the Flame

"At times our own light goes out and is rekindled by a spark from another person. Each of us has cause to think with deep gratitude of those who have lighted the flame within us once again." Albert Schweitzer

In Dance Our Way Home we have a beautiful dance I call '**Passing the Flame.**'

It was inspired by something I once read (somewhere) about Ancient Greek life; a time when all homes and towns had a central hearth-fire. (Hestia, the Greek Hearth Goddess, was a symbol of this sacred fire; the central gathering place where meals and stories were cooked and shared for physical, spiritual and emotional nourishment.)

Story goes that when a daughter left their mother's home to start her own family, they took a burning ember from her family's hearth-fire with them, keeping the familial hearth fire alive - passing the flame from home to home, from generation to generation. The same held true for the establishment of a new city. The hearth fire from one city would light the hearth fire of the new city, ensuring continuity, connection and stability. And so on and so on.

An aside: I've never heard this, nor have I researched this, but I strongly suspect that that is how the tradition of the Olympic Torch was started. It's just a hunch. Makes sense, yes?

In any event, even though families and cities don't practice this passing of the fire any longer (I don't imagine), I love the idea and essence of it. I love the symbolism and the notion of passing the flame.

What images come to mind when you think of this? How does it make you feel? What might this mean to you?

For me, I see flame carriers, torchbearers, light workers, healers, artists, leaders, mentors and teachers. I see coaches, teachers of teachers, facilitators, guides and instructors. I see grandmothers, priestesses, midwives and world leaders.

I see it as a way.

A way to lead. A way to pass on wisdom. A way to pave the path for future generations. A way to role-model what you value, respect and cherish. A way to share from the hearth of your being - the flame of love and joy within - radiating warmth, kindness, inspiration, nourishment, peace, belonging and beauty.

All of us are needed now, in this time of great change, the great turning. Because our dear Mother Earth needs leaders like you - leaders she can entrust with taking responsibility and care for her, who can be guardians and way showers.

Whether you're an introvert or extrovert, you can pass the flame in a way that feels good for you. You may prefer to mentor one-on-one in a quiet, private space. Or perhaps you get high from sharing stories on stage in front of a huge audience. There's no right or wrong way to do it, only what feels right to you.

And **you can pass the flame from exactly where you are right now.** Wherever or however you are in your life, you have something you can teach, show or guide. There's something of value you can pass on, even if it's just a quick smile or a well-loved anecdote.

Many years ago I had clients repeatedly ask me to teach them to be facilitators of my ecstatic dance practice. They wanted to do what I did, and share the healing with their communities. As flattered as I was, and as great that idea was... I repeatedly said no.

Because, a) I didn't really know HOW I did what I did. It was a great mystery to me. My process was intuitive; from the depths of my inner knowing and trust. How could I possibly teach others when I myself wasn't clear on my methods, principles, etc.? And b) I'd never been to a teacher training, nor created one myself, so the whole thing seemed way out of my reach. I had no idea how to do it.

But after a couple years, a reality hit me: If I didn't pass my practice on - pass the flame - my practice would eventually die. The hard truth was that the only other person who knew the practice was Nan, my co-creatrix, but she no longer practiced. I was the ONLY one who was, and at some point, who knows when, I wouldn't facilitate it either (after all, I was in my fifties). And that would be it. The end. I couldn't let that happen.

And so I leaned in. I rallied my two apprentices behind me, and together we figured it out! I found my ten principles, my processes, structures and core values. I dreamed into reality a beautiful thirteen-week facilitator certification training called The DOWH (an acronym for Dance Our Way Home) Immersion.

I opened my home for nights of sharing around the hearth of my fireplace, and we danced in a large bright dance studio. I called in the dancing goddesses, and they came! That was over eight years ago. Little did I know I'd pull back from facilitating sooner than I'd ever imagined.

I never planned or wanted to offer a facilitator training, but I'm grateful for leaning in and saying YES even when it seemed impossible at first. Because of that, many more women experience the sacred gifts it offers. I could never have done that alone.

What do you have to pass on? What great love, truth or joy fires you up? What wisdom, information, tools, ideas, support, or visions can you pass on to your family, friends, community and the world at large? Like your soul's offerings, it's vital that you share it. We need you to step up and lead.

We need you to give the best of yourself, with generosity, depth, fullness and power.
Live, love, give and lead GENEROUSLY. All ways are SACRED.

How can/do/will you PASS THE FLAME?

Heal Our Sisterhood

"Imagine a woman who values the women in her life. A woman who sits in circles of women. Who is reminded of the truth about herself when she forgets." Patricia Lynn Reilly

Sisterhood!

It's a buzz word these days, I know. It might be a foreign concept to you, or something of no interest, or even a turn off. Or maybe you're already immersed in it as your life-mission and can't think of anything better in the world to be in.

Wherever you are at with this, it's all good! You're where you're meant to be, and regardless… I've got chills of excitement just knowing you're here with ME. We have our own little circle of sisterhood right here, right now. You and me, sister. You and me.

Because… I love you. And that's that! You're in!

I've been blessed to have participated in and created and led women's circles for over thirty years, and still do. It's by far one of the most soul-satisfying experiences of my life. It's an honour and a privilege to witness my sisters bringing both their hopes and dreams and their pain and wounds to us.

Powerful stuff. Healing and magic-making. As we heal ourselves we heal each other. As one sister heals, we all heal. As one sister wins, we all win. And as we heal our sisterhood, we heal ALL of humanity. No separation.

You know this, right? But how do we, as women, do this? How do we heal our sisterhood? Where and how does this healing happen? Where does it need to flow to, in relationship to our sisterhood: our birth, step and chosen sisters, female relations, friends, colleagues and neighbours, to our trans sisters, and women beyond our 'inner circle' - across culture, race, sexual orientation and ability?

As I see it… We all come into this world pure, whole and filled with love. But along the way, we fall into spells. Just like in the fairy-tales. As my friend and teacher Michelle Tocher, a story-teller, writer and scholar of fairy-tales, has taught me: At some point in the story, our story, your story - whether from family, media, teachers, community or culture – malevolent forces arrive to put us under their spell, to shape our destiny.

These spells are usually cast through the power of words, often as 'sleeping spells,' like Snow White's curse, to put us to sleep so we will forget who we are, and how much power and beauty we possess. It's a power-over thing often motivated by fear, jealousy, anger or envy.

You know what I'm talking about. You can feel it in your bones, can't you?

Because, the truth is... we've all been touched by them. There are spells that are good for us too, don't get me wrong - spells that protect, empower, support and heal.

But I'm talking about the spells that bind, freeze, hurt and banish. Archaic spells that cause us to doubt, shrink, forget and disconnect. These spells can go deep; so deep that we're unaware we're even under them, like somnolent zombies.

One of those deep and far-reaching soul spells, in my humble opinion, has not only infiltrated our knowing of who we are and our true nature, but how we are with other women! We've been lulled into forgetting one of our greatest and most delicious super powers: US! Together! Inclusive sisterhood as goddesses and divine mirrors for each other.

Smart move, dear shadowy spell of patriarchy! That's the way to do it. Break us up. Disempower us individually and collectively, through jealousy, envy, distrust and comparison. Plant seeds of scarcity in us. Pit us against each other as combatants not lovers, enemies not allies.

Nothing could be further than the truth of who we are, what makes us blossom, and how we create abundance. At the depths of our truest nature and desire, and we're wired for it, we long to be connected, held, loved and celebrated - especially by other women. They are mirrors to our divine feminine essence, after all. This, my dear, is true RESONANCE and RECIPROCITY.

By the way... I'm not immune to the spell either. I can, and do, fall asleep from time to time. Fortunately, because of my heart-centered practices, I wake up quickly. That re-awakening might mean forgiving a friend, mending a bridge, or letting down my guard.

As you can see, **the healing of sisterhood requires us to practice keeping our hearts open, to ourselves and each other.** We need to stop dropping our weapons of mass destruction (and self-destruction) through emotional bombs of shaming, blaming and betraying, and poison arrows of dissing, undermining and distrusting.

We've all been the warrior and the victim. It hurts both ways. I know this from my own stories of soul-wrenching sister blows, and as a mother having witnessed the suffering of my daughter at the hands of one of her friends. It's heart-breaking, soul-shaking, spellbinding. These experiences have shaped me, and remain a core motivator in creating sacred, inclusive and brave spaces for women to unite in sisterhood. It's part of my 'why' in creating this book.

And here's an interesting phenomenon: We can be such great caretakers for each other in our pain and loss, but where are we in our brightest successes and glory? (Going back to my disco story, for example.) **Why aren't we championing, rejoicing, and celebrating each other more often?**

It's time to stop the oppression and unkindness between us... please! Let's all do our part, our inner work, to fully show up to our sisters' bliss without feeling like it takes away from our own light. We need to get busy waking up, and waking each other up. We need loving, healing and creative spaces for us to come together and rise.

It's time to say YES to sister love, compassion and celebration. It's time to redefine, create, play, dance, heal and express ourselves in solidarity, as divine reflections. Through our courageous and authentic sisterhood we'll be carried forward. We'll clear and pave the path for our daughters and granddaughters (and heal our history and lineage). We'll remember our deep feminine power and wisdom. We'll dance our way home - shadow *and* light.

Give yourself permission to see and love the women in your life with more generosity, reverence and kindness. Your life, and mine, depends on it. We ALL need to wake up if there is to be any evolution or revolution. (*If you're in a position of privilege, that means doing the work to be an ally.) We must be advocates for our sisters, to be the kiss that awakens, the fairy godmother and her magic wand, whatever it takes to break the spell.

Let's choose connection over isolation, love over fear, and joy over jealousy. Let's choose sisterhood... Sacred, messy, resonant, rich, diverse, challenging, life-saving and whole-making SISTERHOOD! **And if you don't know where to start, or this task feels too big...**

Here are some ideas: Remember, you're a role model for next generations.

- **Think and speak only kind words to and about other women.** Practice catching your thoughts and words when you begin to judge and criticize women. And that includes <u>gossip</u>: Don't start or listen to it! Shift your heart and mind from comparison to compassion. Think 'Divine Mirrors.' Think love, beauty, oneness.

- **Be a champion and cheerleader for them.** Lend a hand, an ear, a shoulder; in support and solidarity. (Don't assume they don't need your help.) Amplify their voice, especially that of the marginalized. Claim their victory as yours. And practice giving complements - to friends and strangers - often. You might make their day!

- **Ask for help and support.** Rally and gather your allies. Allow us to support and love you when you feel vulnerable, scared or stressed. Let us hold you and remind you of who you really are - whole, beautiful, unique or strong. Let us be your shiny mirror.

- **Reach out to women you adore.** Invite them, individually or together, to join you in a cup of tea, a walk, a party, a meal - with the intention of connecting more honestly, lovingly, generously, courageously. Elevate and deepen your bonds.

- **Reach out to women you don't know, or you're challenged by.** Think of who you feel a jealousy, hurt or anger for, or a sense of 'other' towards. (This may be a hard task, but it's a good one.) Find ways to connect with them, with curiosity, kindness and love. Begin the healing process. They may become your best ally!

- **Keep expanding your heart in resonance with sisterhood.** Go to gatherings where we play, pray, create, etc. Keep practicing flexing your 'sisterhood' muscles, and soon you'll feel the unity, strength and beauty of being in a circle, a sister clan!

Are you with me, sweet sister? Please say yes!

Get Solar Powered, Sun Goddess

We've all experienced shrinking, holding back, playing small or hiding parts of ourselves so we'll fit in, be loved, acceptable, manageable and bite-size-able. So we'll feel safe. So others will feel safe too. All. Of. Us.

It takes great amounts of energy to hold back, to contain, to shrink. Think about it: It takes great pressure and fortitude to compress. It takes great strength and effort to constrict. And what a waste of energy it is, in most cases.

Your life *force* is meant to give life, not take it away.

Imagine putting that same amount of energy into the full embodiment, expansion, and liberation of your being. Imagine giving yourself full permission to do just that. What would that look, feel and be like? Go ahead... I'll give you a minute...

As I've expressed before - WE, me, your sisters, and the world, NEED you. We need your prayers. We need your creations. We need you to pass the flame.

We need your light!!

This was the motivation that called me to design a special training program for women called RADICAL RADIANCE. It exemplifies the seventh principle of my Dance Our Way Home practice which says...

"Radiance is our original state of being: We all were born with a spark of spirit, of life. This spark is called radiance, light, love, beauty. It is our task to shine!"

And yes... It IS your task to shine. It IS your task to unleash the power in your belly - your solar powered love-light. When you do, my friend, you are a force to be reckoned with.

You become a Sun Goddess in your own right!

I know, you've probably been taught in spiritual and esoteric circles that the sun is a 'masculine' symbol and the moon is 'feminine.' But there are always exceptions to the rule. In this case, there are numerous bright solar-powered beings around the world who are embodied in the form of the Divine Feminine, as Goddesses of the Sun.

You already know one, our beloved **Amaterasu**, the ancient Shinto Sun Goddess of Japan, but there are others. These sacred creatrix deities who birth life into existence remind us of our own bright nature - our own radiance, vitality, force, brilliance and power beyond measure.

Call on these deities of sunshine to support your journey and reclamation of your radiance and ever flowing power. For example:

Aditi. She's a Mother and Creatrix Goddess from India who gave birth to the universe, the heavenly bodies, and ALL the Hindu gods and goddesses. She's the Keeper of Light who illuminates all life. Her name means "free from bonds" or "limitless" or "unfettered."

Or **Aine** (pronounced AW-neh). She's an Irish Sun Goddess of Light, Wealth, Fertility and Sovereignty, also known as a Faery Queen and a Love Goddess. Her name means radiance, brightness, glow, splendor and joy, one who represents the spark of life. Her festival was celebrated on Midsummer's Eve.

Bast, an Egyptian Goddess originally known as a Lion Goddess of the sunset, symbolizes the sun's fertilizing force. Over time, her image grew tamer. She became a cat or cat-headed woman carrying the sun. Bast rules dancing, pleasure, music and joy.

And there's **Beiwe**, a Sámi Goddess of Lapland known as a Spring and Summer Goddess of Fertility and Sanity, worshipped for her returning light after the long winter. She causes the plants and animals to grow, especially reindeer, bringing wealth and prosperity to her humans.

Gün Ana is a Turkish Sun Goddess of Life, Fertility, Warmth and Health whose rays connect her to the spirits of plants, animals and humans. Her worshippers turn towards sunrise when praying, and celebrate her feast during the summer solstice.

Saule, a Lithuanian Baltic Goddess of Growth, Fertility and Regeneration of all life on Earth, rides each day across the sky in a chariot of copper wheels, pulled by two white horses with golden manes. As the full light of the sun, she is portrayed as a daisy, wheel or rosette, and as the setting sun, she's a ring or crown.

And **Yhi.** She's a Sun Goddess from Australia who created life after waking up from a deep sleep, yawning light onto the frozen earth. Melting under her steps, and through her desire to see everything dance, she set all of life into motion.

In the quiet of your home, explore this Sun Goddess Visualization:
Approx. 15 minutes

1. **Find a comfortable place to sit, lie down or stand.**

2. **Close your eyes and rest your hands on your solar plexus,** just above your navel. In the chakra system it's called Manipura - the Lustrous Gem, your center of will, power and energy.

3. To ground yourself, **imagine the Earth** below you, holding and supporting you.

4. **Find your breath** and follow its natural flow of inhale and exhale for a few minutes.

5. **Imagine a beautiful ball of light** pulsing and radiating under your hands and in your belly.

6. **See the colour yellow** shining and shimmering. **Feel its warming rays** heating up your belly.

7. With each breath, **see and feel it growing brighter and bigger,** expanding down into your feet, up into your head, and into your hands.

8. **Let the light radiate beyond your skin.** Feel your light expanding, and flowing out through your pores, your breath, your eyes, your heart.

9. **Imagine radiating out the top of your head** and down onto yourself, like a shower of light.

10. **See yourself as a beautiful Sun Goddess,** glowing, pulsing with light and life-force, like a golden star, shining brightly.

11. **Send your love-light out** beyond the walls, up into the sky and down into the Earth.

12. **See your light touching the world,** your loved ones, and those in need. Like Yhi, the Australian Sun Goddess, melt the world with your desire to make life dance.

13. **Send your light back to yourself, saying:** "I am a Goddess of Light. I am powerful beyond measure."

14. **Feel into that truth.**

15. **Add anything you like** to this visualization until you feel it's complete.

16. **Give thanks** and open your bright eyes.

Explore this Sun Goddess Visualization out in the world, in public:

Doing this practice out in public is another really interesting and powerful experience.

The invitation is to connect with your Sun Goddess self while sitting on the bus, waiting in your doctor's office, or walking down the street. As you did in the privacy of your own home, this time do it with **eyes open, hands resting, and the affirmation said silently.** Everything else remains the same.

May you remember your brilliance, strength, fertility, creativity and resilience. May you know yourself as a Sun Goddess - a creatrix, a life-bringer and a force.

Shine on, Sister Sun Goddess! Shine on!

Show & Tell

Did you have 'Show & Tell' in your school when you were a child? You know, that time when you have to go up in front of the teacher and the whole class to 'show' something and 'tell' the class about it - like a map you drew in Geography, or a calculation you made in Math? I did.

And I really didn't like it... at least when it came to my turn. I remember always being nervous, afraid of forgetting what I'd say or fearing my 'show' and/or 'tell' wouldn't be quite good enough. My young girl-self was already learning about the inner and outer judge, and lessons on being vulnerable and sensitive, lessons that we all learn too soon and soon enough.

Transforming those shaky moments of doubt, of unworthiness, of fear, is a life-long journey. But we can, and we do! As you know from some of my personal stories revealed in this book, my healing and courage came when I found my people, and when I practiced listening to my own truth and rhythm, and chose to stand up for myself, in my light, in my own way. Then I was able to truly shine without apology or outside approval.

The best way I know to show up fully, and to test the waters of courage and confidence, is to practice, practice, practice.

That night in Bali when I did my 'Trance Dance' was one of those opportunities. I'm going to call that night **Show & Tell**. (I've personally transmuted any heavy energy that name once held, and have reclaimed it as a beautiful, radiant opportunity for us.)

This practice is an invitation to create and host your own Show & Tell soirée; to invite friends and family to join you in a sacred space of sharing - to practice showing up authentically, generously and willingly - through a story, a poem, a creation or performance, whatever feels delicious to offer.

All that is required is the willingness and commitment to show up and participate. That's it. (Simple, yes? Yes!)

And if any fearful or protective gremlin comes into your psyche - doubting your ability to pull this off - thank them and get back to the business at hand by doing what I did: shake them off. You'll be fine. You'll be great. Because... **You are brilliant, and there's something only YOU can share.**

And I promise you... you don't have to do a Trance Dance. Share only what feels good to share. It can be simple. It can be small. It can be wild. It can be long. Imagine how wonderful it can be to share your light (your gifts, your truth, your heart) with people you love, and to receive them in return.

*And be forewarned: You might love this so much, you'll want to do it again and again!

Create a Show & Tell soirée in your own home. Let's go over the details:

1   **Pick a night** when you'll have the whole night free.

2   **Make a plan.** Will you have dinner first, or drinks or whatever else you wish to embellish the night with to make it special? Will you have a time frame around when the night will end, or not? And how will you choose who goes up when? Names in a hat, or their choice? Once you know the plan…

3   **Choose between 6-10 friends** to invite to your special evening of creativity, love and sharing.

4   **Explain the concept of Show & Tell** to them: Everyone attending must take the floor <u>for at least 10 minutes</u>. All offerings are accepted and welcomed. They can tell stories, do performances, paint, bake cookies, share poetry, do magic tricks, you name it.

5   **Give them all the logistics of time and place.** Specify if there's an ending time, or if it goes until it ends. My preference is to not have an ending time so it can flow as long as needed, but that might not be an option. It's all good.

On the night of:

1   **Prepare the space** with chairs, couches and/or cushions on the floor for the **Show & Tell** part of the evening.

2   **Invite everyone to take a seat** when you're ready to begin. Remind them to receive each friend with open hearts and minds.

3   **Invite someone** (however you decide to choose) to come up to the front to share their offering.

4   **Remind them of the 10-minute minimum rule**, and you'll be the time-keeper. You decide if you need to encourage them to keep going, or if they need to wrap it up if they go over and you have a strict ending time.

5   **When they are finished, invite everyone to rise and give a standing ovation**, so they feel heard, seen, appreciated and honoured. Shower them with love!

6   **Call the next one up**, or take a break. Let the pace and tone of the night be relaxed, easy, delicious and inviting.

7   **Keep going until EVERYONE has had a turn**, including yourself!

8   **Give thanks at the end**, and wrap it up any way that feels good.

Share Your Light in Amaterasu's Circle

Calling all gods and goddesses!

Our dear beloved Amaterasu has gone into hiding.
She needs us. She needs our love.
Meet me at the front of the cave, and bring a piece of polished mirror.
Let's come together to reflect and shine.
Together, life will flourish, for the good of us all.
And may it be so!

The invitation to come together in a circle, **Amaterasu's Circle**, was born and calls you now, to gather friends and loved ones; to practice being divine mirrors AND the reflections in it - like Amaterasu, Uzume and the gods and goddesses - by honouring each other's unique beauty and magnificence through words of love and appreciation. From heart to heart to heart.

Remember the '**Appreciate Your Unique Light**' practice in the Seventh Turn, where you gaze lovingly at yourself in the mirror and shower yourself with loving words? Well, it's like that, but the shower is much bigger and brighter, expanded into a group experience.

You'll see... It's powerful. Deeply healing, regenerative, and light-inducing.

The circle itself takes about thirty minutes, but to make it even more delicious, invite your friends and loved ones to come for <u>two to three hours</u>, giving time pre and post circle to enjoy your connections. Have tea, break bread, and share stories. Take advantage of this 'heart' time together.

OK. Let the healing and celebrations begin. **It's time for all of us to dance out of the cave and into the light.** Here we go...

Amaterasu's Circle: Approx. 30 min.

Prep:

1   **Invite about 6-8 people** (not too big, not too small) to join you at your home, or somewhere private, safe, contained and comfortable. You definitely don't want any interruptions. Explain to them that you have a beautiful idea to do a circle of appreciation. All they need is to show up with an open heart and mind. No experience is necessary.

2   **Set the space up,** either before they arrive or with them. Use chairs or cushions. I personally prefer cushions on the ground. If you're going to be on the ground, make sure the floor or carpet is clean. Arrange the chairs or cushions so they're

touching, in a tight circle. Place a cushion or chair in the middle. (Keep everyone on the same level, so all chairs, or all cushions.)

3   **Have a time-keeping device** ready to track each person's time in the center. I recommend 2 minutes each, and another 2 minutes for transitions and switches. I also suggest finding a <u>soothing timer-alarm</u>, like chimes or birds, or crickets, etc.

When everyone has arrived and you're ready to begin:

1   **Explain what's going to happen.** Tell them that each of them will have the wonderful opportunity to be both a receiver and giver of appreciation. That one at a time, they will sit in the middle of the circle, close their eyes, and receive loving words from everyone, all at the same time.

2   **Ask for a volunteer to be the first to go in the middle.** (*As the hostess of this circle, I suggest that you go last.) Let them get settled, sitting in an open posture, while you invite everyone else to take a seat around the circle.

3   **Set the timer to 2 minutes.** Keep it by your side so you can turn it off easily.

4   <u>**Explain in more detail what they are about to do.**</u> **Tell them...**

"In a minute, the person in the middle is going to **close their eyes,** and relax their body and heart to receive our love and appreciation. Once I've started the timer, I'll say **GO**.

As soon as you hear GO, the rest of us will **lean in**, gazing lovingly at the person in the middle, and **all together** begin **showering them with words of appreciation**, pumping them with love for **2 minutes, non-stop**. For example:

You are ... beautiful, loved, divine.
I love how you ... play, are so generous, laugh.
I love your ... sense of humour, style, joy.
I'm so grateful for your ... presence, kindness, friendship.

The one receiving the love, stay in your heart, keeping your <u>eyes closed</u>, and **allow the words to flow through you**. Invite your love-light to radiate out!

When the timer goes off, slowly, not abruptly, we'll stop our words. The receiver of our love will **slowly open their eyes, and take turns making eye contact** with each of us as they offer a **gesture**, or word, **of thanks**.

And, then we'll switch. A new person will settle into the middle, and we'll begin again. Don't take too long between people, to keep the energy and flow going. <u>Stay in silence</u> through the transitions.

<u>**Also, here are 4 things to remember while you're expressing your appreciation:**</u>

⊙   **Get as close as possible.** Even whispering into their ear from time to time is delicious.

- ◎ **Keep the volume of our voices at a similar level** so everyone is heard.
- ◎ **Be genuine.** Let the words come from your heart.
- ◎ **Don't stop until you hear the timer.** There should be no pauses or silence. If you run out of words, **repeat yourself**, like a mantra, or repeat someone else's words.

Any questions? Okay... Let's begin."

Closing:

1. **After everyone has had a turn**, including you, rearrange the chairs or cushions for everyone to be in circle for a closing.

2. **Create a safe and grounding container or closure.** (This practice can evoke a lot of emotion.) And **give thanks** to the beauty, love and healing just offered and received.

   Below are a few suggestions. Pick one, a combination, or something else. Or, invite someone else to do the closing. Trust your intuition.

   - ◎ **Hold hands.**
   - ◎ **Chant OM.**
   - ◎ **Gaze around the circle with gratitude.**
   - ◎ **Do a short go-around:** Each person shares a word, a sound, a gesture, or all three... of thanks, or a feeling, or say, "I am committed to my full shining."
   - ◎ **Do a longer go-around:** Each one sharing in more depth.
   - ◎ **Share pop-corn style.** (Not in any particular order, allow anyone to share when and as they like.)
   - ◎ **Stand up and have a delicious group hug.**

3. **Invite everyone to stay for tea, or food, or lounge time.** This post-circle time is sweet and powerful because your hearts will be more tender, open and available. Enjoy the AFTER GLOW!

"And as we let our own light shine, we unconsciously give other people permission to do the same. As we are liberated from our fear, our presence automatically liberates others." Marianne Williamson

Share Your Light Playlist

Fill yourself up. Celebrate who you are, and then send it out into the world. Touch the world with your dance, your light, your gifts.

1. **Strength of a Woman**, Strength of a Woman, by Mary J. Blige
2. **Science of a New Time**, Frequencies of the Motherland, by Goddess Alchemy Project
3. **Spirit I Am**, Let Your Heart Be Known, by Steve Gold
4. **Revolution**, Joyful, by Coco Love Alcorn
5. **Golden**, Beautifully Human - Words and Sounds, Vol. 2, by Jill Scott
6. **Jamming**, Legend (Remastered), by Bob Marley & The Wailers
7. **Appreciation**, Essential Levitation - 20 Years of Ibiza Chillout Music, by Levitation & Jelly & Fish
8. **Perfume** (Supervielle Remixed by Campo), Bajofondo Tango Club, by Campo
9. **The Masterplan**, The Masterplan - EP, by Diana Brown & Barrie K Sharpe
10. **The Brave Ones**, Every Opposite, by Zaki Ibrahim
11. **Arrow and Bow** (Marek Hemmann Remix), Arrow and Bow - EP, by Oliver Koletzki & Fran
12. **Share Your Light**, Share Your Light (feat. Paul Randolph) - Single, by Simbad
13. **I'll Take You There** (feat. Jamie Principle) (Dimitri from Paris Re-Edit), I'll Take You There - Single, by Frankie Knuckles & Director's Cut
14. **Say A Prayer For Two**, 12 Inch Classics, by Crown Heights Affair
15. **Fragile**, Branded, by Isaac Hayes
16. **Shining Star**, That's the Way of the World, by Earth, Wind & Fire
17. **Itaipava**, Flight of the Urubus, by Entheogenic
18. **Rafiki** (DNA Remix), A Ma Zone, by Zap Mama
19. **Another Day**, Another Day - Single, by Jahcoustix & the Outsideplayers
20. **Spirit of the Woman**, Grace, by Sasha Butterfly
21. **Gotta Serve Somebody**, Slow Train Coming, by Bob Dylan
22. **Come Together Slow** (feat. Marti Nikko), 4am: Plum Mood, by DJ Drez

Go to: www.EricaRoss.com/playlists

Epilogue: Holding it All

*"The integral seeker is meant neither for total darkness
nor for blinding light. Everywhere he goes, he must see." Sri Aurobindo*

So, how are you?

When I get asked that simple question we all get asked oh-so-many-many times a day, I don't know what to say anymore.

Do I talk about the loss I feel because of my limited mobility - well, at least, for now? About the decline of my father's memory? Do I talk about the deep pain I feel when I see cruelty, violence and injustice in the world?

Or, do I talk about the pleasure in connecting with an old, dear friend? The hope I feel about my healing body? The ecstatic joy of completing this book?

On any given day, I can experience all these feelings - pain, loss, hope and joy within a matter of minutes. We are flickering flames, after all.

So, what do I say?

For me, life has become about holding all of these things together...

The joy and the sorrow. The pain and the ease. The loss and discovery. I no longer try to rid myself of the one in hopes of the other happier feeling taking its place. I don't try to resist the difficult feelings because it's all true. All of these things.

It's a lifetime of experience I hold - 63 years of it - all of which can feel 'lived' in a single moment when the pain in my hip hobbles me while a beam of afternoon light delights me as it passes through stained glass and dances across my living room wall.

It's kind of like having a flashlight and a spotlight shining at the same time: I have the pain, but I also feel joy. The dark and the light dance in us all the time, continuously. Sometimes the light feels more present. Sometimes less.

It's a life-long lesson, learning how to embrace our manifold existence - our paradoxical *and* fluid self - to hold all of these things at once. But, as it is with the ups and downs of day-to-day life, so it is with a whole life: It's messy and rich, complex and exquisitely beautiful, mutable and shape-shifting.

We learn to hold it all.

It is the fullness of life we hold. All. Of. It.

When I was teaching art at Sheena's Place, a client gave me a poem called **'The Cure,'** Author Unknown:

We think we get over things.
We don't get over things.
Or say, we get over the measles but not a broken heart.
We need to make that distinction.
The things that become part of our experience
never becomes less a part of our experience.
How can I say it?
The way to get over a life is to die.
Short of that, you move with it,
let the pain be pain,
Not in the hope that it will vanish
but in the faith that it will fit in,
find its place in the shape of things
and be then not any less pain but true to form.
Because anything natural has an inherent shape
and will flow towards it.
And a life is as natural as a leaf.
That's what we're looking for:
not the end of a thing but the shape of it.
Wisdom is seeing the shape of your life without obliterating,
getting over a single instant of it.

"We think we get over things."

It's not for me to cut it out of my life. It happened, it's a part of me. I see how it fits in with the shape of my life.

"... let the pain be pain, Not in the hope that it will vanish but in the faith that it will fit in, find its place in the shape of things and be then not any less but true to form."

YES! This feels like truth. It feels like home, as I seek the way to hold it all.

May you find peace in the shape of things.

May it be so.

I love you.

Epilogue: Holding it All 299

You are FREE to be and feel as you wish… Your choice. Your way.

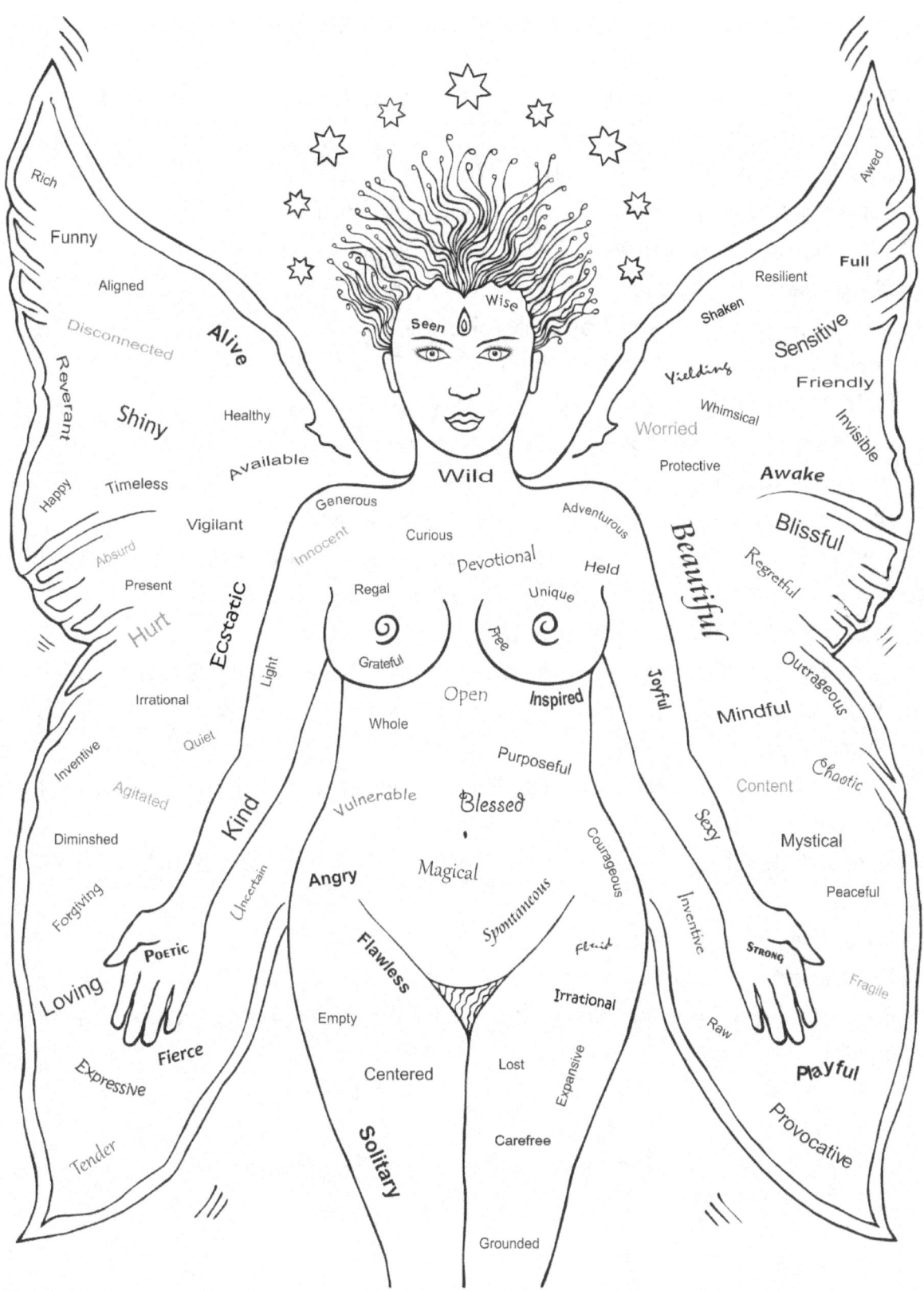

Holding it All Playlist

Dance with everything. Feel, hold and move with it all.
You are whole, fluid and divine.

1. **The Mirror**, A Gift Of Love - Music Inspired By The Love Poems Of Rumi, by Debra Winger
2. **Shiv Shakti**, A Hundred Thousand Angels, by Bliss
3. **Suite da Terra**, O Primeiro Canto, by Dulce Pontes
4. **I Am Whole. Isha Upanishad**, Bodies of Rivers, by Lila
5. **Wholeness**, Wholeness - Single, by Sounds of Isha
6. **Both Sides Now**, Clouds, by Joni Mitchell
7. **Karuna Sagari Ma**, This Is Soul Kirtan!, by C.C. White
8. **Didn't Cha Know**, Mama's Gun, by Erykah Badu
9. **Be Yourself**, Be Yourself - Single, by Peruquois
10. **Tumare Darshan**, Sacred Soul, by Emar
11. **The World Unseen**, Signs & Wonders, by Blue Six
12. **Joy and Pain**, The Greatest Hits: Lifelines, Vol. 1 by Kurtis Blow & Frankie Beverly
13. **The Power**, Believe, by Cher
14. **Shadows And The Light**, All My Life, by Maysa Leak
15. **Here We Are** (Original Mix), Here We Are - EP, by Spiral System & Lottie Child
16. **Stay Human** (Stereo Steambath Remix), Traveler '02, by Michael Franti & Spearhead
17. **The World Is Like a Mirror**, Instinctive Traveler (feat. Bajka), by Dissidenten
18. **Rosalinda**, Bhakti, by Suzanne Sterling
19. **Song Of Gratitude** (Featuring Ian De Souza), Portals Of Sound - EP, by Deborah Brodey
20. **Indu**, The Yoga Sessions, by Masood Ali Khan
21. **Maunaleo**, Melelana, by Keali'i Reichel
22. **Eternal Chant**, Dhyana Aman: Meditation of No Mind, by Manose & Choying Drolma

Go to: www.EricaRoss.com/playlists

Index of Practices

- A Day of Curiosity / **74**
- Accept What Is / See Life as a Sacred Experiment / **251**
- Appreciate Your Unique Light / **264**
- Be a Mirror / **160**
- Be in Silence / **37**
- Be Kind to Yourself / **40**
- Be Moved / **81**
- Be with Your Exhale / **184**
- Become a Wanderer / **83**
- Become an Open Vessel / **195**
- Boast Your Way Out / **135**
- Breathe / **33**
- Connect with the Gifts of Animal Wisdom / **224**
- Consciously Collaborate / **128**
- Create a Gratitude (List &) Collage / **247**
- Create an Altar for Aphrodite / **116**
- Create Beauty / **228**
- Dance with Love, AKA 'Love Comes Dancing' / **122**
- Dance Your Wild / Dance Yourself Free / **231**
- Dare to be Impulsive / **86**
- Design Vows of Self Devotion / **119**
- Divine with Oracle Decks / **89**
- Encounter the Wild Goddess / **219**
- Find Your People / **156**
- Forgive with Metta (Loving Kindness) / **141**
- Form a Healing Circle / **166**
- Free Your Voice / **189**
- Get Playful / Laugh Together / **162**
- Get Solar Powered, Sun Goddess / **288**
- Heal Our Sisterhood / **285**
- Keep Your Heart Open, Regardless / **254**
- Know Your 'Group' Self / **170**
- Let Go with De-Cording / **137**
- Linger at the Threshold / **35**

- ◎ Listen Compassionately to Another / **125**
- ◎ Listen for Answers / Ask Questions / **48**
- ◎ Listen for Signs and Synchronicities / **50**
- ◎ Listen to Your Yoni / **52**
- ◎ Live Life Unscripted / **213**
- ◎ Meander with a Pen / **78**
- ◎ Nourish Your Relationship / **131**
- ◎ Pamper Yourself / **45**
- ◎ Pass the Flame / **283**
- ◎ Shake it Loose / **186**
- ◎ Share Your Light in Amaterasu's Circle / **293**
- ◎ Show & Tell / **291**
- ◎ Slow Down with Body Flow / **42**
- ◎ Support Your Expanding Heart / **258**
- ◎ Tell Your Future Self / **197**
- ◎ Throw a Dance Party / **164**
- ◎ Touch the Wild / **216**
- ◎ Trance Dance with Love / **261**
- ◎ Transform Your 'NEVER!' / **192**
- ◎ What's Your Soul's Offering? / **279**

Other Women's Voices

Here's a small sampling of books to carry you forward on your spiral journey - on creativity, healing, empowerment, sisterhood, goddess mythology and love.

- All About Love: New Visions, by bell hooks
- Beautiful Necessity: The Art and Meaning of Women's Altars, by Kay Turner
- Big Magic: Creative Living Beyond Fear, by Elizabeth Gilbert
- Calling Down the Sky: Canadian Aboriginal Voices, by Rosanna Deerchild
- Goddesses in Everywoman, by Jean Shinoda Bolen
- Heart Talk: Poetic Wisdom for a Better Life, by Cleo Wade
- Her Words: An Anthology of Poetry About the Great Goddess, edited by Burleigh Muten
- Hunger: A Memoir of (My) Body, by Roxane Gay
- Imagine a Woman in Love with Herself: Embracing Your Wisdom and Wholeness, by Patricia Lynn Reilly
- Iron Butterflies: Women Transforming Themselves and the World, by Birute Regine
- Literary Witches: A Celebration of Magical Women Writers, by Taisia Kitaiskaia and Katy Horan
- Love Warrior: A Memoir, by Glennon Doyle Melton
- Maps to Ecstasy: The Healing Power of Movement, by Gabrielle Roth
- Phenomenal Woman: Four Poems Celebrating Women, by Maya Angelou
- salt., by Nayyirah Waheed
- Shakti Woman: Feeling Our Fire, Healing Our World, by Vicki Noble
- she walks for days inside a thousand eyes: a two-spirit story by Sharron Proulx-Turner
- Sister Outsider: Essays and Speeches, by Audre Lorde
- The Artist's Way, by Julia Cameron
- The Complete Persepolis, by Marjane Satrapi
- The Dark Side of the Light Chasers: Reclaiming Your Power, Creativity, Brilliance and Dreams, by Debbie Ford
- The Diary of Anaïs Nin (Seven Volumes), by Anaïs Nin
- The Earth Path: Grounding Your Spirit in the Rhythms of Nature, by Starhawk
- The Great Cosmic Mother: Rediscovering the Religion of the Earth, by Monica Sjöö, Barbara Mor
- The Invitation, by Oriah "Mountain Dreamer" House

- The Language of the Goddess, by Marija Gimbutas
- Upstream: Selected Essays, by Mary Oliver
- Woman Who Glows in the Dark: A Curandera Reveals Traditional Aztec Secrets of Physical and Spiritual Health, by Elena Avila with Joy Parker
- Women Who Run With the Wolves, by Clarissa Pinkola Estes
- Your Body Is Your Subconscious Mind, by Candace B. Pert

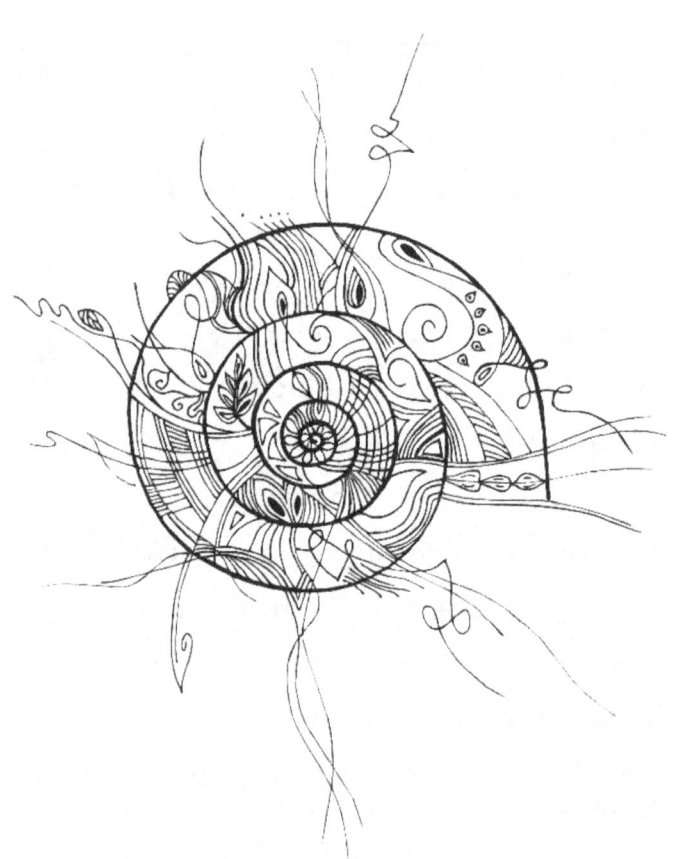

In Praise of Juli

Two invaluable guides accompanied the creation of this book: One seen, one unseen.

The unseen guide was my Muse: the invisible force that inspires my creative flow - both from within and around me, nudging me this way and that; moving my hands as I drew, and whispering in my soul as I wrote.

The other - very much seen and known - came first in the form of a vision. You see... One day near the end of December 2015, while deep in a 'peace' meditation led by Max Ryan via Periscope (a live-streaming platform), there, sitting on my lap was the image of a book, beside the face of my friend, Juli Lyons.

I knew Juli as a stunning photographer from the weekly 'B-School' (Marie Forleo's online business course) mastermind meetup we both attended for a couple years. I'd heard her share, once, that she had the gift to write in the voice of another, but I'd not read anything she'd written.

But there it was. The vision was clear: A book. And Juli. I knew without a doubt that this was the answer to my prayers. I'd been looking for months for my next offering, my next creative work, after letting go of my dance facilitation because of chronic pain. I just didn't know what it was.

This book was it, but IF, and only if, Juli was a part of it. Because, well... I trust my visions. No Juli, no book.

And miraculously, she said yes to my wild invitation to help me birth a book, even when I had no clear idea about it (unfortunately the vision didn't include a cover design or title). Plus, neither one of us had ever created a book before.

And Juli, as my flawless vision showed me, was the perfect person - the perfect mirror, with a bounty of skills and shiny gifts - to help me realize this book.

Through the many months of creating *She Reflects*, her brilliance touched not only my heart and soul, but every page: the molding of the structure, to the crafting of the stories, to the editing of my reflections and practices. Always grounded in generosity, curiosity and kindness.

Thanks to Juli's patient and loving nudges, I found my writer within. She was the best practice partner in consciously collaborating with integrity, discernment and joy. Juli was my trusted mentor, my producer, and ally in creating magic in this sacred experiment.

It's because of this and more...

I say to Juli: Thank you for being a bright light. To you, I bow with the deepest gratitude.

More Gratitude

I could not have endeavored the creation of *She Reflects* if it wasn't for ALL the cheerleaders and mirror holders - the supportive and loving souls who've inspired, encouraged, and believed in me. For that, my gratitude knows no bounds. Deepest thanks go especially to:

My brilliant proofreader, AKA 'word polisher,' Dayna Plummer; Cheryl Antao-Xavier and Pam Lostracco for making *She Reflects* sparkle. And Mary Hynes, Liat Margolis and Nan Keyser, for kindly reviewing sections of the book early on, and Deborah Brodey and Elisa Hatton, for their wise eagle-view at the finish.

My beloved partner, Rob Wright, and my beautiful daughter, Caya Ross-Dalling, for being my unbreakable rock and touch stone, respectively, reminding me of what is home. And my treasured and seriously-talented parents, Honey and Oscar Ross, for offering me unconditional love, inspiration and support, always.

My sister, Lisa Ross, and my soul sisters, expressly: Nan Keyser, Julie Anne Daugherty, Kathy Killinger, Zahra Haji, Deborah Brodey, Marla Slavner, Brenda MacIntyre, Caro Cloutier, Valerie Moysey, Gennie Brukner, Medea Chechik, Wendy Roman, Tanya LeBlanc, ChaCha Chapin, Vanya Laporte, Liz Diaz, Ale Collas, Elisa Hatton, Twyla Kowalenko, Laura Theodor, Roberta Evans, Judy Sunshine, Chandra Rath, Trishka Marek, Ellen Gould Ventura, Lissa M. Cowan, Jill Hewlett and Tabitha Kot, for the best gift I could receive - deep friendship.

My brother, Howard (Howi) Ross, Caya's dad, Gareth Dalling, and soul-brothers, Max Ryan (the catalyst for the vision of this book), Leo and Joseph at Orbital Arts, Raoul Trujillo, Tad Hargrave, Mounir (Moon) Khoury, Victor Morgado and Anthony (Anthos) Reynolds, for being good men in my life.

My birth and chosen family and friends, especially: The 'Wright' family, my niece, Maiyan Ross, my cousins, Sherri and Alan Bergman, and my beloved families in Philadelphia, Wales and Vietnam; and my communities: ecstatic dance, business (B-School), and virtual (including my 'Love in Action' family), for loving me and encouraging me to keep shining my light, tell my stories, and share my gifts.

My many cherished teachers, people and places where I've lived and studied (Canada, USA, Wales, Indonesia) and visited (60+, but in particular, S. E. Asia) and my clients and trainees, for trusting in me and allowing me to learn, lead, stumble and fall, and rise again.

My healers and bodyworkers: Clarissa Pena, Alvaro Esteban, Frances James, ChaCha Chapin, Dr. Larry Feldman, David Peereboom, Adi Kanda, Raje Harwood, Nikki and Zora Singh, and Katarina Bulat, for soothing my weary body. And, the talented musicians, singers and DJs featured in my *She Reflects* Playlists, for sharing their genius with the world.

And lastly… The great big, beautiful and miraculous web of life, for giving me the opportunity to practice being human: with curiosity, compassion, creativity and courage. And YOU, for showing up for yourself, and for all of us. A deep bow!

About the Author

Erica Ross is a left-handed extrovert, wanderer, and lover and maker of beautiful things and sacred spaces.

Growing up in a home of dance, art, love and activism, and with over 40 years in the creative, healing and spiritual arts, Erica offers the wisdom of her life experience as a dancer, artist, DJ, group facilitator, trainer and mother. Erica has followed her wild heart, creative impulses and freedom-loving spirit around the globe since the early 70s, making homes in Canada, the USA, Indonesia and Wales.

For the last 20 years she's dedicated herself to the liberation and healing of the feminine soul; to come home to, and fall in love with, ourselves and each other through her award-winning practice, Dance Our Way Home, plus her facilitator and expressive arts trainings, workshops, retreats and programs (locally, internationally and virtually). Dance Our Way Home is a magical brew of ecstatic dance and sisterhood rooted in divine feminine and earth-based spirituality and teachings, love and creativity.

Erica is the mother of a grown daughter, and lives with her partner in Toronto where she creates art. Wherever she is, Erica finds magic and friends, sees life as a sacred experiment, and practices keeping her heart open, regardless. This is her first book. She is deeply honoured and grateful for you being here with her.

+++

How has *She Reflects* touched your life?

How has the book moved you? What was challenging? What was awesome?

Spread the love by SHARING what you found - what you made, what you healed, what you let go of. Share your photos, art, poetry/written word, videos, and your colouring pages from the *She Reflects Journal & Colouring Book*.

Share with your friends/relatives.
Share with Erica at erica@ericaross.com.
Share on your favourite social platforms using the hashtag: **#shereflects**. On IG: tag Erica with **@She_Reflects**, and on Pinterest: **@EricaRossJoy**.

*When posting/sharing your colouring pages, please credit Erica by adding: "Original artwork by Erica Ross from *She Reflects*." Thank you!

Visit: www.EricaRoss.com

www.ingramcontent.com/pod-product-compliance
Lightning Source LLC
Chambersburg PA
CBHW081718100526
44591CB00016B/2417